AWS®

Certified Cloud Practitioner

Study Guide

CLF-C01 Exam

AWS®
Certified Cloud Practitioner
Study Guide
CLF-C01 Exam

Ben Piper

David Clinton

SYBEX®
A Wiley Brand

Senior Acquisitions Editor: Kenyon Brown
Development Editor: Kathryn Duggan
Production Editor: Lauren Freestone
Copy Editor: Kim Wimpsett
Editorial Manager: Pete Gaughan
Production Manager: Kathleen Wisor
Associate Publisher: Jim Minatel
Proofreader: Tiffany Taylor
Indexer: Johnna VanHoose Dinse
Project Coordinator, Cover: Brent Savage
Cover Designer: Wiley
Cover Image: © Getty Images, Inc./Jeremy Woodhouse

Copyright © 2019 by John Wiley & Sons, Inc., Indianapolis, Indiana

Published simultaneously in Canada

ISBN: 978-1-119-75670-5
ISBN: 978-1-119-49070-8
ISBN: 978-1-119-49069-2 (ebk.)
ISBN: 978-1-119-49071-5 (ebk.)

Manufactured in the United States of America

SKY10032601_011722

Acknowledgments

We would like to thank the following people who helped us create this *AWS Certified Cloud Practitioner Study Guide CLF-C01 Exam.*

First, a special thanks to our friends at Wiley. Kenyon Brown, senior acquisitions editor, got the ball rolling on this project and put all the pieces together. Our project editor Kathi Duggan kept us on track and moving in the right direction. We're also very grateful to our sharp-eyed technical editor John Mueller and Pete Gaughan: we may not know exactly what a "content enablement manager" is, but we do know that this one made a big difference.

Lastly—once again—the authors would like to thank each other!

About the Authors

 **David Clinton** is a Linux server admin who has worked with IT infrastructure in both academic and enterprise environments. He has authored technology books—including *AWS Certified Solutions Architect Study Guide: Associate SAA-C01 Exam, Second Edition* (Sybex, 2019)—and created 20 video courses teaching Amazon Web Services and Linux administration, server virtualization, and IT security for Pluralsight.

In a previous life, David spent 20 years as a high school teacher. He currently lives in Toronto, Canada, with his wife and family and can be reached through his website: https://bootstrap-it.com.

 **Ben Piper** is a cloud and networking consultant who has authored multiple books including the *AWS Certified Solutions Architect Study Guide: Associate SAA-C01 Exam, Second Edition* (Sybex, 2019). He has created more than 20 training courses covering Amazon Web Services, Cisco routing and switching, Citrix, Puppet configuration management, and Windows Server Administration. You can contact Ben by visiting his website: https://benpiper.com.

About the Authors

Contents at a Glance

Contents

Table of Exercises

Introduction

Studying for any certification always involves deciding how much of your studying should be practical hands-on experience and how much should be simply memorizing facts and figures. Between the two of us, we've taken more than 20 different IT certification exams, so we know how important it is to use your study time wisely. We've designed this book to help you discover your strengths and weaknesses on the AWS platform so that you can focus your efforts properly. Whether you've been working with AWS for a long time or you're relatively new to it, we encourage you to carefully read this book from cover to cover.

Passing the AWS Certified Cloud Practitioner exam won't require you to know how to provision and launch complex, multitier cloud deployments. But you will need to be broadly familiar with the workings of a wide range of AWS services. Everything you'll have to know should be available in this book, but you may sometimes find yourself curious about finer details. Feel free to take advantage of Amazon's official documentation, which is generally available in HTML, PDF, and Kindle formats.

Even though the *AWS Certified Cloud Practitioner Study Guide CLF-C01 Exam* skews a bit more to the theoretical side than other AWS certifications, there's still a great deal of value in working through each chapter's hands-on exercises. The exercises here aren't meant to turn you into a solutions architect who knows *how* things work but to help you understand *why* they're so important.

Bear in mind that some of the exercises and figures rely on the AWS Management Console, which is in constant flux. As such, screen shots and step-by-step details of exercises may change. If what you see in the Management Console doesn't match the way it's described in this book, use it as an opportunity to dig into the AWS online documentation or experiment on your own.

Each chapter includes review questions to thoroughly test your understanding of the services you've seen. We've designed the questions to help you realistically gauge your understanding and readiness for the exam. Although the difficulty level will vary between questions, you can be sure there's no "fluff." Once you complete a chapter's assessment, refer to Appendix A for the correct answers and detailed explanations.

The book also comes with a self-assessment exam at the beginning with 25 questions, two practice exams with a total of 100 questions, and flashcards to help you learn and retain key facts needed to prepare for the exam.

Changes to AWS services happen frequently, so you can expect that some information in this book might fall behind over time. To help you keep up, we've created a place where we'll announce relevant updates and where you can also let us know of issues you encounter. Check in regularly to this resource at https://awsccp.github.io/.

What Does This Book Cover?

This book covers topics you need to know to prepare for the Amazon Web Services (AWS) Certified Cloud Practitioner Study Guide exam:

Chapter 1: The Cloud   This chapter describes the core features of a cloud environment that distinguish it from traditional data center operations. It discusses how cloud platforms provide greater availability, scalability, and elasticity and what role technologies such as virtualization and automated, metered billing play.

Chapter 2: Understanding Your AWS Account   In this chapter, you'll learn about AWS billing structures, planning and monitoring your deployment costs, and how you can use the Free Tier for a full year to try nearly any AWS service in real-world operations for little or no cost.

Chapter 3: Getting Support on AWS   This chapter is focused on where to find support with a problem that needs solving or when you're trying to choose between complex options. You'll learn about what's available under the free Basic Support plan as opposed to the Developer, Business, and Enterprise levels.

Chapter 4: Understanding the AWS Environment   In this chapter, we discuss how, to enhance security and availability, Amazon organizes its resources in geographic regions and Availability Zones. You'll also learn about Amazon's global network of edge locations built to provide superior network performance for your applications.

Chapter 5: Securing Your AWS Resources   The focus of this chapter is security. You'll learn how you control access to your AWS-based resources through identities, authentication, and roles. You'll also learn about data encryption and how AWS can simplify your regulatory compliance.

Chapter 6: Working with Your AWS Resources   How will your team access AWS resources so they can effectively manage them? This chapter will introduce you to the AWS Management Console, the AWS Command Line Interface, software development kits, and various infrastructure monitoring tools.

Chapter 7: The Core Compute Services   Providing an alternative to traditional physical compute services is a cornerstone of cloud computing. This chapter discusses Amazon's Elastic Compute Cloud (EC2), Lightsail, and Elastic Beanstalk services. We also take a quick look at various serverless workload models.

Chapter 8: The Core Storage Services   This chapter explores Amazon's object storage services including Simple Storage Service (S3) and Glacier for inexpensive and highly accessible storage, and Storage Gateway and Snowball for integration with your local resources.

Chapter 9: The Core Database Services   Here you will learn about how data is managed at scale on AWS, exploring the SQL-compatible Relational Database Service (RDS), the NoSQL DynamoDB platform, and Redshift for data warehousing at volume.

Chapter 10: The Core Networking Services   AWS lets you control network access to your resources through virtual private clouds (VPCs), virtual private networks (VPNs), DNS routing through the Route 53 service, and network caching via CloudFront. This chapter focuses on all of them.

Chapter 11: Automating Your AWS Workloads   This chapter covers the AWS services designed to permit automated deployments and close DevOps integration connecting your development processes with your Amazon-based application environments.

Chapter 12: Common Use-Case Scenarios   This chapter illustrates some real-world, cloud-optimized deployment architectures to give you an idea of the kinds of application environments you can build on AWS.

Appendix A: Answers to Review Questions   This appendix provides the answers and brief explanations for the questions at the end of each chapter.

Appendix B: Additional Services   To make sure you're at least familiar with the full scope of AWS infrastructure, this appendix provides brief introductions to many of the services not mentioned directly in the chapters of this book.

Interactive Online Learning Environment and Test Bank

The authors have worked hard to create some really great tools to help you with your certification process. The interactive online learning environment that accompanies this *AWS Certified Cloud Practitioner Study Guide* includes a test bank with study tools to help you prepare for the certification exam—and increase your chances of passing it the first time! The test bank includes the following:

Sample tests   All the questions in this book are included online, including the assessment test at the end of this introduction and the review questions printed after each chapter. In addition, there are two practice exams with 50 questions each. Use these questions to assess how you're likely to perform on the real exam. The online test bank runs on multiple devices.

Flashcards   The online text banks include 100 flashcards specifically written to hit you hard, so don't get discouraged if you don't ace your way through them at first. They're there to ensure that you're really ready for the exam. And no worries—armed with the review questions, practice exams, and flashcards, you'll be more than prepared when exam day comes. Questions are provided in digital flashcard format (a question followed by a single correct answer). You can use the flashcards to reinforce your learning and provide last-minute test prep before the exam.

We plan to update any errors or changes to the AWS platform that aren't currently reflected in these questions as we discover them here: https://awsccp.github.io/.

Should you notice any problems before we do, please be in touch.

Glossary   A glossary of key terms from this book is available as a fully searchable PDF.

Go to www.wiley.com/go/sybextestprep to register and gain access to this interactive online learning environment and test bank with study tools.

Exam Objectives

According to the *AWS Certified Cloud Practitioner Exam Guide* (version 1.4), the AWS Certified Cloud Practitioner (CLF-C01) examination is "intended for individuals who have the knowledge and skills necessary to effectively demonstrate an overall understanding of the AWS Cloud, independent of specific technical roles addressed by other AWS certifications" (for example, solution architects or SysOps administrators).

To be successful, you'll be expected to be able to describe the following:

- The AWS Cloud and its basic global infrastructure
- AWS Cloud architectural principles
- The AWS Cloud value proposition
- Key AWS services along with their common use cases (for example, highly available web applications or data analysis)
- The basic security and compliance practices relating to the AWS platform and the shared security model
- AWS billing, account management, and pricing models
- Documentation and technical assistance resources
- Basic characteristics for deploying and operating in the AWS Cloud

AWS recommends that "candidates have at least six months of experience with the AWS Cloud in any role, including technical, managerial, sales, purchasing, or financial." They should also possess general knowledge of information technology and application servers and their uses in the AWS Cloud.

Objective Map

The exam covers four domains, with each domain broken down into objectives. The following table lists each domain and its weighting in the exam, along with the chapters in the book where that domain's objectives are covered.

Domain	Percentage of Exam	Chapter(s)
Domain 1: Cloud Concepts	28%	
1.1 Define the AWS Cloud and its value proposition		1, 12
1.2 Identify aspects of AWS Cloud economics		1, 12
1.3 List the different cloud architecture design principles		1, 9, 10, 11, 12

Domain	Percentage of Exam	Chapter(s)
Domain 2: Security	24%	
2.1 Define the AWS Shared Responsibility model		4
2.2 Define AWS Cloud security and compliance concepts		5, 6, 8, 10
2.3 Identify AWS access management capabilities		5, 8, 10, 11
2.4 Identify resources for security support		3, 6
Domain 3: Technology	36%	
3.1 Define methods of deploying and operating in the AWS Cloud		6, 7, 8, 9, 10, 11, 12
3.2 Define the AWS global infrastructure		4, 10
3.3 Identify the core AWS services		6, 7, 8, 9, 10
3.4 Identify resources for technology support		3
Domain 4: Billing and Pricing	12%	
4.1 Compare and contrast the various pricing models for AWS		2, 7
4.2 Recognize the various account structures in relation to AWS billing and pricing		2, 7
4.3 Identify resources available for billing support		2, 3, 6

Assessment Test

1. Which of the following describes the cloud design principle of scalability?

    A. The ability to automatically increase available compute resources to meet growing user demand

    B. The ability to route incoming client requests between multiple application servers

    C. The ability to segment physical resources into multiple virtual partitions

    D. The ability to reduce production costs by spreading capital expenses across many accounts

2. Which of the following best describes the cloud service model known as infrastructure as a service (IaaS)?

    A. End user access to software applications delivered over the internet

    B. Access to a simplified interface through which customers can directly deploy their application code without having to worry about managing the underlying infrastructure

    C. Customer rental of the use of measured units of a provider's physical compute, storage, and networking resources

    D. Abstracted interfaces built to manage clusters of containerized workloads

3. How does AWS ensure that no single customer consumes an unsustainable proportion of available resources?

    A. AWS allows customers to consume as much as they're willing to pay for, regardless of general availability.

    B. AWS imposes default limits on the use of its service resources but allows customers to request higher limits.

    C. AWS imposes hard default limits on the use of its service resources.

    D. AWS imposes default limits on the use of its services by Basic account holders; Premium account holders face no limits.

4. The AWS Free Tier is designed to give new account holders the opportunity to get to know how their services work without necessarily costing any money. How does it work?

    A. You get service credits that can be used to provision and launch a few typical workloads.

    B. You get full free access to a few core AWS services for one month.

    C. You get low-cost access to many core AWS services for three months.

    D. You get free lightweight access to many core AWS services for a full 12 months.

5. AWS customers receive "production system down" support within one hour when they subscribe to which support plan(s)?

    A. Enterprise.

    B. Business and Enterprise.

    C. Developer and Basic.

    D. All plans get this level of support.

6. AWS customers get full access to the AWS Trusted Advisor best practice checks when they subscribe to which support plan(s)?

   A. All plans get this level of support.

   B. Basic and Business.

   C. Business and Enterprise.

   D. Developer, Business, and Enterprise.

7. The AWS Shared Responsibility Model illustrates how AWS itself (as opposed to its customers) is responsible for which aspects of the cloud environment?

   A. The redundancy and integrity of customer-added data

   B. The underlying integrity and security of AWS physical resources

   C. Data and configurations added by customers

   D. The operating systems run on EC2 instances

8. Which of these is a designation for two or more AWS data centers within a single geographic area?

   A. Availability Zone

   B. Region

   C. Network subnet

   D. Geo-unit

9. How, using security best practices, should your organization's team members access your AWS account resources?

   A. Only a single team member should be given any account access.

   B. Through a jointly shared single account user who's been given full account-wide permissions.

   C. Through the use of specially created users, groups, and roles, each given the fewest permissions necessary.

   D. Ideally, resource access should occur only through the use of access keys.

10. Which of the following describes a methodology that protects your organization's data when it's on-site locally, in transit to AWS, and stored on AWS?

    A. Client-side encryption

    B. Server-side encryption

    C. Cryptographic transformation

    D. Encryption at rest

11. What authentication method will you use to access your AWS resources remotely through the AWS Command Line Interface (CLI)?

    A. Strong password

    B. Multifactor authentication

    C. SSH key pairs

    D. Access keys

12. Which of these is the primary benefit from using resource tags with your AWS assets?

    A. Tags enable the use of remote administration operations via the AWS CLI.

    B. Tags make it easier to identify and administrate running resources in a busy AWS account.

    C. Tags enhance data security throughout your account.

    D. Some AWS services won't work without the use of resource tags.

13. What defines the base operating system and software stack that will be available for a new Elastic Compute Cloud (EC2) instance when it launches?

    A. The Virtual Private Cloud (VPC) into which you choose to launch your instance.

    B. The instance type you select.

    C. The Amazon Machine Image (AMI) you select.

    D. You don't need to define the base OS—you can install that once the instance launches.

14. Which of the following AWS compute services offers an administration experience that most closely resembles the way you would run physical servers in your own local data center?

    A. Simple Storage Service (S3)

    B. Elastic Container Service (ECS)

    C. Elastic Compute Cloud (EC2)

    D. Lambda

15. Which of the following AWS object storage services offers the lowest ongoing charges, but at the cost of some convenience?

    A. Glacier

    B. Storage Gateway

    C. Simple Storage Service (S3)

    D. Elastic Block Store (EBS)

16. Which of the following AWS storage services can make the most practical sense for petabyte-sized archives that currently exist in your local data center?

    A. Saving to a Glacier Vault

    B. Saving to a Simple Storage Service (S3) bucket

    C. Saving to an Elastic Block Store (EBS) volume

    D. Saving to an AWS Snowball device

17. Which of the following will provide the most reliable and scalable relational database experience on AWS?

    A. Relational Database Service (RDS)

    B. Running a database on an EC2 instance

    C. DynamoDB

    D. Redshift

18. What's the best and simplest way to increase reliability of an RDS database instance?

    A. Increase the available IOPS.

    B. Choose the Aurora database engine when you configure your instance.

    C. Enable Multi-AZ.

    D. Duplicate the database in a second AWS Region.

19. How does AWS describe an isolated networking environment into which you can launch compute resources while closely controlling network access?

    A. Security group

    B. Virtual private cloud (VPC)

    C. Availability Zone

    D. Internet gateway

20. What service does AWS use to provide a content delivery network (CDN) for its customers?

    A. VPC peering

    B. Internet gateway

    C. Route 53

    D. CloudFront

21. What is Amazon's Git-compliant version control service for integrating your source code with AWS resources?

    A. CodeCommit

    B. CodeBuild

    C. CodeDeploy

    D. Cloud9

22. Which AWS service allows you to build a script-like template representing complex resource stacks that can be used to launch precisely defined environments involving the full range of AWS resources?

    A. LightSail

    B. EC2

    C. CodeDeploy

    D. CloudFormation

23. What is Amazon Athena?

    A. A service that permits queries against data stored in Amazon S3

    B. A service that permits processing and analyzing of real-time video and data streams

    C. A NoSQL database engine

    D. A Greece-based Amazon Direct Connect service partner

24. What is Amazon Kinesis?

   A. A service that permits queries against data stored in Amazon S3

   B. A service that permits processing and analyzing of real-time video and data streams

   C. A NoSQL database engine

   D. A Greece-based Amazon Direct Connect service partner

25. What is Amazon Cognito?

   A. A service that can manage authentication and authorization for your public-facing applications

   B. A service that automates the administration of authentication secrets used by your AWS resources

   C. A service that permits processing and analyzing of real-time video and data streams

   D. A relational database engine

Answers to Assessment Test

1. **A.** A scalable deployment will automatically "scale up" its capacity to meet growing user demand without the need for manual interference. See Chapter 1.

2. **C.** IaaS is a model that gives customers access to virtualized units of a provider's physical resources. IaaS customers manage their infrastructure much the way they would local, physical servers. See Chapter 1.

3. **B.** AWS applies usage limits on most features of its services. However, in many cases, you can apply for a limit to be lifted. See Chapter 2.

4. **D.** The Free Tier offers you free lightweight access to many core AWS services for a full 12 months. See Chapter 2.

5. **B.** "Production system down" support within one hour is available only to subscribers to the Business or Enterprise support plans. See Chapter 3.

6. **D.** All support plans come with full access to Trusted Advisor except for the (free) Basic plan. See Chapter 3.

7. **B.** According to the Shared Responsibility Model, AWS is responsible for the underlying integrity and security of AWS physical resources, but not the integrity of the data and configurations added by customers. See Chapter 4.

8. **A.** An Availability Zone is one of two or more physical data centers located within a single AWS Region. See Chapter 4.

9. **C.** Team members should each be given identities (as users, groups, and/or roles) configured with exactly the permissions necessary to do their jobs and no more. See Chapter 5.

10. **A.** End-to-end encryption that protects data at every step of its life cycle is called client-side encryption. See Chapter 5.

11. **D.** AWS CLI requests are authenticated through access keys. See Chapter 6.

12. **B.** Resource tags—especially when applied with consistent naming patterns—can make it easier to visualize and administrate resources on busy accounts. See Chapter 6.

13. **C.** The AMI you select while configuring your new instance defines the base OS. See Chapter 7.

14. **C.** You can administrate EC2 instances using techniques that are similar to the way you'd work with physical servers. See Chapter 7.

15. **A.** Amazon Glacier can reliably store large amounts of data for a very low price but requires CLI or SDK administration access, and retrieving your data can take hours. See Chapter 8.

16. D. You can transfer large data stores to the AWS cloud (to S3 buckets) by having Amazon send you a Snowball device to which you copy your data and which you then ship back to Amazon. See Chapter 8.

17. A. RDS offers a managed and highly scalable database environment for most popular relational database engines (including MySQL, MariaDB, and Oracle). See Chapter 9.

18. C. Multi-AZ will automatically replicate your database in a second Availability Zone for greater reliability. It will, of course, also double your costs. See Chapter 9.

19. B. A VPC is an isolated networking environment into which you can launch compute resources while closely controlling network access. See Chapter 10.

20. D. CloudFront is a content delivery network (CDN) that distributes content through its global network of edge locations. See Chapter 10.

21. A. CodeCommit is a Git-compliant version control service for integrating your source code with AWS resources. See Chapter 11.

22. D. CloudFormation templates can represent complex resource stacks that can be used to launch precisely defined environments involving the full range of AWS resources. See Chapter 11.

23. A. Amazon Athena is a managed service that permits queries against S3-stored data. See Chapter 13.

24. B. Amazon Kinesis allows processing and analyzing of real time video and data streams. See Chapter 13.

25. A. Amazon Cognito can manage authentication and authorization for your public-facing applications. See Chapter 13.

Chapter

1

The Cloud

THE AWS CERTIFIED CLOUD PRACTITIONER
EXAM OBJECTIVES COVERED IN THIS
CHAPTER MAY INCLUDE, BUT ARE NOT
LIMITED TO, THE FOLLOWING:

Domain 1: Cloud Concepts

✓ 1.1 Define the AWS Cloud and its value proposition

✓ 1.2 Identify aspects of AWS Cloud economics

✓ 1.3 List the different cloud architecture design principles

Introduction

If you want to make smart choices about how your organization is going to use Amazon Web Services' cloud platform, you'll first need to properly understand it. To get there, you'll need to figure out just what the cloud is, what technologies it's built on, what kinds of cost savings and operational advantages it can bring you, and how cloud-based applications work differently than their traditional cousins.

This chapter will introduce you to the basics. The rest of the book will fully flesh out the details.

What Is Cloud Computing?

Using a public cloud is about using other people's servers to run your digital workloads.

In a sense, there's no significant difference between running a software application on servers hosted in your own office versus locating it within Amazon's infrastructure. In both cases, you need to make sure you've got sufficient compute, memory, network, and storage resources. In both cases, fast deployments and avoiding over-provisioning are key goals.

But, particularly when it comes to the largest cloud providers, there are important differences. You see, the sheer size of a platform like AWS (and right now there's no platform on Earth that's bigger) means it can offer you service, cost, and reliability performance that you could probably never hope to re-create on your own.

Let's see how some of that works.

Highly Available and Scalable Resources

There's an awful lot a successful company like AWS can get done with a few hundred thousand networked servers and hundreds of the best trained engineers in the business:

- Design multiple layers of redundancy so that whenever one component fails, its workload is automatically and instantly moved to a healthy replacement.

- Connect resources in geographically remote locations so that the failure of one complete region could trigger a predefined relocation. This relocation can be supported by a similarly automated rerouting of network requests.

- Provide customers with access to as much compute power as they could possibly need, and deliver that power on-demand.
- Because of the scale and efficiency of the platform, AWS can do all that at a price that's often far below what it would cost to run comparable workloads locally.

Professionally Secured Infrastructure

IT security is a constantly moving target. As difficult as it's been to manage last year's threats, you know there's a whole new batch coming right behind them. As a business, you're already responsible for protecting the workstations and networking hardware running in your office along with securing your organization's data and code your developers put into your apps. The integrity of your underlying server infrastructure is just one more potential area of vulnerability for you to worry about.

No matter how good your IT security team is, they're probably not better informed, equipped, and trained than their counterparts at a major cloud provider. Because AWS is so good at what it does—and because it takes responsibility for the security of its platform's underlying networking and compute infrastructure—this is one area where outsourcing will usually make sense.

This won't relieve you of all worries. As you'll see in Chapter 4, "Understanding the AWS Environment," the terms of the AWS Shared Responsibility Model mean that, in many cases, the security and integrity of the resources you run *on* the cloud are still your problem. But *the cloud itself* is managed by AWS.

Metered Payment Model

One of the defining characteristics of any public cloud computing platform is the way it automatically allocates resources to meet client requests. Practically, this means that you can, for instance, log in to the AWS browser console, and define and launch a virtual server (called an *instance* in the AWS world), and moments later your new instance will be ready for you. There's no need to wait for manual intervention by AWS employees.

The flexibility of the self-serve system permits usage patterns that would have been impossible using traditional compute paradigms. Let's say you need to quickly test a possible application configuration you're working on. In the old days, even if the test lasted only an hour, you would still need to find free capacity on a physical server in the server room. Once the test ended, you'd still be paying the maintenance and ownership costs of that server capacity even if it was idle.

In the cloud, by contrast, you fire up an instance, run it for the length of time your test requires, and then shut it down. You'll be billed for only that testing time, which, in some cases, could cost you a fraction of a penny.

Since there's no human processing involved in cloud compute billing, it's as easy for a provider to charge a few pennies as it is thousands of dollars. This metered payment makes it possible to consider entirely new ways of testing and delivering your applications, and it often means your cost-cycle expenses will be considerably lower than they would if you were using physical servers running on-premises.

Comparing the costs of cloud deployments against on-premises deployments requires that you fully account for both capital expenses (*capex*) and operating expenses (*opex*). On-premises infrastructure tends to be very capex-heavy since you need to purchase loads of expensive hardware up front. Cloud operations, on the other hand, involve virtually no capex costs at all. Instead, your costs are ongoing, consisting mostly of per-hour resource "rental" fees.

You'll learn more about AWS billing in Chapter 2, "Understanding Your AWS Account."

Server Virtualization: The Basics

The secret sauce that lets cloud providers give their customers on-demand compute resources in such a wide range of configurations is virtualization. When you request a *virtual machine* (VM) with a particular processor speed, memory capacity, and storage size, AWS doesn't send some poor engineer running through the halls of its data center looking for an available machine with exactly that profile. Rather, as you can see illustrated in Figure 1.1, AWS carves the necessary resources from larger existing devices.

FIGURE 1.1   VMs accessing storage and compute resources from their host server

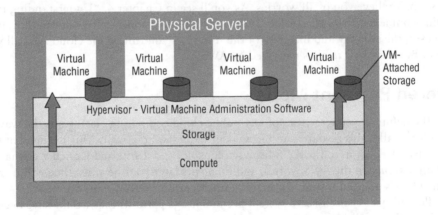

A 5 TB storage drive could, for instance, be divided into dozens of smaller virtual volumes, each associated with a different virtual server (or instance). And the resources of a single physical server could be invisibly shared between multiple instances. The operating systems installed on each of those instances could run, blissfully unaware that they're actually only masters over a small subset of a much larger server environment.

The virtualization model offers two compelling benefits:

- **Speed:** Defining, purchasing, provisioning, testing, and launching a new physical server can take months. Even a simple reboot can keep you waiting for a couple of minutes. The time lag between requesting a new cloud-based VM and logging in and getting to work can be seconds, but never more than a few minutes. Restarting a VM can sometimes happen faster than you can type your login details.

- **Efficiency:** It's rare to find a nonvirtualized physical server that utilizes anywhere near 100 percent of its capacity. More likely, either it'll spend its time running mostly empty or it'll be badly overused while you wait for more capacity to come online. Multiple virtual machines, on the other hand, can be tightly packed onto a physical server running a hypervisor (a common technology for hosting VMs). When space opens up on one server, you can quickly fill it with another virtual workload. When a server reaches capacity, overflow workloads can be moved to another machine. And the more workloads you're managing, the more flexible everything gets.

Amazon's formidable scale and logistical abilities mean that it's often able to leverage the benefits of virtualization to provide both superior performance and pricing.

Cloud Platform Models

Cloud services come in more than one flavor. Choosing the one that's right for your project will depend on your specific needs and how much fine control you'll need over the underlying gears and levers.

Infrastructure as a Service

Infrastructure as a Service (IaaS) products generally simulate the look and feel you'd get from managing physical resources. IaaS products give you direct access to a provider's compute, storage, and networking assets. Because it's you that's in there playing around at the hardware level, you—rather than the IaaS provider—are responsible for the consequences of any bad configurations. The trade-off is that you get to closely configure every layer of your operating stack.

You'll learn much more about these examples later in the book, but AWS IaaS products include Elastic Cloud Compute (EC2) for virtual machine instances, Elastic Block Store (EBS) for storage volumes, and Elastic Load Balancing.

Platform as a Service

Unlike IaaS, Platform as a Service (PaaS) products simplify the process of building an application by *hiding the complexity* of the infrastructure that runs it. You're given an interface through which you define the behavior and environment you want for your application. This will often include the code that will run your application.

AWS PaaS products include Elastic Beanstalk and Elastic Container Service (ECS).

Software as a Service

Software as a Service (SaaS) products offer services meant to be accessed by end users. An easily recognizable illustration is Google's Gmail service, which allows users to manage their email by logging in to a browser interface or through an email client (like Microsoft Outlook) that's running locally.

While some may disagree with the designation, AWS SaaS products arguably include Simple Email Service and Amazon WorkSpaces.

Figure 1.2 compares the scope of responsibility you have on IaaS, PaaS, and SaaS platforms with the way it works for on-premises deployments.

FIGURE 1.2 The breakdown of responsibility across multiple infrastructure types

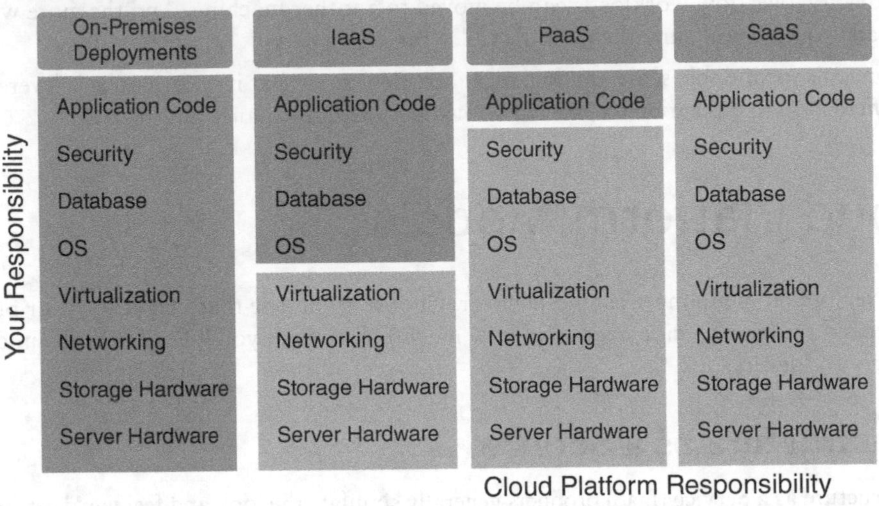

Serverless Workloads

Besides doing an excellent job emulating traditional server behavior, cloud providers can also enable entirely new ways to administrate applications and data. Perhaps the most obvious example is serverless computing.

Now don't be fooled by the name. You can't run a compute function without a computer environment (a "server") somewhere that'll host it. What "serverless" does allow is for individual developers to run their code for seconds or minutes at a time on some else's cloud servers.

The serverless model—as provided by services like AWS Lambda—makes it possible to design code that *reacts* to external events. When, for instance, a video file is uploaded to a repository (like an AWS S3 bucket or even an on-premises FTP site), it can trigger a Lambda function that will convert the file to a new video format. There's no need to maintain and pay for an actual instance running 24/7, just for the moments your code is actually running. And there's no administration overhead to worry about.

Scalability and Elasticity

The world's largest public cloud providers can accomplish a great deal through combining the wonders of server virtualization with the power that comes from owning vast data centers filled with racks upon racks of hardware resources. Elasticity and scalability are the two key principles through which a lot of this happens, and understanding exactly what they mean can help you optimize your design choices so you'll get the most bang for your cloud buck.

Note that there really are no precise and authoritative definitions for scalability and elasticity in the context of cloud computing—and any definitions you do see are bound to involve at least some overlap. Nevertheless, building some kind of picture in your mind of how these two principles work can be valuable.

Scalability

A scalable service will automatically grow in capacity to seamlessly meet any changes in demand. A well-designed cloud-based operation will constantly monitor the health of its application stack and respond whenever preset performance metrics might soon go unmet. The response might include automatically launching new server instances to add extra compute power to your existing cluster. But it will probably also involve prepopulating those instances with the application data and configuration settings they'll need to actually serve your application to your clients.

A large cloud provider like AWS will, for all practical purposes, have endless available capacity so the only practical limit to the maximum size of your application is your organization's budget (and default service limits imposed by AWS that you'll learn about later in Chapter 2).

Just how big is AWS? Well, if it can handle the capacity stresses required to keep millions of Netflix customers happy—and if you've ever watched a movie on the AWS-hosted Netflix, then you know it can—then AWS will surely be able to keep up with whatever trouble your applications send its way.

Elasticity

You can stretch an elastic band far beyond its resting state. But part of what makes it truly elastic is the fact that, when you let go of it, it immediately returns to its original size. The reason the word *elastic* is used in the names of so many AWS services (Elastic Compute Cloud, Elastic Load Balancing, Elastic Beanstalk, and so on) is because those services are built to be easily and automatically resized.

Generally, you set the maximum and minimum performance levels you want for your application, and the AWS service(s) you're using will automatically add or remove resources to meet changing usage demands. By way of illustration, a scalable ecommerce website could be configured to function using just a single server during low-demand periods, but any number of additional servers could be automatically brought online as demand spikes. When demand drops back down, unused servers will be shut down automatically.

Assuming you don't already have one, now is the time to create your own AWS account. Working through the rest of this book will be pretty much impossible without an active account. You will have to provide a credit card, but you won't be charged anything unless you actually launch an actual resource. Work through Exercise 1.1 to make this happen.

EXERCISE 1.1

Create an AWS Account

1. Go to https://aws.amazon.com, and choose the Create An AWS Account button. If, instead, you see a Sign In button, you might have previously logged into an existing account using this browser. If you'd still like to create a new account, choose Sign In and then create a new, different account.

2. Enter the email address you want to associate with the account, a (strong) password, and a new AWS account name you'd like to use. Choose Continue.

3. Select an account type (either Professional or Personal—the only difference is the Company Name field) and the other requested information. Then agree to the AWS terms and choose Create Account And Continue. You will receive a confirmation email, after which you can continue with the activation process.

4. Enter a payment method and, if the payment address is different from the address you used in the previous step, enter a new address and choose Secure Submit.

5. On the Phone Verification page, enter the phone number AWS can use for an auto-mated authentication call. After you choose Call Me Now, enter the PIN that will be displayed in the browser page on your phone's keypad.

6. One last step: on the Support Plan page, select an AWS support plan. If you're not sure which plan you want, just go with the Basic plan for now. It's free, and you can always upgrade later. You'll learn more about AWS support in Chapter 3, "Getting Support on AWS."

Once you're fully activated, you'll receive another email, this one confirming that your account is ready for you.

Summary

The size and quality of a major cloud provider like AWS means that its customers can often benefit from higher-quality security, availability, and reliability than they could provide locally.

While AWS customers are still responsible for the applications they run in the cloud, they don't need to worry about the underlying physical infrastructure that's managed by AWS.

Much of the attraction of cloud computing is the ability to pay for only the services you use, and only as you use them. This allows the provisioning of sophisticated applications with virtually no capital expenses (capex). You will, of course, need to assess and manage the operating expenses (opex).

Server virtualization makes it possible to more densely pack software operations on physical hardware, potentially driving down the costs and improving the time-to-deployment of compute workloads. An even more "virtualized" kind of virtualization is serverless computing, where customers are aware their code and the network events that trigger it.

Cloud-optimized workloads are designed to take advantage of the scalability and elasticity of cloud platforms.

Exam Essentials

Understand how a large and geographically dispersed infrastructure improves service quality. The sheer scale and geographic redundancy of the physical compute and networking resources owned by AWS mean that the company is able to guarantee a level of reliability and availability that would be hard to reproduce in any other environment.

Understand how metered, pay-per-use pricing makes for flexible compute options. Access to cloud infrastructure—sometimes for pennies per hour—makes it possible to experiment, sandbox, and regularly reassess and update application stacks.

Understand that cloud services come on a wide range of forms. IaaS gives you near-full control over virtualized hardware resources, closely emulating the way you would administrate actual physical servers. PaaS products abstract the underlying infrastructure, providing a simplified interface for you to add your application code. SaaS products provide services over a public network directly to end users.

Understand how serverless computing can be both cheap and efficient. Serverless services like AWS Lambda allow you access to AWS compute power for up to 15 minutes for a single function. This lets you operate code in response to real-time event triggers.

Understand how scalability allows applications to grow to meet need. A cloud-optimized application allows for automated provisioning of server instances that are designed from scratch to perform a needed compute function within an appropriate network environment.

Understand how elasticity matches compute power to both rising and falling demand. The scaling services of a cloud provider—like AWS Auto Scaling—should be configured to force compliance with your budget and application needs. You set the upper and lower limits, and the scaler handles the startups and shutdowns to optimize operations in between those limits.

Review Questions

1. Which of the following does not contribute significantly to the operational value of a large cloud provider like AWS?

   A. Multiregional presence

   B. Highly experienced teams of security engineers

   C. Deep experience in the retail sphere

   D. Metered, pay-per-use pricing

2. Which of the following are signs of a highly available application? (Select TWO.)

   A. A failure in one geographic region will trigger an automatic failover to resources in a different region.

   B. Applications are protected behind multiple layers of security.

   C. Virtualized hypervisor-driven systems are deployed as mandated by company policy.

   D. Spikes in user demand are met through automatically increasing resources.

3. How does the metered payment model make many benefits of cloud computing possible? (Select TWO.)

   A. Greater application security is now possible.

   B. Experiments with multiple configuration options are now cost-effective.

   C. Applications are now highly scalable.

   D. Full-stack applications are possible without the need to invest in capital expenses.

4. Which of the following are direct benefits of server virtualization? (Select TWO.)

   A. Fast resource provisioning and launching

   B. Efficient (high-density) use of resources

   C. Greater application security

   D. Elastic application designs

5. What is a hypervisor?

   A. Hardware device used to provide an interface between storage and compute modules

   B. Hardware device used to provide an interface between networking and compute modules

   C. Software used to log and monitor virtualized operations

   D. Software used to administrate virtualized resources run on physical infrastructure

6. Which of the following best describes server virtualization?

    A. "Sharding" data from multiple sources into a single virtual data store

    B. Logically partitioning physical compute and storage devices into multiple smaller virtual devices

    C. Aggregating physical resources spread over multiple physical devices into a single virtual device

    D. Abstracting the complexity of physical infrastructure behind a simple web interface

7. Which of the following best describes Infrastructure as a Service products?

    A. Services that hide infrastructure complexity behind a simple interface

    B. Services that provide a service to end users through a public network

    C. Services that give you direct control over underlying compute and storage resources

    D. Platforms that allow developers to run their code over short periods on cloud servers

8. Which of the following best describes Platform as a Service products?

    A. Services that hide infrastructure complexity behind a simple interface

    B. Platforms that allow developers to run their code over short periods on cloud servers

    C. Services that give you direct control over underlying compute and storage resources

    D. Services that provide a service to end users through a public network

9. Which of the following best describes Software as a Service products?

    A. Services that give you direct control over underlying compute and storage resources

    B. Services that provide a service to end users through a public network

    C. Services that hide infrastructure complexity behind a simple interface

    D. Platforms that allow developers to run their code over short periods on cloud servers

10. Which of the following best describes scalability?

    A. The ability of an application to automatically add preconfigured compute resources to meet increasing demand

    B. The ability of an application to increase or decrease compute resources to match changing demand

    C. The ability to more densely pack virtualized resources onto a single physical server

    D. The ability to bill resource usage using a pay-per-user model

11. Which of the following best describes elasticity?

   A. The ability to more densely pack virtualized resources onto a single physical server

   B. The ability to bill resource usage using a pay-per-user model

   C. The ability of an application to increase or decrease compute resources to match changing demand

   D. The ability of an application to automatically add preconfigured compute resources to meet increasing demand

12. Which of the following characteristics most help AWS provide such scalable services? (Select TWO.)

   A. The enormous number of servers it operates

   B. The value of its capitalized assets

   C. Its geographic reach

   D. Its highly automated infrastructure administration systems

Chapter

2

Understanding Your AWS Account

THE AWS CERTIFIED CLOUD PRACTITIONER EXAM OBJECTIVES COVERED IN THIS CHAPTER MAY INCLUDE, BUT ARE NOT LIMITED TO, THE FOLLOWING:

Domain 4: Billing and Pricing

✓ **4.1 Compare and contrast the various pricing models for AWS**

✓ **4.2 Recognize the various account structures in relation to AWS billing and pricing**

✓ **4.3 Identify resources available for billing support**

Introduction

Amazon Web Services is a really big place. Each account has access to more than 100 distinct services, which can each be deployed in hundreds or even thousands of permutations. Anyone with the right account credentials can—legitimately or otherwise—launch new service instances without anyone else knowing. For the most part, resources running within one AWS Region will be invisible to you when you've got any one of the nearly 20 other regions selected in your console.

With all that going on all the time, there are going to be two account-level things you want to be clear about:

- What's it all going to cost you? Because cloud services are scalable, there's virtually no limit to how much of them you can purchase, or to how much they can cost you. If something isn't going according to plan, you'll want to know what it is and how to pull its plug as soon as possible.

- Who's running the show? In other words, who has the authority to make the big decisions about firing up and shutting down account resources? In addition to the fact that those decisions will have significant financial implications, they'll also define your organization's public presence.

Maintaining control over access to administration resources will be the primary focus of Chapter 5, "Securing Your AWS Resources." But monitoring and keeping a lid on costs is what you're going to learn about here. What you'll see will include the following:

- Taking advantage of the AWS Free Tier

- Understanding how AWS services are priced and how to model pricing for complicated combinations (or stacks) of resources

- Understanding the usage limits AWS places on some services and how to raise those limits

- Keeping on top of your actual account costs

The Free Tier

AWS figures that the more comfortable you feel working with its services, the more likely you'll eventually start moving serious workloads to its cloud. So, AWS offers a generous Free Tier for the first 12 months after opening a new account. Under the Free Tier, you can freely experiment with light versions of most AWS services without being billed.

How Does the Free Tier Work?

It's remarkable how much you can do with the Free Tier. Since, for instance, you're allowed to run a t2.micro Elastic Cloud Compute (EC2) instance—powered by either Linux or Windows—for up to 750 hours per month, you can effectively keep a low-demand website going without interruption for your full first year. In fact, you'd be surprised how much you can get done with such a resource.

You don't have to consume those 750 Free Tier EC2 hours by running a single instance 24/7. You could instead choose to experiment with something more complex, such as a high-availability deployment involving running two or four concurrent instances for a few hours to test resilient failover architectures. As long as the total monthly hours of run time don't exceed 750, your credit card won't be billed.

Similarly, you can run lightweight relational database workloads under Amazon's Relational Database Service (RDS) in any combination for up to 750 hours per month, and you can store up to 5 GB of data within Simple Storage Service (S3) buckets.

Should you actually go over your limit at any point, you'll be billed for the excess amount at normal AWS billing rates. Just to give you an idea what that might cost in real terms, Free Tier–eligible t2.micro instances (using Linux) on EC2 running in the US East region for, say, 850 hours through a single month would cost you only $1.16 USD at current rates ($0.0116/hour). That's because you would be billed only for the hours your usage exceeded the Free Tier maximum.

Tracking Your Free Tier Usage

Of course, accidentally leaving AWS resources running—whether you're enjoying the Free Tier or not—can cost you much more than $1.16. Firing up a synchronously replicated RDS database instance to test your new website backend and then forgetting all about it can easily cost you thousands of dollars a month. You definitely want to keep an eye or two on your account.

You'll learn a lot more about dealing with this problem later in this chapter when we talk about cost management. But right now, we'll show you two ways to monitor your usage specifically in relation to your Free Tier limits.

The first approach involves nothing more than waiting for messages to arrive in your email box. By default, Free Tier–related email alerts are automatically sent whenever account activity approaches or has passed Free Tier limits. Besides turning them off from the Preferences page in the Billing Dashboard in the AWS Management Console, the only thing you can do about alerts is to choose a different email address. You can access the Billing Dashboard from the account drop-down menu that's illustrated in Figure 2.1.

FIGURE 2.1   The account drop-down menu that includes a link to your Billing Dashboard

The second tracking tool will appear toward the bottom of the Billing Dashboard for any account that's still Free Tier–eligible. Figure 2.2 shows you what such a usage tracking tool will look like. The thirstiest services on this account aren't all that active just yet, but you can see how Amazon S3 *storage* (currently at 0.06 percent) is only one of the usage metrics that are tracked; Put and Get requests into and out of S3 buckets also have their own limits.

FIGURE 2.2   The Free Tier usage tracking table displaying an account's busiest AWS services

Top Free Tier Services by Usage		View all
Service	Free Tier usage limit	Month-to-date usage
Amazon Simple Storage Service	2,000 Put Requests of Amazon S3	33.15% (663.00/2,000 Requests)
Amazon Simple Storage Service	20,000 Get Requests of Amazon S3	1.24% (249.00/20,000 Requests)
Amazon Simple Storage Service	5 GB of Amazon S3 standard storage	0.06% (0.00/5 GB-Mo)
Amazon Elastic Compute Cloud	2 million I/Os of Amazon Elastic Block Storage(with EBS Magnetic)	0.02% (374.00/2,000,000 I/O)
Amazon Elastic Compute Cloud	750 hours of Amazon EC2 Linux t2.micro instance usage	0.01% (0.04/750 Hrs)

Choosing the View All button will take you to a page displaying all current Free Tier usage. Even if you haven't been doing much with your account yet, you might be surprised how much is already going on behind the scenes. Don't worry, though: it's just a few monitoring notifications being sent back and forth.

Until you actively launch some services, there won't be anything happening that will actually generate billable events.

What's Available Under the Free Tier?

There are actually two kinds of free services:

- Light implementations of most AWS services that are available through the first 12 months of a new AWS account
- Light usage of certain AWS services that are always available—even after your initial 12 months are up

You can get a detailed rundown of everything that's available for both classes at https://aws.amazon.com/free. To give you some sense of what's out there, the following are some highlights.

The 12-Month Free Tier

We've already discussed running low-powered EC2 and RDS instances and using 5 GB of S3 storage capacity under the Free Tier. Other available free service features include the following:

- 30 GB of either magnetic or solid-state drive (SSD) volumes from Amazon Elastic Block Storage (EBS). EBS volumes are usually used as the primary data drives for EC2 instances. For context, 8 GB is normally more than enough space to run the Linux OS driving a busy web server.
- 500 MB/month of free storage on the Amazon Elastic Container Registry (ECR). ECR is a service for storing and managing Docker container images. 500 MB is enough space to satisfy the needs of nearly any use case.
- 50 GB of outbound data transfers and 2 million HTTP or HTTPS requests for Amazon CloudFront distributions. (These are annual rather than monthly amounts.) CloudFront is Amazon's content delivery network that you can use to serve cached copies of your content to remote users at low latency rates.
- One million API calls/month on Amazon API Gateway. API Gateway is a tool for managing your organization's application programming interfaces (APIs). APIs allow users and applications to connect with mobile and web-based resources.

Permanently Free Services

Some AWS services can be useful even when consumed at levels so low that they don't need to be billed. In such cases, AWS makes them available at those low levels over any time span. These use cases include the following:

- 10 custom monitoring metrics and 10 alarms on Amazon CloudWatch active at any given time. You use CloudWatch either directly or in combination with other tools to track resource performance and costs.

- 10 GB of data retrievals from Amazon Glacier per month. Glacier is a low-cost storage service that's ideal for long-term storage where you're not likely to require quick access to your data.

- 62,000 outbound email messages per month using Amazon Simple Email Service (SES). SES is an enterprise-scale email service geared to organizations that regularly send large volumes of emails.

- One million requests and 3.2 million seconds of compute time for AWS Lambda functions. Lambda lets you run code in response to network-based triggers without having to worry about provisioning any underlying server infrastructure.

One more note on the Free Tier: AWS Free Tier benefits do not apply to resources launched in the GovCloud (US) region or through an AWS Organizations member account. (You'll learn more about AWS Organizations later in this chapter.)

Product Pricing

As you plan, launch, and then manage your AWS deployments, keeping costs within your organization's budget is going to demand a lot of your attention. You'll need to understand how AWS bills for each of the services you're considering, and you'll need to know how to quickly get your hands on accurate pricing information.

Finding AWS Pricing Documentation

We'll get to the understanding part soon enough, but we can definitely help you with the accurate pricing information right now. Each AWS service has its own web page dedicated to pricing. For example, bearing in mind that the URL for an introductory overview of the S3 service is https://aws.amazon.com/s3, to get to the pricing page, you simply add a slash and the word pricing, like this: https://aws.amazon.com/s3/pricing.

Once on the page, you'll find easy-to-read tables displaying pricing levels per hour, month, or some other measured unit that's appropriate to the service. Pricing can vary between AWS Regions, so there's usually some kind of drop-down menu to display only the details you need to see.

As an example, the S3 page lists the cost of usage measured by metrics such as storage, requests, data transfers, and cross-region replication. You'll learn more about how those work in Chapter 8, "The Core Storage Services," but here we're focusing on billing issues. Selecting a different AWS Region from the drop-down will sometimes display significant differences across the global AWS infrastructure. Note the costs of the various storage tiers and—when applicable—how those rates change at various volume levels like 0–50 TB/month or 50–500 TB/month. You will often find yourself paying less for each unit of what AWS produces that you consume when you "buy in bulk."

Similarly, the EC2 pricing page (https://aws.amazon.com/ec2/pricing) lets you choose between on-demand, spot, reserve instances, and dedicated hosts pricing (you'll get the lowdown on those in Chapter 7, "The Core Compute Services"). You'll also need to select the operating system you'll be using with your instance. Microsoft Windows, Red Hat Enterprise Linux, and SUSE Linux Enterprise Server licensing costs are included in the hourly EC2 rates. With those choices made, you'll be shown the per-hour cost for each instance type.

AWS is pretty good about updating its pricing pages, which, considering how often the prices change, is important. Why not work through Exercise 2.1 to get a feel for figuring out the costs of an EC2 instance?

EXERCISE 2.1

Calculate Monthly Costs for an EC2 Instance

Even though you may not yet fully understand EC2 instances—that'll come in Chapter 7— try using the EC2 pricing page to figure out how much it would cost you to run an on-demand compute-optimized c5.18xlarge instance type with a 20 GB EBS storage volume in the US East region. Compare the costs of both Linux and Windows instances:

1. Open the EC2 pricing page (https://aws.amazon.com/ec2/pricing), and select See On-Demand Pricing.

2. Select the US East (N. Virginia) region.

3. Select the Linux tab.

4. Scroll down the list until you get to the c5.18xlarge line. Note the Per Hour value.

5. Multiply that value by 750, which is (more or less) the number of hours in a month.

6. Open the EBS pricing page (https://aws.amazon.com/ebs/pricing), and select the US East (N. Virginia) region.

7. Find the Amazon EBS General Purpose SSD line, and note the Per GB-Month value.

8. Multiply that value by 20 (the desired size of your storage volume), and add that to the EC2 instance type value.

9. Repeat steps 1–8, but select the Windows tab in step 3.

10. Compare the results.

Working with Online Calculators

There's another way to visualize the true cost of a complicated multilevel deployment. If you just had to enter all the configuration parameters you'd need to get your workload running in AWS, and an easy-to-read itemized cost sheet came out the other end, modeling alternate stack profiles would be a breeze.

AWS provides two regularly updated modeling tools: the Simple Monthly Calculator to help you understand what running any combination of AWS resources will cost you, and the Total Cost of Ownership Calculator to closely compare what you're currently paying for on-premises servers with what the same workload would cost on AWS.

AWS Simple Monthly Calculator

You'll find the Simple Monthly Calculator on the internet at http://calculator .s3.amazonaws.com/index.html. Down the left side of the page are tabs for each of the AWS services for which the calculator works. All the basics are covered. When you choose a tab, you'll find forms where you can input data representing the usage you plan for that service.

The default EC2, for example, offers input fields for EC2 instances. You start by choosing the green + button to add a new row, and then enter the number of instances you'll be running, the estimated proportion of time your instance will be running, the instance type (choosing inside the field will display a list of available types), and the billing model. The monthly cost for that instance will appear to the right, while the running total monthly amount will be updated in the Estimate tab at the top of the page.

Don't forget that, as you saw on the AWS pricing documentation pages a bit earlier, you can select an AWS Region from the drop-down menu near the top of the page. You can also select or deselect the Free Usage Tier option to tailor results to the current status of your account—the calculator isn't connected to and doesn't get any data from your account.

Down the column on the right side of the page is a small collection of templates for common deployment scenarios. The Disaster Recovery And Backup sample, for instance, estimates costs for running Linux database servers on EC2 in four geographically distinct regions and maintaining 500 GB of storage in Amazon S3. The stack would seem to be intended to maintain regular copies of database and object storage resources in a way that, in an emergency, can be quickly and reliably restored to a production deployment.

When you've entered data for all the fields on all the service pages necessary to represent your plans, you can choose the Estimate tab at the top, and you'll be shown a fully itemized breakdown of the estimated monthly cost of your resource stack. Choosing the Export To CSV button will allow you to download a comma-separated values spreadsheet containing your profile data. You can use this to show colleagues and clients or to compare this particular model with alternate iterations. The Save And Share button will provide you with a web address pointing to a permanent copy of your results. You can use this to share with those same colleagues and clients.

Generate your own resource stack estimate by completing Exercise 2.2.

EXERCISE 2.2

Build a Deployment Cost Estimate Using the AWS Simple Monthly Calculator

1. Open the calculator page at http://calculator.s3.amazonaws.com/index.html.

2. Deselect the Free Usage Tier check box at the top.

3. Choose the US West (Oregon) region from the drop-down menu.

---

4. With the Amazon EC2 tab on the left selected, choose the green + button to add a new row to the Compute: Amazon EC2 Instances.

5. Type a description in the Description field (perhaps something like **WordPress web server**).

6. Enter **2** in the Instances field to tell the calculator that you'll be running two identical instances.

7. Choose the Usage drop-down and select Hours/Month, and then enter **750** as the value. This means you'll be running the servers 24/7 through the entire month.

8. Choose in the Type field, and select the Linux radio button at the top and then c5.large in the list below. You might need to scroll down a bit to get to it. Choose Close And Save.

9. Choose in the Billing Option field, and select 3 Yr No Upfront Reserved to set the way you'll be paying. Choose Close And Save. You should see your Monthly cost at about $26.28.

10. Choose the Add New Row button in the Storage: Amazon EBS Volumes row, enter **2** for Volumes, and leave the General Purpose SSD default value as it is. Enter **100 GB** for Storage (that will be the size of the EBS volume you'll have attached to each instance).

11. Feel free to add other features either on the EC2 page or on any other page. Then choose the Estimate tab at the top and view your cost breakdown by maximizing each item. When you're done, export the estimate to a CSV file, and then choose Save And Share to get a shareable URL.

Figure 2.3 shows the calculator's spreadsheet output.

FIGURE 2.3   The output of a calculator profile in CSV format

	A	B	C	D	E
1	**Your Estimate**				
2	**Service Type**	Components	Region	Component Price	Service Price
3	Amazon EC2 Service (US West (Oregon))				$36.28
4		Compute:	US West (Oregon)	$26.28	
5		EBS Volumes:	US West (Oregon)	$10	
6		EBS IOPS:	US West (Oregon)	$0	
7		Reserved Instances (One-time Fee):	US West (Oregon)	$0	
8	AWS Support (Basic)				$0
9		Support for all AWS services:		$0	
10			Total Monthly Payment:		$36.28

AWS Total Cost of Ownership Calculator

You can get things going by pointing your browser to https://aws.amazon.com/tco-calculator and then choosing the Launch The TCO Calculator button on the intro page. The idea is that you enter the configuration specifications of your current on-premises or colocation deployment, and the calculator will produce a detailed, itemized estimate of what that workload is costing you in its current location and what it would cost on AWS.

A simple configuration we recently ran as an illustration compared a deployment of 10 physical application servers and two physical database servers along with 20 TB of storage with its AWS equivalent. The calculator's 25-page PDF report included a three-year total cost of ownership price tag for AWS of $310,778 against the equivalent on-premises cost of $554,715. Table 2.1 shows the top-level breakdown.

TABLE 2.1   AWS TCO Calculator Output from a Sample Deployment Configuration

	On-premises	AWS
Server	$373,457	$229,848
Storage	$78,070	$18,633
Network	$96,303	$37,525
IT-Labor	$6,885	$24,772
Total	$554,715	$310,778

We are not convinced that the Amazon-supplied on-premises IT-Labor cost isn't a calculation mistake, by the way. If you've ever worked with data centers of about that size, then you'll know that labor costs were higher by orders of magnitude.

What did all those numbers represent? The calculator incorporates estimates of capital infrastructure expenses including the amortized costs of servers, networking hardware, electricity, cooling, and maintenance, as well as the costs of an AWS business support plan.

The report includes descriptions of the calculator's methodology and assumptions along with some frequently asked questions. Exercise 2.3 will take you through your own use of the calculator.

EXERCISE 2.3

Compare the On-Premises Costs of Running Your Application with AWS Costs

1. Select a currency and either On-Premises or Colocation to describe who is currently hosting your servers.

2. Select the AWS Region that would make the most sense for your cloud deployment and then whether you're currently running your workload on physical severs or on virtual machines (like VMware virtual machines or Docker containers, which, of course, are themselves running on physical machines).

3. Enter the hardware configuration of your nondatabase servers in the Servers row, and then choose Add Row to display a second row where you can enter your database

---

servers' configuration, including the database engine (MySQL, Oracle, SQL Server, etc.) you're running.

4. Enter the type and amount of data storage you're currently using. When you're done, choose the Calculate TCO button.

5. Read through the output and, if you like, choose the Download Report button to get a permanent copy. You'll have to provide your personal information so AWS and its partners can contact you. This isn't necessarily a bad thing, because you'll likely end up getting a serious conversation with a solutions architect out of the deal.

Service Limits

The total scope of the AWS cloud is vast. It's hard to even visualize just how much compute and storage capacity is available for its customers. And the scalability of its design means that there shouldn't be a practical ceiling on how much infrastructure any customer is able to access on demand.

Nevertheless, for various reasons, AWS imposes limits on the scope of resources you can use. That's why if you don't properly plan ahead, your service requests might sometimes push your share of AWS resources past your account limit and fail.

So, for instance, you're allowed to run only 20 on-demand and 20 reserved instances of the EC2 m5.large instance type at any one time within a single AWS Region. Other instance types are limited to similar maximums. This would seem to reflect Amazon's desire to ensure that all classes of resources should be reliably available to meet new demand and not all held by a few large customers. But it can also protect customers from having automated processes accidentally (or maliciously) launch resources that generate unsustainable costs.

Most service limits are *soft* (or adjustable)—meaning that you can manually request that AWS increase a limit for your account. However, some limits are hard and can't be increased no matter how long you threaten to hold your breath.

You can find the complete and up-to-date list of service limits on this AWS documentation page:

https://docs.aws.amazon.com/general/latest/gr/aws_service_limits.html

Billing and Cost Management

All things considered, the health of your organization's finances and operations can depend a great deal on the ins and outs of your AWS account. So, besides the performance of your infrastructure resources like EC2 instances, you'll want to keep a close watch on the account itself. The various tools found in your Billing Dashboard can help with this account oversight. The Dashboard itself, as you saw earlier, is accessible through the account drop-down menu at the top of the AWS Management Console.

The AWS Billing Dashboard

The main Billing & Cost Management Dashboard contains a helpful visual Spend Summary that displays your costs from the previous and current months so far, along with a forecast of the costs you'll likely face through the end of the month. There's also a Month-to-Date Spend By Service display from which choosing the Bill Details button will take you to an itemized breakdown of your current spending.

The Billing Dashboard also includes links to pages where you can set payment methods and enter your organization's tax information. The Payment History link provides records of your previous transactions.

All of this is pretty standard account administration stuff. From here, though, you're going to learn how to protect and optimize your account spend through budgets and monitoring.

AWS Budgets

An AWS budget is a tool for tracking a specified set of events so that when a preset threshold is approached or passed, an alert—perhaps an email—is triggered. You can create one of three budget types:

- Cost budget to monitor costs being incurred against your account
- Usage budget to track particular categories of resource consumption
- Reservation budget to help you understand the status of any active EC2, RDS, Redshift, or Elasticache reserve instances you might have

The budget setup process has two parts:

1. Set the terms of your budget—meaning, what it is that you're tracking.
2. Define how and when you want alerts sent.

Exercise 2.4 will guide you through the process of creating a budget on your account.

EXERCISE 2.4

Create a Cost Budget to Track Spending

In this exercise, you'll configure a budget that will alert you by email whenever your monthly account spend threatens to exceed your limit. This can be particularly useful to protect your account against an attack that launches unauthorized resources:

1. While logged into your account as the root user, choose Create Budget on the Budgets page and select Cost Budget.

2. Give your budget a name, leave Period at Monthly, and enter a Budgeted amount that's a bit higher than the maximum monthly spend you want to permit your account. You can leave the rest of the settings at their defaults, which will track all account costs. Choose Configure Alerts.

---

3. Leave the Alert Based On value as Actual Costs, and add a percentage of **80%** to the % Of Budgeted Amount field. This will trigger the alert when your actual monthly spend hits 80 percent of your maximum.

4. Enter at least one email contact, and then choose Confirm Budget. Review the settings and, if you're happy, choose Create.

Monitoring Your Costs

In-depth deployment planning and properly configured budgets are important tools, but they're not enough. Just like smart security professionals will build layers of firewalls, permissions, and physical controls around their application infrastructure, account administrators will also watch events from multiple perspectives. Ongoing monitoring is a key part of that mix, and that means getting to know Amazon's Cost Explorer and its cost and usage reports.

Cost Explorer

Cost Explorer (https://aws.amazon.com/aws-cost-management/aws-cost-explorer) lets you build graphs to visualize your account's historical and current costs. If you're in a hurry, you can select one of the preconfigured views provided by the service (including spending over the most recent three months by service).

Alternatively, you can launch the Cost Explorer tool to open a heavily customizable view that lets you filter account cost events by date, region, Availability Zone, instance type, platform (Linux, Windows, and so on), and others. CSV-formatted files based on customized views can also be downloaded.

You can save report views to ensure they'll be quickly available whenever you want to drop in for this particular combination of information.

Cost and Usage Reports

Cost and usage reports are (right now, at least) accessed from the Reports link on the Billing Dashboard. You can configure reports to be created that include the full range of activity on your account, including what resources you have running and how much they're costing you. You can control for the level of detail and enable support for Redshift and/or Amazon QuickSight (a managed, pay-per-user business intelligence tool) to handle the visualization and analysis of what can become significant volumes of data.

The reports, once generated at preset intervals, are compressed, saved using the CSV format, and sent to an S3 bucket you've already created. From there, it's up to you to configure Redshift or QuickSight to access and process the data as it's generated.

Cost Allocation Tags

Tags are metadata identification elements representing a resource and its actions. Tags can be used to organize and track your resources, allowing you to visualize and better understand how resources are being used. Just to confuse things, however, AWS offers two distinct kinds of tags that actually have nothing to do with each other.

Resource tags   Resource tags are often used in busy accounts to help administrators quickly identify the purpose and owner of a particular running resource. With hundreds of instances, security groups, buckets, and service definitions scattered through your account, being able to instantly understand what each one is supposed to do will make it a lot easier for you to know how you should manage it.

Cost allocation tags   Cost tags are only meant to interact with billing tools and won't show up in the context of any other AWS resource or process. Like resource tags, cost allocation tags help you efficiently identify your resources, but only for the purpose of tracking your account spending.

You'll learn more about resource tags in Chapter 6, "Working with Your AWS Resources." For now, you should simply be aware of the role that cost allocation tags play in your cost planning. You should also know that there are two kinds of cost allocation tags: AWS-generated cost allocation tags, which AWS automatically generates when resources are created, and user-defined cost allocation tags.

AWS Organizations

Formerly known as Consolidated Billing, AWS Organizations allows you to centralize the administration of multiple AWS accounts owned or controlled by a single company. This can make a lot of sense, since many companies will own more than one account—or might share AWS resources with vendors and clients. Being able to control the allocation of resource permissions, security, and spending from a single pane of glass is a big deal. It's also a convenient way to manage payments.

Just remember that, once accounts are linked, maintaining a secure profile and following best practices becomes even more critical than for stand-alone accounts. After all, a security breach of any one linked account runs the risk of spreading the vulnerability to everything running in *any* of your accounts.

Summary

The Free Tier offers new accounts a full year of free access to light configurations of most AWS services. It's meant as an opportunity to experiment and learn how your organization's needs can be met in the cloud. You can track how close you are to "outspending" your Free Tier allowance from the Billing Dashboard.

You can find pricing information online by adding /pricing to the URL of an AWS service. aws.amazon.com/s3/, for instance, would become aws.amazon.com/s3/pricing. It's important to understand both the billing rates and the specific metrics used to measure them.

The AWS Simple Monthly Calculator and AWS Total Cost of Ownership Calculator let you anticipate real-world usage costs for AWS deployments and (in the case of the TCO calculator) compare your spend with its on-premises equivalent.

Resource requests will sometimes be refused (and launches will fail) if your request would have pushed your consumption past a service limit.

The AWS Billing Dashboard is the hub for accessing account administration, payment and tax status management, cost monitoring, and cost control.

Exam Essentials

Understand the value of the 12-month Free Tier.   The Free Tier lets you run light services such as the t2.micro EC2 instance type and a 30 GB SSH EBS volume. The goal is to get you comfortable with the AWS environment so you can learn how it can be used to host your applications.

Understand the value of permanent Free Tier services.   Low-volume consumption includes the retrieval of up to 10 GB of stored objects from Glacier or 62,000 outbound emails through Amazon SES. The goal is to give you the opportunity to launch proof-of-concept deployments.

Know how to access Amazon's resource pricing online documentation.   To accurately calculate the true costs of an AWS deployment, you must understand the pricing for the particular level of resource you launch within a particular AWS Region. Each service resource (like an EC2 instance) is billed by metrics unique to its characteristics.

Use the AWS Simple Monthly Calculator to accurately model multitiered application stack pricing.   Pricing for all variations of the core AWS services is prebuilt into the calculator, allowing you to model pricing for multiple resource configurations.

Use the AWS Total Cost of Ownership Calculator to compare on-premises with AWS deployment costs.   You can conveniently compare apples to apples—capital expenses for on-premises versus operating expenses for cloud—to know whether the AWS cloud is really right for your workload.

Understand how your use of AWS services is limited by default.   Access to all service resources is restricted by default limits. In many cases, you can manually request limit increases from AWS support.

Understand the value of cost management tools for avoiding costly cloud overspends.   AWS budgets can be configured to send alerts when your resource consumption approaches or passes a preset limit. Cost Explorer provides visualizations to more easily monitor historical and current costs. Cost and usage reports can send in-depth and ongoing CSV-formatted data to Redshift or QuickSight for analysis. You can use cost allocation tags to more effectively track and manage the source of account costs. The security and operations of multiple AWS accounts controlled by a single company can be managed through AWS Organizations.

Review Questions

1. Which of the following EC2 services can be used without charge under the Free Tier?

   A. Any single EC2 instance type as long as it runs for less than one hour per day

   B. Any single EC2 instance type as long as it runs for less than 75 hours per month

   C. A single t2.micro EC2 instance type instance for 750 hours per month

   D. t2.micro EC2 instance type instances for a total of 750 hours per month

2. You want to experiment with deploying a web server on an EC2 instance. Which two of the following resources can you include to make that work while remaining within the Free Tier? (Select TWO.)

   A. A 5 GB bucket on S3

   B. A t2.micro instance type EC2 instance

   C. A 30 GB solid-state Elastic Block Store (EBS) drive

   D. Two 20 GB solid-state Elastic Block Store (EBS) drives

3. Which of the following usage will always be cost-free even after your account's Free Tier has expired? (Select TWO.)

   A. One million API calls/month on Amazon API Gateway

   B. 10 GB of data retrievals from Amazon Glacier per month

   C. 500 MB/month of free storage on the Amazon Elastic Container Registry (ECR)

   D. 10 custom monitoring metrics and 10 alarms on Amazon CloudWatch

4. Which of the following tools are available to ensure you won't accidentally run past your Free Tier limit and incur unwanted costs? (Select TWO.)

   A. Automated email alerts when activity approaches the Free Tier limits

   B. The Top Free Tier Services by Usage section on the Billing & Cost Management Dashboard

   C. Billing & Cost Management section on the Top Free Tier Services Dashboard

   D. The Billing Preferences Dashboard

5. Which of the following is likely to be an accurate source of AWS pricing information?

   A. Wikipedia pages relating to a particular service

   B. The AWS Command Line Interface (AWS CLI)

   C. AWS online documentation relating to a particular service

   D. The AWS Total Cost of Ownership Calculator

6. Which of the following will probably not affect the pricing for an AWS service?

   A. Requests for raising the available service limit

   B. AWS Region

   C. The volume of data saved to an S3 bucket

   D. The volume of data egress from an Amazon Glacier vault

7. Which of the following is a limitation of the AWS Simple Monthly Calculator?

   A. You can calculate resource use for only one service at a time.

   B. Not all AWS services are included.

   C. The pricing is seldom updated and doesn't accurately reflect current pricing.

   D. You're not able to specify specific configuration parameters.

8. Which of the following Simple Monthly Calculator selections will likely have an impact on most other configuration choices on the page? (Select TWO.)

   A. Calculate By Month Or Year

   B. Include Multiple Organizations

   C. Free Usage Tier

   D. Choose Region

9. Which of the following is not an included parameter in the AWS Total Cost of Ownership Calculator?

   A. The tax implications of a cloud deployment

   B. Labor costs of an on-premises deployment

   C. Networking costs of an on-premises deployment

   D. Electricity costs of an on-premises deployment

10. Which of the following AWS Total Cost of Ownership Calculator parameters is likely to have the greatest impact on cost?

    A. Currency

    B. AWS Region

    C. Guest OS

    D. Number of servers

11. Which of the following AWS documentation URLs points to the page containing an up-to-date list of service limits?

    A. https://docs.aws.amazon.com/general/latest/gr/limits.html

    B. https://docs.aws.amazon.com/general/latest/gr/aws_service_limits.html

    C. https://aws.amazon.com/general/latest/gr/aws_service_limits.html

    D. https://docs.aws.amazon.com/latest/gr/aws_service_limits.html

12. Which of the following best describes one possible reason for AWS service limits?

    A. To prevent individual customers from accidentally launching a crippling level of resource consumption

    B. To more equally distribute available resources between customers from different regions

    C. To allow customers to more gradually increase their deployments

    D. Because there are logical limits to the ability of AWS resources to scale upward

13. Is it always possible to request service limit increases from AWS?

    A. Yes. All service limits can be increased.

    B. No. A limit can never be increased.

    C. Service limits are defaults. They can be increased or decreased on demand.

    D. No. Some service limits are hard.

14. Which is the best place to get a quick summary of this month's spend for your account?

    A. Budgets

    B. Cost Explorer

    C. Cost and usage reports

    D. Billing & Cost Management Dashboard

15. What is the main goal for creating a Usage budget type (in AWS Budgets)?

    A. To correlate usage per unit cost to understand your account cost efficiency

    B. To track the status of any active reserved instances on your account

    C. To track particular categories of resource consumption

    D. To monitor costs being incurred against your account

16. Which of the following is not a setting you can configure in a Cost budget?

    A. Period (monthly, quarterly, etc.)

    B. Instance type

    C. Start and stop dates

    D. Owner (username of resource owner)

17. What is the main difference between the goals of Cost Explorer and of cost and usage reports?

    A. Cost Explorer displays visualizations of high-level historical and current account costs, while cost and usage reports generate granular usage reports in CSV format.

    B. Cost and usage reports display visualizations of high-level historical and current account costs, while Cost Explorer generates granular usage reports in CSV format.

    C. Cost Explorer lets you set alerts that are triggered by billing events, while cost and usage reports help you visualize system events.

    D. Cost and usage reports are meant to alert you to malicious intrusions, while Cost Explorer displays visualizations of high-level historical and current account costs.

18. What is the purpose of cost allocation tags?

    A. To associate spend limits to automatically trigger resource shutdowns when necessary

    B. To help you identify the purpose and owner of a particular running resource to better understand and control deployments

    C. To help you identify resources for the purpose of tracking your account spending

    D. To visually associate account events with billing periods

19. Which of the following scenarios would be a good use case for AWS Organizations? (Select TWO.)

  A. A single company with multiple AWS accounts that wants a single place to administrate everything

  B. An organization that provides AWS access to large teams of its developers and admins

  C. A company that's integrated some operations with an upstream vendor

  D. A company with two distinct operational units, each with its own accounting system and AWS account

20. Which of these tools lets you design graphs within the browser interface to track your account spending?

  A. Budgets

  B. Cost Explorer

  C. Reports

  D. Consolidating Billing

Chapter

3

Getting Support on AWS

THE AWS CERTIFIED CLOUD PRACTITIONER EXAM OBJECTIVES COVERED IN THIS CHAPTER MAY INCLUDE, BUT ARE NOT LIMITED TO, THE FOLLOWING:

Domain 2: Security

✓ 2.4 Identify resources for security support

Domain 3: Technology

✓ 3.4 Identify resources for technology support

Domain 4: Billing and Pricing

✓ 4.3 Identify resources available for billing support

Introduction

Preparing and securing effective on-premises server workloads can be complicated and stressful. Forget about enterprise workloads: most people probably still get nervous configuring port forwarding on a home router. Of course, much of the anxiety can be blamed on the fact that you're not doing these things every day. Experience breeds confidence.

So when AWS tells you that it has made it easy to provision and launch robust, multilevel application environments, there's no reason not to believe it. You really can do remarkable things with little more than a couple of mouse clicks. But breaking through the experience barrier can be nearly as hard in the cloud as it was for your engineers working years ago in your own data center.

Well, at least you're not on your own. AWS provides layers of support designed to help you as you take your first confusing steps on the platform, learn about the many ways you can use AWS services, and struggle to optimize and secure your increasingly complex resources.

This chapter will show you the kinds of AWS support that are available and how to find them. You'll learn about the four AWS support plans, what professional services are available, what kinds of online documentation and forums are out there, and what Amazon's Trusted Advisor tool is.

Support Plans

When you create a new AWS account, you're required to select a support plan. Depending on the kinds of projects you plan to run with your account, the $15,000/month and up that you'll pay for the Enterprise Support plan might feel a bit excessive, so the free Basic Support plan is always an option while you're getting started. But you should understand how each plan works and, more importantly, when it's time to change to something more appropriate.

Support Plan Pricing

We'll dive deeply into what you get from each plan later, but first, let's see what they cost per month. Table 3.1 shows how the price you'll pay for support will depend on the amount your account is billed for AWS resource usage in a given month.

TABLE 3.1   Monthly Pricing for Amazon Paid Support Plans (All prices in U.S. Dollars)

Developer	Business	Enterprise
Greater of $29 or...	Greater of $100 or...	Greater of $15,000 or...
3% of monthly account usage	10% of usage up to $10,000	10% of AWS usage for the first $0–$150,000
	7% of usage up to $80,000	7% of AWS usage from $150,000–$500,000
	5% of usage up to $250,000	5% of AWS usage from $500,000–$1,000,000
	3% of usage over $250,000	3% of AWS usage over $1,000,000

Let's see what this might look like in a real-world scenario. Suppose a company enrolled its AWS account in the Business Support plan and, in its first full month, consumed $25,000 in AWS resources. That amount might have covered a pair of highly available r5d.24xlarge Elastic Cloud Compute (EC2) Microsoft Windows instances for a Microsoft SharePoint Server 2016 farm and a SQL Server RDS instance on a db.r3.2xlarge multi-AZ database instance.

Since the monthly usage fell within the $10,000 to $80,000 range, it's billed at 7 percent. For $25,000, that'll definitely come out higher than the $100 minimum. In fact, 7 percent of $25,000 is $1750, which is a lot of money. But it might make more sense when you consider the overall amount of money you're spending and the kinds of cost savings and security hardening you can get from having 24/7 email, chat, and phone access to AWS cloud support engineers. Compare it to the cost of hiring a full-time solutions architect who's got that level of experience. Better yet, compare it to the cost of cleaning up after a major—and preventable—data breach wipes out your backend servers and spills your customers' private information all over the internet.

The same considerations would apply to the Enterprise Support plan at the high usage end. The bigger your infrastructure, the more there is that can go wrong, and the more you've got to lose. A large organization spending $750,000 each month should probably protect that investment with a 3 percent support "surcharge" of $22,500. That's probably less than you'd pay for two experienced and competent administrators.

On the other hand, if you're still in the planning stages for your project and you're not yet running expensive resources 24/7, you can get full Developer or Business Support for the minimum rates ($29 or $100 per month, respectively) to help as you ramp up. That can be a great deal.

What kind of support do you get for your money? We'll dive into the details in the coming sections, but Table 3.2 summarizes some of the highlights.

TABLE 3.2   Some Key Benefits of the AWS Support Plans

Basic	Developer	Business	Enterprise
7 Trusted Advisor (TA) checks	7 TA checks	All TA checks	All TA checks
	8 a.m. to 6 p.m. (local time) email access to associate	24/7 email, chat, phone access to engineer	24/7 email, chat, phone access to senior engineer
	General guidance within 24 business hours	General guidance within 24 hours	General guidance within 24 hours
	System impaired help within 12 business hours	System impaired help within 12 hours	System impaired help within 12 hours
		Production system down help within 1 hour	Production system down help within 1 hour
			Business-critical system down help within 15 minutes

In addition, an Enterprise Support plan will provide access to architectural and operational reviews, recommendations, and reporting. You'll find a complete comparison of support plans at this address: https://aws.amazon.com/premiumsupport/compare-plans.

We'll now explore the plan levels one at a time.

The Basic Support Plan

On the Basic plan, you're not paying anything beyond the regular costs of consuming AWS resources. However, for the most part, you're given access only to publicly available documentation, including white papers, tutorials, and support forums. In addition, you'll be able to contact customer service at any time of the day or night for account-related issues (such as bill payment).

You also get limited access to the Trusted Advisor tool. You'll learn much more about Trusted Advisor a bit later in this chapter. Finally, you'll receive alerts concerning interruptions to any AWS services you're currently using through the Personal Health Dashboard (PHD). When relevant, PHD alerts are visible from the top bar on the AWS Management Console page.

The Developer Support Plan

AWS recommends the Developer Support plan for organizations running nonproduction workloads. What's a nonproduction workload? It's a website or application that's still in the development stages and isn't yet handling critical transactions or heavy traffic. In other words, it's a workload that could fail for extended periods of time without bringing about the sudden violent end to all life as we know it.

Why is the Developer plan not ideal for critical applications? Because your direct access to AWS cloud support associates is limited to emails during business hours and to asking their advice on general information about AWS use cases. The associates you contact when you open a support ticket won't be able to discuss specific problems you're having or details about the way your particular application should be deployed. So if you are running infrastructure that simply *must* remain active, then you should seriously consider signing up for a higher support level.

The Business Support Plan

The Business Support plan can meet the needs of many organizations by offering relatively fast and detailed answers to your technical questions. Is your production system down? The Business plan guarantees a response from a cloud support engineer via email, chat, or phone within one hour. Less severe issues can take longer—up to 24 hours for what AWS calls general guidance.

This level of support can include help troubleshooting interoperability between AWS resources and third-party software and operating systems. For an additional fee, you can also get in-depth guidance while you're still in your project's design stage through Infrastructure Event Management.

The Enterprise Support Plan

As you can easily tell from the price tag (starting at $15,000/month), the Enterprise plan is appropriate only for large operations whose scope is global and for whom downtime is simply unthinkable. For example, can you imagine an evening without Netflix (which is, after all, a key AWS customer)?

What does that $15,000 get you? The detail that most stands out is the technical account manager (TAM) who is assigned as a dedicated "guide and advocate" for your account. Your TAM is more than just a technical resource; the TAM becomes closely involved in your deployment, guiding your team through planning, launches, and proactive reviews—all optimized using best practices. As your advocate within AWS, a TAM can open doors and make innovative solutions possible.

Besides a TAM, Enterprise customers get 24/7 access to senior cloud support engineers and a 15-minute response time for business-critical troubleshooting.

More details on all AWS support plans are available at https://aws.amazon.com/premiumsupport.

AWS Professional Services

Support is also available through the AWS Professional Services organization. The Professional Services team provides "offerings"—detailed guides to achieving specific outcomes—and work with third-party consultants from the AWS Partner Network (APN) to actively help you build your deployments. The Professional Services team also makes tech talk webinars, white papers, and blog posts publicly available.

For more details, contact AWS support. You can read more about the program at https://aws.amazon.com/professional-services.

Documentation and Online Help

Even if you decide not to sign up for a paid support plan, there are still many places to look for help—it's just that, for the most part, it'll be *self-help*. In this section, we'll introduce you to some rich collections of written content that are spread across multiple websites and presented in multiple formats. If you're sufficiently determined and motivated, there's little you *won't* be able learn from those sources.

Documentation

AWS provides a lot of documentation resources. By "a lot" we mean there's so much of it that you'll probably never have enough time to read through the whole thing. Instead, you'll be better off learning how to navigate to the page containing the information you're really after and then to the section within that page that answers your specific question.

While the precise layout and organization will change over time, as of this writing the main AWS documentation page can be found at https://docs.aws.amazon.com. There you'll find links to more than 100 AWS services along with tutorials and projects, software development kits (SDKs), toolkits, and general resources.

When you choose one of the service links, you'll usually find more links to individual documentation resources available as HTML (for browser viewing), PDF (offline and printing), Kindle (eBook), and GitHub (MarkDown formatted) versions. You can also access documentation from links on AWS service pages or, of course, through search engine queries.

The pages themselves tend to be nicely divided by topic, each accessible from a table of contents at the top. The instructions include plenty of code snippets and console-based instructions along with outbound links to other pages containing related information. Intuitive navigation within a topic is possible through links in the left panel. As these pages can be rather long, you might want to try searching through the page using part of an error message you're getting or a relevant phrase.

The AWS documentation team does a pretty good job keeping their content organized and updated. One important trick—especially if you've landed on a page based on the results of an internet search engine—is to look for the word *latest* in the web page's URL. This tells you that you're on the page that accurately reflects the most recent version of the software. Here's an example of a page that includes the *latest* identifier:

https://docs.aws.amazon.com/AmazonS3/latest/user-guide/what-is-s3.html

AWS documentation comes in some other forms, as you'll discover in the next sections.

Knowledge Center

The AWS Knowledge Center (https://aws.amazon.com/premiumsupport/knowledge-center) is basically a frequently asked questions (FAQ) page that accidentally swallowed a family pack–sized box of steroids and then walked through the radioactive core of a nuclear power plant wearing wet pajamas. Or, in simpler terms, there's a lot of information collected here.

The Knowledge Center page contains links to nearly 1,000 questions arranged by service, each representing a fairly common problem encountered by real AWS customers. You'll find questions like, "How can I install the AWS CloudFormation helper scripts on Ubuntu or Red Hat Enterprise Linux?" and "What happens when my reserved instance expires?"

Choosing a question will take you to a page with a proposed resolution and more links to related information. If you're ever stuck, it's probably worth taking a quick look to see whether there's a solution in the Knowledge Center.

EXERCISE 3.1

Find Out How to Copy Files from One S3 Bucket to Another

You're looking for the most efficient and reliable way to copy files between S3 buckets. You're not going to actually do that in this exercise, but you will find a guide that will tell you how:

1. Navigate to the Knowledge Center (https://aws.amazon.com/premiumsupport/knowledge-center), and scroll down a little until you can see the link to Amazon S3. When you choose that link, you'll find yourself about halfway down the page at the start of the Amazon Simple Storage Service (Amazon S3) section.

2. You should visually scan through the section looking for an appropriate link, but it might be faster to use your browser's Find tool (Ctrl+F) to search for a related word. Copy might work here.

3. If you see your search term highlighted within the S3 section, you might have struck gold. In this case, you should see a link entitled "How do I create and copy an Amazon Machine Image (AMI) from one AWS Region to another?" When you choose it, you'll be taken to a page containing a full guide to setting up the AWS Command Line Interface (AWS CLI), copying your files, and then verifying that the copy worked.

Security Resources

AWS makes it perfectly clear that it wants your deployments to be as secure as possible. One way it makes this easier to accomplish is by maintaining a dedicated documentation page with links to useful and practical security-related resources. The page, found at https://aws.amazon.com/security/security-resources, points to AWS blogs, white papers, articles, and tutorials covering topics such as security best practices and encrypting your data in transit and at rest.

AWS often adds new content to the collection, and the links to blogs will always lead to fresh content.

Discussion Forums

When things don't work the way you expected, it's generally safe to assume you're not the first person to hit this particular brick wall. Even if this is something only a couple dozen people have experienced, there's a good chance that at least one of them asked about it on some online forum. While many of those questions were probably asked on Stack Overflow or another public site, the AWS discussion forums have also addressed their share of problems.

The site—found at https://forums.aws.amazon.com—is divided into categories including Amazon Web Services (which is further divided into individual services), AWS Startups (focused on newcomers to the platform), AWS Web Site and Resources (topics like Java Development and High Performance Computing), and a number of areas serving non-English speakers using languages like Japanese and German. You can search the entire site or individual forums to see whether your question might already have been answered.

To post on the forum, you'll need to be signed into your AWS account *and* have a forum nickname and email.

Trusted Advisor

You use Trusted Advisor to visually confirm whether your account resource configurations are sound and are compliant with best practices. Trusted Advisor organizes its compliance alerts across five categories, which are described in Table 3.3.

TABLE 3.3   The Five Trusted Advisor Alert Categories

Category	Purpose	Examples
Cost Optimization	Identifies any resources that are running and costing you money but are either underutilized or inactive	EC2 instances or Redshift clusters that, over time, are mostly idle
Performance	Identifies configuration settings that might be blocking performance improvements	Inappropriate reliance on slower magnetic or low-throughput Elastic Block Store (EBS) volumes
Security	Identifies any failures to use security best-practice configurations	Simple Storage Service (S3) buckets with publicly accessible permissions or security groups permitting unrestricted access

Category	Purpose	Examples
Fault Tolerance	Identifies any running resources that, through poor configuration, are unnecessarily vulnerable to service disruptions	Data volumes that aren't properly backed up or instances that aren't replicated
Service Limits	Identifies resource usage that's approaching AWS Region or service limits (as described in Chapter 2, "Understanding your AWS Account")	Your account is currently using close to the 100 Simple Storage Service (S3) buckets limit

The status of an advisor *check* is illustrated by the icon next to a particular item. Figure 3.1 shows what a healthy service limit status might look like. However, if, for instance, you haven't configured multifactor authentication for your root account, you'll get a red alert icon suggesting that you should seriously consider attending to the problem. Each item can be expanded to provide contextual information.

FIGURE 3.1   The green "healthy" icon indicating that these services are not approaching their service limits

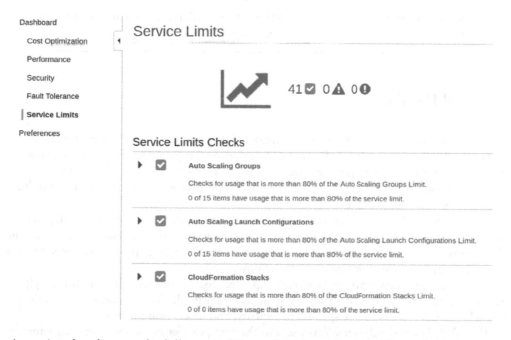

As you've already seen, the full range of Trusted Advisor alerts is only available for users signed on to either the Business or Enterprise Support service tier. For everyone else—including those on the free Basic Support plan—access is limited to service limits and some

of the security alerts. All users are able to browse through inactive versions of the entire range of alerts to at least see what they're missing.

This is an automated service, so, as you may see for yourself as you work through Exercise 3.2, you should expect to encounter some false positives. For instance, Trusted Advisor will flag any S3 bucket that permits public access. A lot of the time, that's a signal of a serious problem, but sometimes—as when you're using the bucket to host a static website—that's exactly what you want. So, don't think you have to blindly follow all the suggestions you're shown. This is an *advisor*, after all, not your mother.

EXERCISE 3.2

Confirm That Your Account Security Settings Are Compliant with Best Practices

1. While logged into your account, navigate to the Trusted Advisor home page (https://console.aws.amazon.com/trustedadvisor).

2. Note any recommended actions that may be displayed on the main page, and then choose the Security icon at the top of the screen to focus on just security items.

3. If there are any red "action recommended" items (like a root account that isn't config-ured for MFA), then expand the item to see your options.

4. Similarly, expand and explore any yellow "investigation recommended" icons to see whether there's anything you should take care of.

Summary

AWS requires you to select one of four support plans. The Basic plan is free, Developer starts at $29, Business starts at $100, and Enterprise starts at $15,000. Nonfree plans (beyond the minimum charge) are billed as a percentage of total monthly resource usage. The higher the support level, the more responsive and personalized the technical trouble-shooting and planning support you get.

The Developer Support plan is aimed at organizations still testing and planning deploy-ments. The Business Support plan is for smaller operations running relatively light produc-tion infrastructure. The Enterprise Support plan is ideal for large production deployments with a global footprint that cannot tolerate downtime.

AWS provides exhaustive and regularly updated documentation using multiple styles across a number of web platforms. Those include user guide documentation pages, the Knowledge Center, resources specific to security, and discussion forums.

The AWS Trusted Advisor alerts users to the best-practice compliance of their running account resources. Basic Support and Developer Support plan users get service limit and some security information, while Business and Enterprise customers get access to all alerts.

Exam Essentials

Know how to choose a support plan that reflects your operational needs.   The more complex and expensive your AWS deployments get, the more costly a configuration mistake becomes. You can think about more expensive AWS support levels much the same way you already think about hiring experienced and reliable admins. Whatever it takes to design and deploy a lean and security-hardened application is a justifiable business expense.

Understand the benefits of the Enterprise Support plan's technical account manager (TAM). The ongoing, personalized attention your account deployments receive from a TAM can make a significant difference in the quality of support. There's nothing like having an expert insider involved in the planning and execution of your complex infrastructure.

Understand how to find AWS resource usage guidance through official AWS documentation. The AWS user guides are available in multiple formats (including HTML, PDF, Kindle, and, on GitHub, MarkDown) and methodically explain practical usage for AWS services at all levels. The Knowledge Center is a large collection of FAQs covering hundreds of common problems and their solutions.

Understand how to use Trusted Advisor for alerts to common system misconfigurations. The Trusted Advisor alerts are divided into five categories: Cost Optimization, Performance, Security, Fault Tolerance, and Services Limits. You should set up an administration routine that includes regular visits to the Trusted Advisor to see whether any important status checks have changed.

Review Questions

1. Your company is planning a major deployment on AWS. While the design and testing stages are still in progress, which of the following plans will provide the best blend of support and cost savings?

   A. Basic

   B. Developer

   C. Business

   D. Enterprise

2. Your web development team is actively gearing up for a deployment of an ecommerce site. During these early stages of the process, individual developers are running into frustrating conflicts and configuration problems that are highly specific to your situation. Which of the following plans will provide the best blend of support and cost savings?

   A. Basic

   B. Developer

   C. Business

   D. Enterprise

3. Your corporate website was offline last week for more than two hours—which caused serious consequences, including the early retirement of your CTO. Your engineers have been having a lot of trouble tracking down the source of the outage and admit that they need outside help. Which of the following will most likely meet that need?

   A. Basic

   B. Developer

   C. Business

   D. Enterprise

4. For which of the following will AWS provide direct 24/7 support to all users—even those on the Basic Support plan?

   A. Help with infrastructure under a massive denial-of-service (DoS) attack

   B. Help with failed and unavailable infrastructure

   C. Help with making a bill payment to AWS

   D. Help with accessing your infrastructure via the AWS CLI

5. The primary purpose of an AWS technical account manager is to:

   A. Provide 24/7 customer service for your AWS account

   B. Provide deployment guidance and advocacy for Enterprise Support customers

C. Provide deployment guidance and advocacy for Business Support customers

D. Provide strategic cost estimates for Enterprise Support customers

6. Your Linux-based EC2 instance requires a patch to a Linux kernel module. The problem is that patching the module will, for some reason, break the connection between your instance and data in an S3 bucket. Your team doesn't know if it's possible to work around this problem. Which is the most cost-effective AWS plan through which support professionals will try to help you?

A. Developer.

B. Business.

C. Enterprise.

D. No plan covers this kind of support.

7. Your company enrolled in the Developer Support plan and, through the course of one month, consumed $4,000 USD of AWS services. How much will the support plan cost the company for the month?

A. $120

B. $29

C. $100

D. $480

8. Your company enrolled in the Business Support plan and, through the course of three months, consumed $33,000 of AWS services (the consumption was equally divided across the months). How much will the support plan cost the company for the full three months?

A. $4,000

B. $100

C. $1,100

D. $2,310

9. Which of the following AWS support services does not offer free documentation of some sort?

A. AWS Professional Services

B. The Basic Support plan

C. AWS Partner Network

D. The Knowledge Center

10. What is the key difference between the roles of AWS Professional Services and a technical account manager (TAM)?

A. The Professional Services product helps AWS Partner Network cloud professionals work alongside your own team to help you administrate your cloud infrastructure. The TAM is a cloud professional employed by AWS to guide you through the planning and execution of your infrastructure.

B. The TAM is a cloud professional employed by AWS to guide you through the planning and execution of your infrastructure. The Professional Services product provides cloud professionals to work alongside your own team to help you administrate your cloud infrastructure.

C. The TAM is a member of your team designated as the point person for all AWS projects. The Professional Services product provides consultants to work alongside your own team to help you administrate your cloud infrastructure.

D. The Professional Services product is a network appliance that AWS installs in your data center to test cloud-bound workloads for compliance with best practices. The TAM is a cloud professional employed by AWS to guide you through the planning and execution of your infrastructure.

11. AWS documentation is available in a number of formats, including which of the following? (Select TWO.)

A. Microsoft Word (DOC)

B. Kindle

C. HTML

D. DocBook

12. Which of the following documentation sites are most likely to contain code snippets for you to cut and (after making sure you understand exactly what they'll do) paste into your AWS operations? (Select TWO.)

A. https://aws.amazon.com/premiumsupport/knowledge-center

B. https://aws.amazon.com/premiumsupport/compare-plans

C. https://docs.aws.amazon.com

D. https://aws.amazon.com/professional-services

13. What is the primary function of the content linked from the Knowledge Center?

A. To introduce new users to the functionality of the core AWS services

B. To explain how AWS deployments can be more efficient and secure than on-premises

C. To provide a public forum where AWS users can ask their technical questions

D. To present solutions to commonly encountered technical problems using AWS infrastructure

14. On which of the following sites are you most likely to find information about encrypting your AWS resources?

A. https://aws.amazon.com/premiumsupport/knowledge-center

B. https://aws.amazon.com/security/security-resources

C. `https://docs.aws.amazon.com`

D. `https://aws.amazon.com/security/encryption`

15. When using AWS documentation pages, what is the best way to be sure the information you're reading is up-to-date?

A. The page URL will include the word *latest*.

B. The page URL will include the version number (i.e., 3.2).

C. The page will have the word *Current* at the top right.

D. There is no easy way to tell.

16. Which of the following is not a Trusted Advisor category?

A. Performance

B. Service Limits

C. Replication

D. Fault Tolerance

17. "Data volumes that aren't properly backed up" is an example of which of these Trusted Advisor categories?

A. Fault Tolerance

B. Performance

C. Security

D. Cost Optimization

18. Instances that are running (mostly) idle should be identified by which of these Trusted Advisor categories?

A. Performance

B. Cost Optimization

C. Service Limits

D. Replication

19. Within the context of Trusted Advisor, what is a false positive?

A. An alert for a service state that was actually intentional

B. A green OK icon for a service state that is failed or failing

C. A single status icon indicating that your account is completely compliant

D. Textual indication of a failed state

20. Which of the following Trusted Advisor alerts is available only for accounts on the Business or Enterprise Support plan? (Select TWO.)

A. MFA on Root Account

B. Load Balancer Optimization

C. Service Limits

D. IAM Access Key Rotation

Chapter

4

Understanding the AWS Environment

THE AWS CERTIFIED CLOUD PRACTITIONER EXAM OBJECTIVES COVERED IN THIS CHAPTER MAY INCLUDE, BUT ARE NOT LIMITED TO, THE FOLLOWING:

Domain 2: Security

✓ 2.1 Define the AWS Shared Responsibility model

Domain 3: Technology

✓ 3.2 Define the AWS global infrastructure

Introduction

The way you'll use AWS services for your cloud workloads will be largely defined by the way AWS itself organizes its hardware, networking, and security infrastructure. So, the best way to learn how to configure things as efficiently and effectively as possible is to understand exactly how AWS infrastructure works.

This chapter will help you map out the "lay of the AWS land" in your mind. You'll learn about how—and why—Amazon's hundreds of globally distributed data centers are divided into regions that, in turn, are further divided into Availability Zones. You'll explore how you can design your own applications to take the best advantage of those divisions.

You'll also learn about how AWS can extend the network reach of your applications through its globally distributed edge locations that make up the front end of CloudFront, Amazon's content delivery network (CDN). Finally, you'll learn how the ways you use and rely on Amazon's resources are governed by the terms of both the AWS Shared Responsibility Model and the AWS Acceptable Use Policy. Failing to properly understand those two frameworks will, at best, lead you to make expensive mistakes and, at worst, lead to disaster.

AWS Global Infrastructure: AWS Regions

AWS performs its cloud magic using hundreds of thousands of servers maintained within physical data centers located in a widely distributed set of geographic regions. As Amazon's global footprint grows, the number of regions grows with it. You'll soon see why having as wide a choice of regions as possible is a valuable feature of cloud computing.

As of the time of this writing, Table 4.1 represents the full list of available regions. But by the time you read this, there will probably be more. The documentation page at https://aws.amazon.com/about-aws/global-infrastructure should always contain the latest information available.

TABLE 4.1   The Current List of AWS Regions and Their Designations

Region	Designation
US West (Oregon) Region	us-west-2
US West (N. California) Region	us-west-1
US East (Ohio) Region	us-east-2
US East (N. Virginia) Region	us-east-1
Asia Pacific (Mumbai) Region	ap-south-1
Asia Pacific (Osaka-Local)	ap-northeast-3
Asia Pacific (Seoul) Region	ap-northeast-2
Asia Pacific (Singapore) Region	ap-southeast-1
Asia Pacific (Sydney) Region	ap-southeast-2
Asia Pacific (Tokyo) Region	ap-northeast-1
Canada (Central) Region	ca-central-1
China (Beijing) Region	cn-north-1
EU (Frankfurt) Region	eu-central-1
EU (Ireland) Region	eu-west-1
EU (London) Region	eu-west-2
EU (Paris) Region	eu-west-3
South America (São Paulo) Region	sa-east-1
AWS GovCloud (US)	us-gov-west-1

Not all of those regions are accessible from regular AWS accounts. Deploying resources into the U.S. government GovCloud region (or the AWS secret region designed for the U.S. intelligence community), for instance, requires special permission.

Regionally Based Services

When you request an instance of an AWS service, the underlying hardware of that instance will be carved out of a server running in one—and only one—AWS Region. This is true whether you're talking about an Elastic Compute Cloud (EC2) virtual machine instance, its Elastic Block Store (EBS) storage volume, a bucket within Simple Storage Service (S3), or a new Lambda "serverless" function. In all those cases, although that anyone anywhere in the world can be given access to your resources, their underlying physical host can exist in no more than one region.

Of course, that's not to say you can't choose to run parallel resources in multiple regions—or that there aren't sometimes edge-case scenarios where it makes sense to do so. But you must always be aware of the region that's active for any resource launch you're planning.

We should emphasize that point since it's something that can, if forgotten, cause you grief. Through no fault of the AWS designers, it's surprisingly easy to accidentally launch a new resource into the wrong region. Doing this can make it impossible for mutually dependent application components to find each other and, as a result, can cause your application to fail. Such accidental launches can also make it hard to keep track of your running resources, leading to the avoidable expense caused by unused and unnecessary instances not being shut down. Of course, as you saw in Chapter 2, "Understanding Your AWS Account," the Billing & Cost Management Dashboard can provide helpful insights into all this.

Checking your current region should become a second-nature reflex—much like the quick mirror checks (we hope) you regularly perform while you're driving a car. Figure 4.1 shows how your region status is displayed in the top right of the AWS Management Console page and how it can easily be changed from the drop-down menu.

FIGURE 4.1 The AWS Management Console feature indicating the region that's currently active and permitting you to switch to a different available region

What's in all this for you? Dividing resources among regions lets you do the following:

- Locate your infrastructure geographically closer to your users to allow access with the lowest possible latency

- Locate your infrastructure within national borders to meet regulatory compliance with legal and banking rules

- Isolate groups of resources from each other and from larger networks to allow the greatest possible security

Globally Based Services

Remember that absolute, immutable, and fundamental law we mentioned a bit earlier about all AWS resources existing in one and only one region? Well, rest assured, dear friend, that it is indeed absolutely, immutably, and fundamentally true.

Except where it isn't.

You see, some AWS resources are not visibly tied to any one region. Even if those resources are, technically, running on hardware that must exist within a single region, AWS presents them as global. As a rule, their global status will generally make sense from a structural perspective. Here are some examples of global services:

- AWS Identity and Access Management (IAM) is the service for managing the way access to your account resources is achieved by way of users and groups, roles, and policies. You'll learn much more about IAM in Chapter 5, "Securing Your AWS Resources."

- Amazon CloudFront is the content delivery network you can use to lower access latency for your application users by storing cached versions of frequently requested data at AWS edge locations.

- While Amazon S3 buckets must, as we mentioned earlier, exist within a single region, S3 is nevertheless considered a global service (open the S3 Console page and look at the region indicator).

The region indicated on the AWS Management Console pages for each of those services will be Global.

Service Endpoints

To work with or access the resources you're running within AWS Regions, you'll have to know how they're identified. Your developers or administrators will, for instance, want to connect with resources through their application code or shell scripts. For such access, they'll often authenticate into your account and list and administrate resources and objects by referring to the endpoint that's specific to a particular region and service.

For example, the correct endpoint for an EC2 instance in the us-east-1 (Northern Virginia) region would be

```
ec2.us-east-1.amazonaws.com
```

The endpoint for the Amazon Relational Database Service (RDS) in the eu-west-3 (Paris) region is

```
rds.eu-west-3.amazonaws.com
```

For a long, up-to-date, and complete list of endpoints for all AWS services, see this page:

```
https://docs.aws.amazon.com/general/latest/gr/rande.html
```

AWS Global Infrastructure: Availability Zones

An AWS Region (with the current exception of the Osaka-Local region) encompasses at least two distinct Availability Zones connected to each other with low-latency network links. Although, for security reasons, Amazon zealously guards the street addresses of its data centers, we do know that a single AZ is made up of at least one fully independent data center that's built on hardware and power resources used by no other AZ.

As shown in Figure 4.2, AWS resources based in a single region can be requested and run within any AZ in the region.

FIGURE 4.2   A representation of AWS infrastructure divided among multiple regions and Availability Zones

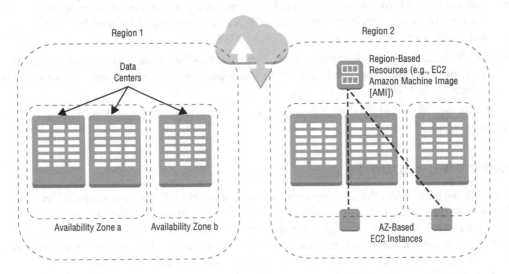

The advantage of this level of separation is that if one AZ loses power or suffers some kind of catastrophic outage, the chances of it spreading to a second AZ in the region are minimal. You can assume that no two AZs will ever share resources from a single physical data center.

Availability Zone Designations

Understanding how Availability Zones work has immediate and practical importance. Before launching an EC2 instance, for example, you'll need to specify a network subnet associated with an AZ. It's the subnet/AZ combination that will be your instance's host environment. Unsure about that subnet business? You'll learn more in just a few moments.

For now, though, you should be aware of how AZs are identified within the AWS resource configuration process. Recall from earlier in this chapter that the Northern Virginia region is described as us-east-1. With that in mind, us-east-1a would be the first AZ within the us-east-1 region, and us-east-1d would be the fourth. Working through Exercise 4.1 will help you picture all this in action.

EXERCISE 4.1

Select a Subnet and AZ for an EC2 Instance

In this exercise, you'll work through the process of selecting a subnet and Availability Zone, but you won't actually launch an EC2 instance:

1. Choose the EC2 link from the AWS services menu, and then choose Launch Instance. Confirm that the region indicator at the top right of the page shows N. Virginia. If it doesn't, select that region.

2. Choose the Select button next to the Amazon Linux 2 AMI entry (it should be the first entry listed on the Quick Start tab).

3. Leave the default t2.micro (Free Tier–eligible) instance type selected, and choose the Next: Configure Instance Details button.

4. Hover your mouse over the information ("i") icon next to the Subnet item, and read the description. Then choose the adjoining drop-down menu. You will probably see around six subnet IDs, each one associated with its default AZ.

5. This exercise will not continue any further with the instance launch process, so you can choose Cancel to abort. Nothing will have been launched, and you will incur no costs.

You may have noticed that the AZs weren't listed in order in the subnet drop-down menu. For example, us-east-1a was probably not first and, equally probably, it wasn't immediately followed by us-east-1b. The reason for this strange setup reflects Amazon's familiarity with human nature: faced with two, three, or six choices that all appear equal, which one do you suppose most people will select? Did you vote for "whichever one appears first on the list"? Good call.

The problem with consistently listing the AZs in order is that the vast majority of users would always go for us-east-1a. But launching so many resources in just that first AZ would place unmanageable stress on the resources in poor old us-east-1a and leave all the others underutilized. So, Amazon solves the problem by displaying the AZs out of order.

Availability Zone Networking

You'll only get the full value out of the resources you run within an AWS Region by properly organizing them into network segments (or *subnets*). You might, for instance, want to isolate your production servers from your development and staging servers to ensure that there's no leakage between them. This can free your developers to confidently experiment with configuration profiles without having to worry about accidentally bringing down your public-facing application. Distributing production workloads among multiple subnets can also make your applications more highly available and fault tolerant. We'll talk more about that in the next section.

A subnet is really nothing more than a single block of Internet Protocol (IP) addresses. Any compute device that requires network connectivity must be identified by an IP address that's unique to the network. The servers or other networked devices that are assigned an IP address within one subnet are generally able to communicate with each other by default but might have traffic coming into and/or out of the subnet restricted by firewall rules.

Private networks—including AWS subnets—using the IPv4 protocol are allowed to use all the addresses within the three address ranges shown in Table 4.2.

TABLE 4.2   Available Private IPv4 Address Ranges

From	To	Total Available Addresses
192.168.0.0	192.168.255.255	65,536
172.16.0.0	172.31.255.255	1,048,576

There's nothing preventing a private network manager from subdividing those addresses into hundreds of smaller subnets. The default subnets provided by AWS as part of its Availability Zones are, in fact, just such subdivided networks. AWS, as a matter of fact, permits up to 200 subnets per AZ.

Calculating netmasks for those ranges to properly understand their Classless Inter-Domain Routing (CIDR) notation goes way beyond the scope of this chapter—and of the AWS Cloud Practitioner exam objectives. But it can't hurt to consider that AWS might describe the address range available to a particular subnet as something like 172.31.16.0/20 or 172.31.48.0/20. Whenever you see such a notation in an AWS configuration dialog, you'll now know that you're looking at the IP address range for a subnet.

Availability Zones and High Availability

One of the key principles underlying the entire business of server administration is that all hardware (and most software) will eventually fail. It may be an important router today or a storage volume tomorrow, but nothing can last forever. And when something does break, it usually takes your application down with it. A resource running without backup is known as a *single point of failure*.

The only effective protection against failure is redundancy, which involves provisioning two or more instances of whatever your workload requires rather than just one. That way, if one suddenly drops off the grid, a backup is there to immediately take over. But it's not enough to run parallel resources if they're going to be sitting right next to each other in the same data center. That wouldn't do you a lot of good in the event of a building-wide blackout or a malicious attack, leaving your backup just as dead as the instance it was supposed to replace. So, you'll also need to distribute your resources across remote locations.

In this context, it really makes no difference whether your workload is running in your on-premises data center or in the Amazon cloud. In either case, you'll need resource redundancy that's also geographically parallel. What *is* different is how much *easier*—and sometimes cheaper—it can be to build resilience into your *cloud* infrastructure.

Since the AWS cloud is already available within dozens and dozens of Availability Zones spread across all continents (besides, for now at least, Antarctica), deploying or, at least, preparing quick-launch templates for remote backup instances is easy. And since AWS workloads can be requested and launched on-demand, the job of efficiently provisioning parallel resources is built into the platform's very DNA.

The configuration and automation stage can be a bit tricky, but that's for your developers and administrators to figure out, isn't it? They're the ones who took and passed the AWS Solutions Architect Associate (or Professional) certification, right?

You should at least be aware that AWS slays the application failure dragon using autoscaling and load balancing:

- Autoscaling can be configured to replace or replicate a resource to ensure that a predefined service level is maintained regardless of changes in user demand or the availability of existing resources.

- Load balancing orchestrates the use of multiple parallel resources to direct user requests to the server resource that's best able to provide a successful experience. A common use case for load balancing is to coordinate the use of primary and (remote) backup resources to cover for a failure.

AWS Global Infrastructure: Edge Locations

The final major piece of the AWS infrastructure puzzle is its network of edge locations. An *edge location* is a site where AWS deploys physical server infrastructure to provide low-latency user access to Amazon-based data.

That definition is correct, but it does sound suspiciously like the way you'd define any other AWS data center, doesn't it? The important difference is that your garden-variety data centers are designed to offer the full range of AWS services, including the complete set of EC2 instance types and the networking infrastructure customers would need to shape their compute environments. Edge locations, on the other hand, are much more focused on a smaller set of roles and will therefore stock a much narrower set of hardware.

So, what actually happens at those edge locations? You can think of them as a front-line resource for directing the kind of network traffic that can most benefit from speed.

Edge Locations and CloudFront

Perhaps the best-known tenant of edge locations is CloudFront, Amazon's CDN service. How does that work? Let's say you're hosting large media files in S3 buckets. If users would have to retrieve their files directly from the bucket each time they were requested, delivery—especially to end users living continents away from the bucket location—would be relatively slow. But if you could store cached copies of the most popular files on servers located geographically close to your users, then they wouldn't have to wait for the original file to be retrieved but could be enjoying the cached copy in a fraction of the time.

 Not all content types are good candidates for CloudFront caching. Files that are frequently updated or that are accessed by end users only once in a while would probably not justify the expense of saving to cache.

In addition to CloudFront, there are other AWS services that make use of edge locations. Here are few examples:

Amazon Route 53   Amazon's Domain Name System (DNS) administration tool for managing domain name registration and traffic routing

AWS Shield   A managed service for countering the threat of distributed denial-of-service (DDoS) attacks against your AWS-based infrastructure

AWS Web Application Firewall (WAF)   A managed service for protecting web applications from web-based threats

Lambda@Edge   A tool designed to use the serverless power of Lambda to customize CloudFront behavior

So all this talk will make more sense, we suggest you explore the configuration process for a CloudFront distribution by following Exercise 4.2.

EXERCISE 4.2

Take a Quick Look at the Way CloudFront Distributions Are Configured

1. Choose the CloudFront link from the AWS services menu, choose Create Distribution, and then choose the Get Started button underneath the Web Distribution section of the "Select a delivery method for your content" page.

2. Once you're on the Create Distribution page, choose inside the box next to the Origin Domain Name item. If you have any content (like a publicly available S3 bucket), it should appear as an option. Either way, since you're not planning to actually launch anything right now, it doesn't matter what—if any—value you enter.

3. Scroll down the page and note, for instance, the Distribution Settings section. Choose the Price Class drop-down arrow to see the available options for the scope of your distribution (the number of edge locations where your content will be saved).

---

4. Note the Distribution State settings at the bottom of the page.

5. When you're done exploring, choose the Cancel link at the bottom to ensure you don't accidentally launch a distribution for no purpose.

Regional Edge Cache Locations

In addition to the fleet of regular edge locations, Amazon has further enhanced CloudFront functionality by adding what it calls a *regional edge cache*. The idea is that CloudFront-served objects are maintained in edge location caches only as long as there's a steady flow of requests. Once the rate of new requests drops off, an object will be deleted from the cache, and future requests will need to travel all the way back to the origin server (like an S3 bucket).

Regional edge cache locations—of which there are currently nine worldwide—can offer a compromise solution. Objects rejected by edge locations can be moved to the regional edge caches. There aren't as many such locations worldwide, so the response times for many user requests won't be as fast, but that'll still probably be better than having to go all the way back to the origin. By design, regional edge cache locations are more capable of handling less-popular content.

The AWS Shared Responsibility Model

The AWS cloud—like any large and complex environment—is built on top of a stack of rules and assumptions. The success of your AWS projects will largely depend on how well you understand those rules and assumptions and on how fully you adopt the practices that they represent. The AWS Shared Responsibility Model is a helpful articulation of those rules and assumptions, and it's worth spending some time thinking about it.

Amazon distinguishes between the security and reliability *of* the cloud, which is its responsibility, and the security and reliability of what's *in* the cloud, which is up to you, the customer.

The cloud itself consists of the physical buildings, servers, and networking hardware used by AWS data centers. AWS is responsible for making sure that its locations are secure, reliably powered, and properly maintained. AWS is also on the hook for patching, encrypting (where relevant), and maintaining the operating systems and virtualization software running its physical servers and for the software running its managed services.

But that's where things can get a bit complicated. What exactly is "managed" and what's "unmanaged"? Figure 4.3 (which you saw previously in Chapter 1, "The Cloud") compares the "of the cloud/in the cloud" mix as it applies across the three key cloud models: Infrastructure as a Service, Platform as a Service, and Software as a Service.

FIGURE 4.3 A general comparison between local and managed deployments

On-Premises Deployments	IaaS	PaaS	SaaS
Application Code	Application Code	Application Code	Application Code
Security	Security	Security	Security
Database	Database	Database	Database
OS	OS	OS	OS
Virtualization	Virtualization	Virtualization	Virtualization
Networking	Networking	Networking	Networking
Storage Hardware	Storage Hardware	Storage Hardware	Storage Hardware
Server Hardware	Server Hardware	Server Hardware	Server Hardware

Your Responsibility

Cloud Platform Responsibility

Figure 4.4 illustrates the way responsibility for the integrity and security of AWS infrastructure is divided between Amazon and its customers.

FIGURE 4.4 A representation of the AWS Shared Responsibility Model

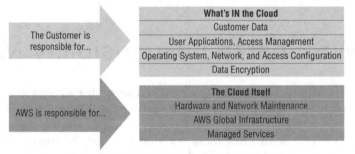

The Customer is responsible for...

What's IN the Cloud
Customer Data
User Applications, Access Management
Operating System, Network, and Access Configuration
Data Encryption

AWS is responsible for...

The Cloud Itself
Hardware and Network Maintenance
AWS Global Infrastructure
Managed Services

The AWS Shared Responsibility Model

Managed Resources

A managed cloud service will "hide" all or some of the underlying configuration and administration work needed to keep things running, leaving you free to focus on the "business" end of your project. For example, an application running on an EC2 instance might need a database in the backend. You could install and configure a MySQL database engine on the instance itself, but you'd be responsible for patches, updates, and all the regular care and feeding (not to mention letting it out for its morning walks).

Alternatively, you could point your application to a stand-alone database you launch on Amazon's Relational Database Service (RDS). AWS is responsible for patching an RDS database and ensuring its data is secure and reliable. You only need to worry about populating the database and connecting it to your application.

RDS, therefore, is a good example of a partially managed service. How would the next level of managed service work? Look no further than Elastic Beanstalk, which hides just about all the complexity of its runtime environment, leaving nothing for you to do beyond uploading your application code. Beanstalk handles the instances, storage, databases, and networking headaches—including ongoing patches and administration—invisibly.

Unmanaged Resources

The most obvious example of an unmanaged AWS service is EC2. When you launch an EC2 instance, you're expected to care for the operating system and everything that's running on it exactly the way you would for a physical server in your on-premises data center. Still, even EC2 can't be said to be entirely unmanaged since the integrity of the physical server that hosts it is, of course, the responsibility of AWS.

Think of it as a sliding scale rather than a simple on-off switch. Some cloud operations will demand greater involvement from you and your administration team, and some will demand less. Use this simple rule of thumb: *if you can edit it, you own it*. The key—especially during a project's planning stages—is to be aware of your responsibilities and to always make security a critical priority.

Service Health Status

As part of its end of the bargain, AWS makes regularly updated, region-by-region reports on the status of its services publicly available. Any service outages that could affect the performance of anyone's workload will appear on Amazon's Service Health Dashboard (https://status.aws.amazon.com)—often within a minute or two of the outage hitting.

While configuration errors are always a possible cause of a failure in your infrastructure, you should always make the Service Health Dashboard one of your first stops whenever you dive into a troubleshooting session.

AWS Acceptable Use Policy

Because they're so easy to scale up, cloud computing services are powerful tools for accomplishing things no one had even dreamed of just a decade ago. But for that same reason, they're also potential weapons that can be used to commit devastating crimes.

The AWS Acceptable Use Policy (https://aws.amazon.com/aup) makes it abundantly clear that it does not permit the use of its infrastructure in any illegal, harmful, or offensive way. Amazon reserves the right to suspend or even terminate your use of its services should you engage in illegal, insecure, or abusive activities (including the sending of spam and related mass mailings). Even running penetration testing operations against your own AWS infrastructure can cause you trouble if you don't get explicit permission from Amazon in advance.

You should take the time to read the document and keep its terms in mind as you deploy on AWS.

Summary

An AWS Region connects at least two Availability Zones located within a single geographic area into a low-latency network. Because of the default isolation of their underlying hardware, building secure, access-controlled regional environments is eminently possible.

An Availability Zone is a group of one or more independent (and fault-protected) data centers located within a single geographic region.

It's important to be aware of the region that's currently selected by your interface (either the AWS Management Console or a command-line terminal), as any operations you execute will launch specifically within the context of that region.

The design structure of Amazon's global system of regions allows you to build your infrastructure in ways that provide the best possible user experience while meeting your security and regulatory needs.

AWS offers some global resources whose use isn't restricted to any one region. Those include IAM, CloudFront, and S3.

You can connect to AWS service instances using their endpoint addresses, which will (generally) incorporate the host region's designation.

EC2 virtual machine instances are launched with an IP address issued from a network subnet that's associated with a single Availability Zone.

The principle of high availability can be used to make your infrastructure more resilient and reliable by launching parallel redundant instances in multiple Availability Zones.

AWS edge locations are globally distributed data servers that can store cached copies of AWS-based data from which—on behalf of the CloudFront service—they can be efficiently served to end users.

The elements of the AWS platform that you're expected to secure and maintain and those whose administration is managed by Amazon are defined by the AWS Shared Responsibility Model.

Exam Essentials

Understand the importance of resource isolation for cloud deployments.   Properly placing your cloud resources within the right region and Availability Zone—along with carefully setting appropriate access controls—can improve both application security and performance.

Understand the role of autoscaling in a highly available deployment.   The scalability of AWS resources means you can automate the process of increasing or decreasing the scale of a deployment based on need. This can automate application recovery after a crash.

Understand the role of load balancing in a highly available deployment.   The ability to automatically redirect incoming requests away from a nonfunctioning instance and to a backup replacement is managed by a load balancer.

Understand the principles of the AWS Shared Responsibility Model.   AWS handles security and administration for its underlying physical infrastructure and for the full stack of all its managed services, while customers are responsible for everything else.

Understand the principles of the AWS Acceptable Use Policy.   Using AWS resources to commit crimes or launch attacks against any individual or organization will result in account suspension or termination.

Review Questions

1. Which of the following designations would refer to the AWS US West (Oregon) region?

   A. us-east-1

   B. us-west-2

   C. us-west-2a

   D. us-west-2b

2. Which of the following is an AWS Region for which customer access is restricted?

   A. AWS Admin

   B. US-DOD

   C. Asia Pacific (Tokyo)

   D. AWS GovCloud

3. When you request a new virtual machine instance in EC2, your instance will automatically launch into the currently selected value of which of the following?

   A. Service

   B. Subnet

   C. Availability Zone

   D. Region

4. Which of the following are *not* globally based AWS services? (Select TWO.)

   A. RDS

   B. Route 53

   C. EC2

   D. CloudFront

5. Which of the following would be a valid endpoint your developers could use to access a particular Relational Database Service instance you're running in the Northern Virginia region?

   A. us-east-1.amazonaws.com.rds

   B. ecs.eu-west-3.amazonaws.com

   C. rds.us-east-1.amazonaws.com

   D. rds.amazonaws.com.us-east-1

6. What are the most significant architectural benefits of the way AWS designed its regions? (Select TWO.)

   A. It can make infrastructure more fault tolerant.

   B. It can make applications available to end users with lower latency.

   C. It can make applications more compliant with local regulations.

   D. It can bring down the price of running.

7. Why is it that most AWS resources are tied to a single region?

   A. Because those resources are run on a physical device, and that device must live somewhere

   B. Because security considerations are best served by restricting access to a single physical location

   C. Because access to any one digital resource must always occur through a single physical gateway

   D. Because spreading them too far afield would introduce latency issues

8. You want to improve the resilience of your EC2 web server. Which of the following is the most effective and efficient approach?

   A. Launch parallel, load-balanced instances in multiple AWS Regions.

   B. Launch parallel, load-balanced instances in multiple Availability Zones within a single AWS Region.

   C. Launch parallel, autoscaled instances in multiple AWS Regions.

   D. Launch parallel, autoscaled instances in multiple Availability Zones within a single AWS Region.

9. Which of the following is the most accurate description of an AWS Availability Zone?

   A. One or more independently powered data centers running a wide range of hardware host types

   B. One or more independently powered data centers running a uniform hardware host type

   C. All the data centers located within a broad geographic area

   D. The infrastructure running within a single physical data center

10. Which of the following most accurately describes a subnet within the AWS ecosystem?

   A. The virtual limits imposed on the network access permitted to a resource instance

   B. The block of IP addresses assigned for use within a single region

   C. The block of IP addresses assigned for use within a single Availability Zone

   D. The networking hardware used within a single Availability Zone

11. What determines the order by which subnets/AZ options are displayed in EC2 configuration dialogs?

   A. Alphabetical order

   B. They (appear) to be displayed in random order.

   C. Numerical order

   D. By order of capacity, with largest capacity first

12. What is the primary goal of autoscaling?

    A. To ensure the long-term reliability of a particular physical resource

    B. To ensure the long-term reliability of a particular virtual resource

    C. To orchestrate the use of multiple parallel resources to direct incoming user requests

    D. To ensure that a predefined service level is maintained regardless of external demand or instance failures

13. Which of the following design strategies is *most* effective for maintaining the reliability of a cloud application?

    A. Resource isolation

    B. Resource automation

    C. Resource redundancy

    D. Resource geolocation

14. Which of the following AWS services are *not likely* to benefit from Amazon edge locations? (Select TWO.)

    A. RDS

    B. EC2 load balancers

    C. Elastic Block Store (EBS)

    D. CloudFront

15. Which of the following is the primary benefit of using CloudFront distributions?

    A. Automated protection from mass email campaigns

    B. Greater availability through redundancy

    C. Greater security through data encryption

    D. Reduced latency access to your content no matter where your end users live

16. What is the main purpose of Amazon Route 53?

    A. Countering the threat of distributed denial-of-service (DDoS) attacks

    B. Managing domain name registration and traffic routing

    C. Protecting web applications from web-based threats

    D. Using the serverless power of Lambda to customize CloudFront behavior

17. According to the AWS Shared Responsibility Model, which of the following are responsibilities of AWS? (Select TWO.)

    A. The security of the cloud

    B. Patching underlying virtualization software running in AWS data centers

    C. Security of what's in the cloud

    D. Patching OSs running on EC2 instances

18. According to the AWS Shared Responsibility Model, what's the best way to define the status of the software driving an AWS managed service?

    A. Everything associated with an AWS managed service is the responsibility of AWS.

    B. Whatever is added by the customer (like application code) is the customer's responsibility.

    C. Whatever the customer can control (application code and/or configuration settings) is the customer's responsibility.

    D. Everything associated with an AWS managed service is the responsibility of the customer.

19. Which of the following is one of the first places you should look when troubleshooting a failing application?

    A. AWS Acceptable Use Monitor

    B. Service Status Dashboard

    C. AWS Billing Dashboard

    D. Service Health Dashboard

20. Where will you find information on the limits AWS imposes on the ways you can use your account resources?

    A. AWS User Agreement Policy

    B. AWS Acceptable Use Policy

    C. AWS Acceptable Use Monitor

    D. AWS Acceptable Use Dashboard

Chapter

5

Securing Your AWS Resources

**THE AWS CERTIFIED CLOUD PRACTITIONER
EXAM OBJECTIVES COVERED IN THIS
CHAPTER MAY INCLUDE, BUT ARE NOT
LIMITED TO, THE FOLLOWING:**

Domain 2: Security

✓ **2.2 Define AWS Cloud security and compliance concepts**

✓ **2.3 Identify AWS access management capabilities**

Introduction

Everyone in the IT world knows that application and infrastructure security are critically important elements of any deployment. Unfortunately, the constant stream of news about catastrophic data breaches suggests that some of us may not yet realize just *how* important.

No matter what role you play within your organization's cloud deployment life cycle, ensuring that your assets are properly protected is part of your job. This chapter will help you explore the tools AWS provides to help you with that responsibility.

You'll learn how to use the *Identity and Access Management* (IAM) service to control which people and processes get past the wall guarding your resources (authentication) and what they're allowed to do once they're in (authorization). You'll learn how IAM does that through the smart use of users, groups, roles, and federated identities.

We'll discuss applying *encryption* to your cloud data—both while it's on its way from your local data center and after it's comfortably settled into its AWS home—and managing the encryption keys that do all that heavy lifting. Finally, we'll talk about all the work AWS has done ensuring that its infrastructure is compliant with as wide a range of regulatory frameworks as possible.

AWS Identity and Access Management

We'll start with IAM, whose management dashboard (https://console.aws.amazon.com/iam) connects you to all the administration tools you'll need to manage the basics of account security. As you can see in Figure 5.1, the Security Status section of that page provides a friendly reminder that there might be some issues requiring your attention.

Those suggestions include protecting your account by locking down the root user (the user identity that was generated when you first created your AWS account) and replacing the *effective* functionality of root by setting up IAM users and groups for your day-to-day administration tasks. The coming sections will explain both why and how these changes are made.

FIGURE 5.1   The Security Status section of the IAM Dashboard includes important configuration advice that's especially important for new accounts

Security Status   0 out of 5 complete.

- ⚠ Delete your root access keys   ⌄
- ⚠ Activate MFA on your root account   ⌄
- ⚠ Create individual IAM users   ⌄
- ⚠ Use groups to assign permissions   ⌄
- ⚠ Apply an IAM password policy   ⌄

Protecting the Root User

For practical reasons, the root user has the permissions necessary to perform any task on your account. That includes launching any resources in any region and authorizing any expenses. The problem is that actively using the root user over the long term with only minimal protections presents a significant security risk. Should the root credentials ever be compromised through an attack, there will be no limit to the potential for mischief. All your data could be stolen or deleted or the attacker could run up hundreds of thousands of dollars of charges running a rogue crypto mining operation.

The recommended best practice is, therefore, to protect the root user by creating a complex password and implementing multifactor authentication and, for most administration activities, use IAM users instead. That will be covered next.

Authentication

Whether you're logging in to work with your AWS account via the AWS Management Console, running a command from the terminal of your personal laptop, or connecting a remote application to AWS resources at the programming code level, you'll need to prove you are who you claim to be and that "who you claim to be" has a right to the access you're after. Often that will mean providing some kind of user ID and password. In the case of programmatic or command-line access, you'll need a set of access keys. Opening a remote login session to a Linux instance on Elastic Compute Cloud (EC2) will require a valid key pair. Let's look at those one at a time.

Passwords

While you're still learning your way around AWS, you'll probably do most of your work from the browser's AWS Management Console. As you'll learn in Chapter 6, "Working with Your AWS Resources," using the command line (specifically, AWS CLI) can be a far more efficient way to get things done, but the AWS Management Console works too.

The root user logs into the AWS Management Console with the associated email address along with the password set when the account was created (or subsequently updated). But as you're no doubt already well aware, not all passwords are created equal. If you want your account to have any chance of surviving an attack, you should avoid passwords that can be easily guessed. Instead, choose complex and long passwords that include uppercase and lowercase characters, numbers, and symbols. Even better, use only randomly generated strings that aren't even distantly based on the stuff going on in your life (like your birthday). And never (ever) reuse passwords across multiple accounts.

> Don't think you can remember passwords like those? Welcome to the club. The simplest and most effective solution is to use a password manager like LastPass, Dashlane, or KeePass2.

As mentioned, the first step in protecting your root user is to give it a high-quality password. But that doesn't mean you should let other users off the hook. You'll soon see how to create such users. But before that happens, you should have an appropriate *password policy* already in place. You can configure a policy from the Account Settings section of the IAM Dashboard that will require the passwords used by all users on the account to conform with minimum complexity. Figure 5.2 shows the policy options available to you on the Password Policy page.

FIGURE 5.2   The IAM Account Settings page where you can set an account-wide password policy

▾ Password Policy

A password policy is a set of rules that define the type of password an IAM user can set. For more information about password policies, go to Managing Passwords in Using IAM.

Currently, this AWS account does not have a password policy. Specify a password policy below.

Minimum password length: [6]

☐ Require at least one uppercase letter ❶
☐ Require at least one lowercase letter ❶
☐ Require at least one number ❶
☐ Require at least one non-alphanumeric character ❶
☑ Allow users to change their own password ❶
☐ Enable password expiration ❶
    Password expiration period (in days):   [   ]
☐ Prevent password reuse ❶
    Number of passwords to remember: [   ]
☐ Password expiration requires administrator reset ❶

[Apply password policy]   [Delete password policy]

Multi-factor authentication (MFA) adds a second layer of security to your logins. Once it's enabled, a user will need to provide not only a password to authenticate ("something you know") but also, as a second factor, a temporary digital token sent through a preset device ("something you have"), like a smartphone running an Authenticator app.

MFA works by associating a physical device—either a Universal 2nd Factor (U2F) or MFA-compliant device like YubiKey or a smartphone with the Authenticator app installed—with your account. When you try to log in, you'll first enter a password, and then a short-lived code (usually a six-digit number) will be sent to your MFA device. You only need to read the number and enter it into the appropriate field on the login page, and you'll be allowed in.

While complex passwords and MFA are important for any account user, they're both especially critical for your root user. Exercise 5.1 will walk you through some of the possible settings for creating a password policy for your users from the IAM Dashboard.

EXERCISE 5.1

Create a Password Policy for Your IAM Users

1. From the IAM Dashboard, choose Account Settings, which will take you to a page that includes the Password Policy tool.

2. If appropriate for your account, change the value of Minimum Password Length from 6 to 8. This will require all new passwords to contain at least eight characters.

3. Again, if appropriate, check these boxes:

   - Require At Least One Uppercase Letter

   - Require At Least One Lowercase Letter

   - Require At Least One Number

   - Require At Least One Non-alphanumeric Character

 Since recent thinking in the security industry has questioned the value of forcing users to regularly change their passwords, unless we had no choice, we wouldn't set a password expiration period.

4. Choose Apply Password Policy.

Access Keys

As we mentioned, programmatic and command-line access to many AWS resources is authenticated by access keys (without the option of MFA). You can generate a new set of keys while logged into the AWS Management Console from the *Security Credentials* page—which is accessed from the account drop-down menu at the top right of the AWS Management Console page.

Choosing the Create New Access Key button will get you there. You'll then have the option of downloading the key to your computer as a text file or showing the actual Access

Key ID and Secret Access Key values in the dialog where you can copy and paste them somewhere safe. Just make sure you choose one of those options, because you'll never be shown the secret access key itself again. You should also remember that it's never a good idea to expose the Secret Access Key in plain text—as part of an email, for example.

The Security Credentials page also lists all your keys and allows you to deactivate, activate, or delete existing keys. This is where, while logged in as the root user, you should take the time to delete all keys associated with the root account.

Secure Shell Key Pairs

The industry-standard tool for safely encrypting remote login sessions is the Secure Shell (SSH) protocol. Without encryption, all commands and keystrokes you enter during a terminal session run over an insecure network will be easily readable by anyone with access to that network. When that "network" is the internet, that can add up to a lot of unfriendly eyes on your data.

Encryption converts those plain-text data packets into what looks like gibberish. Indeed, ideally—assuming no one has yet cracked the encryption algorithm you're using—that text is and will remain gibberish, unless you happen to have the decryption key required to decrypt it. The SSH protocol manages the encryption and decryption steps in the process as long as compatible keys are present at both ends of the connection.

When you launch a new EC2 Linux instance (and a heavy majority of EC2 instances are running one flavor or another of Linux), you'll be prompted either to use an existing SSH key pair or to create a new one. Similar to access keys, you'll get only one opportunity to download the private half of the SSH key pair to your own computer. Again, do so without publicly exposing the file.

Once the private key is downloaded (and, for Linux and macOS, given appropriate permissions), you open SSH sessions to your instances by invoking the key in a connection command that might look something like this:

```
ssh -i keyname.pem ec2-user@<public_ip_address_of_instance>
```

Since the release of Windows 10, you can even launch SSH sessions into remote Linux servers natively from Windows machines.

Users, Groups, and Roles

We think it's safe to assume that the readers of this book are a pretty sharp bunch. But even if you haven't been paying all that much attention, we're pretty sure that, by now, you'd have picked up on our theme that you shouldn't be using the root user for regular administration duties. Instead, as you've seen, you're better off creating users to whom you can assign only the permissions needed for a specific set of tasks (thus adhering to the *principle of least privilege*) and then having your team authenticate with those user identities.

IAM Users

Curious to see how creating and managing IAM users happens in the real world? Follow the steps in Exercise 5.2—it won't cost you anything.

EXERCISE 5.2

Create an IAM User and Assign Limited Permissions

1. Choose the Users link in the IAM Dashboard, and then choose the Add User button.

2. Give your user a name (we'll use **Steve** for this exercise), and select one or both of the access types shown. Selecting the Programmatic Access option will guide you to create an access key ID and secret access key as part of the process, while the AWS Management Console Access option will let you set a login password. For this exercise, just select AWS Management Console Access.

3. Choose the Custom Password radio button that will appear, and enter a password for your user that meets any password policy requirements you set for your account earlier. Leave the Require Password Reset box checked so your user will be forced to create a new password when signing in for the first time. Choose the Next: Permissions button.

4. On the Set Permissions page, select the Attach Existing Policies Directly tab, and enter **ec2** into the Filter Policies search field. Scroll down a bit through the results, and choose the box next to the AmazonEC2FullAccess entry. This will give your user the authority to create, launch, and destroy EC2 instances (for this exercise, we'll assume that those are all the permissions you want to give this user). Choose the Next: Tags button.

5. You don't need to create a tag for your user, but it can help you keep track of things as your account gets busier. So, for this example, enter **Unit** as the key and then **EC2-admin** as its value. (If you were to add a different user for managing Simple Storage Service [S3] resources at some point, you could enter a key-value combination of Unit/S3-admin.) Choose Next: Review.

6. When you've confirmed that everything is set the way you want, choose Create User. You'll be shown a URL (that looks something like https://291976716973.signin. aws.amazon.com/console) that your new user can access to log in with the user name (Steve in this example) and the password you've created. The number at the start of the address portion is your AWS account number. You could also have AWS send the new user an email with login instructions.

If you wanted to create a primary admin to replace your root user for day-to-day administration, you would select the AdministratorAccess policy, which would provide enough permissions to get most admin tasks done without exposing your account to unnecessary risk.

IAM Groups

As your organization devotes more team members to your AWS infrastructure, manually assigning permissions to each individual user one at a time will become a tedious and time-consuming chore. Using groups to administrate the permissions associated with multiple users in batches can get all that done much more efficiently.

You could, for instance, have one group called EC2-admins and a second called S3-admins. When someone new signed up to your team, you would only need to create an IAM user and then attach it to the appropriate group. The user would automatically inherit all the permissions of that group. And if at some time down the line you needed to add to or reduce the group's permissions, editing the group itself would instantly apply the changes to all the group's members. Try it for yourself in Exercise 5.3.

EXERCISE 5.3

Assign Multiple Users to an IAM Group

1.   Choose the Groups link in the IAM Dashboard and then the Create New Group button. Give your group a name (we'll use **S3-admins** for this example).

2.   Enter **s3** in the Policy Type filter field, and then select AmazonS3FullAccess from the policies that will be displayed. Review and create the group.

3.   From the Groups page, select the S3-admins group, and choose the Group Actions drop-down menu button. Choose Add Users To Group. Select the user Steve you created in Exercise 5.2 (or the name of any other user you might want to include), and then choose the Add Users button. Your user will now have full admin powers over all S3 resources in your account.

IAM Roles

Like users and groups, IAM roles define the limits for what can be done within your AWS account. The important difference is that, unlike users and groups, roles are, for the most part, used by applications and services rather than people.

When creating a role, you begin by defining a *trusted entity*—the entity (or beneficiary) that will be trusted to use the role. That entity could be an AWS service (like EC2), an identity provided by a third-party federated identify provider (like Google or Amazon Cognito—which allow a digital identity to be linked across multiple identity management systems), or a different AWS account.

You might, for instance, need to give users logged in to your mobile application through their Google accounts access to specific resources on AWS services (such as data kept on S3). You'll have to specify exactly what permissions you want to give the role or, in other words, what you want the beneficiary processes to be able to do. You'll then choose the policy that best fits your anticipated needs and associate it with the role. From that point any authenticated mobile app users will have access to those S3 resources.

Providing Federated Access

Well, now that we've brought up this whole business of federated identities, we should discuss how you can incorporate them into your authentication profile. Federation expands the available tools for managing authentication beyond the simple IAM options you've already seen.

You can integrate third-party standards like the *Security Assertion Markup Language 2.0* (SAML) or Microsoft's Active Directory into your infrastructure. This lets you use users' existing login sessions to add *single sign-on* (SSO) across your AWS infrastructure and enable seamless access between your mobile apps and backend resources like DynamoDB databases or S3-based objects.

Besides the IAM role configuration options you saw a bit earlier in this chapter, federated access to AWS resources can be handled through the AWS Single Sign-On service. For Active Directory integration with cloud-based MS SharePoint, .NET, and SQL Server–based workloads, you would use the AWS Directory Service for Microsoft Active Directory (more commonly known as AWS Microsoft AD).

Credential Report

There's one more IAM resource you should know about: credential reports. Accessed from the IAM Dashboard, a credential report displays a simple interface with no more (or less) than one lonely button: Download Report. We'll let you handle the practical details from there.

But we strongly suggest you make a point of regularly downloading the comma-separated values (CSV) files the service generates. Reports contain important information about the state of your account security, listing all current IAM users and giving you key intelligence, such as when each of them last logged in, whether they have MFA enabled, whether they have active access keys, and when those keys were last rotated.

This is a quick and (fairly) painless way to monitor your account for security holes that you shouldn't ignore.

Encryption

We've already mentioned data encryption and, in general terms, how it works in the context of SSH connectivity. But the need to protect the integrity of your data goes well beyond remote login sessions. You should consider encrypting your data just about wherever you store or consume it. Whether or not your particular use cases and privacy needs justify the effort, AWS provides a number of enterprise-strength encryption tools that are conveniently and effectively integrated into relevant services.

Encryption keys—the data files used to control an object's cryptographic transformation—are mostly managed on AWS by the AWS *Key Management Service* (KMS). When you select to encrypt an AWS resource, KMS will apply encryption using a customer master key (CMK) that's been generated especially for your account. You can manage your keys—including creating new keys or scheduling the deletion of old ones—through either the KMS Dashboard or the Encryption Keys page within IAM.

What can be encrypted? Just about any data managed by an AWS service, including Relational Database Service (RDS) and DynamoDB databases. Elastic Block Store (EBS) volumes that you attach to EC2 instances can also be encrypted when you create them. When they're encrypted, those resources will, for all practical purposes, be unreadable without the decryption key. AWS will invisibly decrypt your data only when the access request is accompanied by successful authentication.

Encryption for S3 works in much the same way, but there's a twist. You can have S3 encrypt the objects of a bucket at any time—during or after bucket creation. You can select either S3-managed server-side encryption keys (SSE-S3) or KMS-managed keys (SSE-KMS). Either way, the process will often all take place "under the hood" without requiring any further input from you.

But besides ensuring that the wrong people won't be able to read the objects living in your S3 buckets (*server-side encryption*), you also have to worry about the bad guys intercepting those objects while in transit from your local infrastructure (*client-side encryption*).

Client-side encryption is a bit more complicated. You'll need to encrypt your data before uploading it to S3 using either a *KMS-managed customer master key* or a *client-side master key*. That key will then be used to manage the encryption and decryption throughout the data's life cycle on the S3 platform.

Regulatory Compliance (AWS Artifact)

Will the application you plan to run on AWS be processing credit card transactions? What about private health records, personal employment histories, or restricted military information? Are you sure the AWS security and reliability environment is good enough to meet the regulatory standards required by your industry and government?

Those are questions you'll need to answer *before* you dive too deeply into your deployment planning. But where can you find authoritative answers? AWS Artifact.

At this point, you may be wondering, what's with the name Artifact? Well, the service home page is a set of links to documents describing various regulatory standards and how AWS meets them. Each of those documents is referred to by Amazon as an *artifact*.

When you choose a link, you're first asked to agree to the terms and conditions included in an AWS Artifact nondisclosure agreement. When you choose the agreement box, the actual artifact will be generated, opening a download pop-up.

What's available? There are national documents like the U.S. government's Federal Risk and Authorization Management Program (FedRAMP), the Government of Canada (GC) Partner Package, and the Australian Prudential Regulation Authority (APRA) "Management of Security Risk in Information and Information Technology" workbook. You'll also find industry standards like the PCI DSS Attestation of Compliance (AOC) and Responsibility Summary for handling credit card transaction data.

You'll also find official reports of Service Organization Controls (SOC) 1, 2, and 3 audits of AWS infrastructure. Those documents can, for instance, be used by AWS customers in the United States as part of their Sarbanes–Oxley compliance reporting.

Summary

You should enforce the use of strong passwords by your users by creating a password policy in IAM. Ideally, you should also require multi-factor authentication (MFA).

Programmatic and command-line access to resources is authenticated using security credentials consisting of an access key ID and a secret access key. SSH access to EC2 Linux instances must be authenticated using a key pair generated by AWS—the private key must be installed on the client (user) computer.

You can efficiently control resource access for large numbers of users with different access needs through IAM groups. The principle of least privilege supports giving your users and groups only the minimum permissions they'll need to do their jobs.

An IAM role is a set of permissions permitting access to a beneficiary process to a defined set of resources. This is an important tool for securely enabling functionality between parts of your AWS infrastructure.

You can review important information on the security status of your users from the credential report in IAM and read about AWS compliance with regulatory and industry standards in AWS Artifact.

Exam Essentials

Know how to lock down your account's root user to reduce your exposure to risk.   Make sure your root user has a strong password that is MFA-enabled and is never used for day-to-day administration tasks.

Know how to enforce the use of strong passwords for all your users.   Set an IAM password policy to force longer passwords using uppercase and lowercase letters, numbers, and nonstandard characters.

Understand how AWS manages access credentials for EC2 key pairs, secret access keys, and encryption keys.   Whether you're looking to secure terminal connections to your EC2 servers, API access, or the privacy of your data, you'll need to make use of AWS encryption services of one sort or another.

Know how to provide (federated) access to your AWS resources based on third-party authentication systems like Google.   Using standards such as SAML 2.0 and Microsoft's Active Directory, you can incorporate external authentication into your AWS infrastructure, making it easy, for instance, for users of your mobile application to retrieve data from a DynamoDB database.

Be aware that AWS Key Management Service (KMS) manages encryption keys.   KMS-managed keys are used across a wide range of AWS services, including EBS, RDS, DynamoDB, and S3.

Be aware that AWS Artifact is a compliance information resource.   AWS Artifact provides access to official documentation on the compliance of AWS infrastructure relating to any one of dozens of government or industry security standards.

Review Questions

1. What is the primary function of the AWS IAM service?

   A. Identity and access management

   B. Access key management

   C. SSH key pair management

   D. Federated access management

2. Which of the following are requirements you can include in an IAM password policy? (Select THREE.)

   A. Require at least one uppercase letter.

   B. Require at least one number.

   C. Require at least one space or null character.

   D. Require at least one nonalphanumeric character.

3. Which of the following should you do to secure your AWS root user? (Select TWO.)

   A. Assign the root user to the "admins" IAM group.

   B. Use the root user for day-to-day administration tasks.

   C. Enable MFA.

   D. Create a strong password.

4. How does multi-factor authentication work?

   A. Instead of an access password, users authenticate via a physical MFA device.

   B. In addition to an access password, users also authenticate via a physical MFA device.

   C. Users authenticate using tokens sent to at least two MFA devices.

   D. Users authenticate using a password and also either a physical or virtual MFA device.

5. Which of the following SSH commands will successfully connect to an EC2 Amazon Linux instance with an IP address of 54.7.35.103 using a key named mykey.pem?

   A. `echo "mykey.pem ubuntu@54.7.35.103" | ssh -i`

   B. `ssh -i mykey.pem ec2-user@54.7.35.103`

   C. `ssh -i mykey.pem@54.7.35.103`

   D. `ssh ec2-user@mykey.pem:54.7.35.103 -i`

6. What's the most efficient method for managing permissions for multiple IAM users?

   A. Assign users requiring similar permissions to IAM roles.

   B. Assign users requiring similar permissions to IAM groups.

   C. Assign IAM users permissions common to others with similar administration responsibilities.

   D. Create roles based on IAM policies, and assign them to IAM users.

7. What is an IAM role?

    A. A set of permissions allowing access to specified AWS resources

    B. A set of IAM users given permission to access specified AWS resources

    C. Permissions granted a trusted entity over specified AWS resources

    D. Permissions granted an IAM user over specified AWS resources

8. How can federated identities be incorporated into AWS workflows? (Select TWO.)

    A. You can provide users authenticated through a third-party identity provider access to backend resources used by your mobile app.

    B. You can use identities to guide your infrastructure design decisions.

    C. You can use authenticated identities to import external data (like email records from Gmail) into AWS databases.

    D. You can provide admins authenticated through AWS Microsoft AD with access to a Microsoft SharePoint farm running on AWS.

9. Which of the following are valid third-party federated identity standards? (Select TWO.)

    A. Secure Shell

    B. SSO

    C. SAML 2.0

    D. Active Directory

10. What information does the IAM credential report provide?

    A. A record of API requests against your account resources

    B. A record of failed password account login attempts

    C. The current state of your account security settings

    D. The current state of security of your IAM users' access credentials

11. What text format does the credential report use?

    A. JSON

    B. CSV

    C. ASCII

    D. XML

12. Which of the following IAM policies is the best choice for the admin user you create in order to replace the root user for day-to-day administration tasks?

    A. AdministratorAccess

    B. AmazonS3FullAccess

    C. AmazonEC2FullAccess

    D. AdminAccess

13. What will you need to provide for a new IAM user you're creating who will use "programmatic access" to AWS resources?

A. A password

B. A password and MFA

C. An access key ID

D. An access key ID and secret access key

14. What will IAM users with AWS Management Console access need to successfully log in?

A. Their username, account_number, and a password

B. Their username and password

C. Their account number and secret access key

D. Their username, password, and secret access key

15. Which of the following will encrypt your data while in transit between your office and Amazon S3?

A. DynamoDB

B. SSE-S3

C. A client-side master key

D. SSE-KMS

16. Which of the following AWS resources *cannot* be encrypted using KMS?

A. Existing AWS Elastic Block Store volumes

B. RDS databases

C. S3 buckets

D. DynamoDB databases

17. What does KMS use to encrypt objects stored on your AWS account?

A. SSH master key

B. KMS master key

C. Client-side master key

D. Customer master key

18. Which of the following standards governs AWS-based applications processing credit card transactions?

A. SSE-KMS

B. FedRAMP

C. PCI DSS

D. ARPA

19. What is the purpose of the Service Organization Controls (SOC) reports found on AWS Artifact?

    A. They can be used to help you design secure and reliable credit card transaction applications.

    B. They attest to AWS infrastructure compliance with data accountability standards like Sarbanes–Oxley.

    C. They guarantee that all AWS-based applications are, by default, compliant with Sarbanes–Oxley standards.

    D. They're an official, ongoing risk-assessment profiler for AWS-based deployments.

20. What role can the documents provided by AWS Artifact play in your application planning? (Select TWO.)

    A. They can help you confirm that your deployment infrastructure is compliant with regulatory standards.

    B. They can provide insight into various regulatory and industry standards that represent best practices.

    C. They can provide insight into the networking and storage design patterns your AWS applications use.

    D. They represent AWS infrastructure design policy.

Chapter

6

Working with Your AWS Resources

THE AWS CERTIFIED CLOUD PRACTITIONER EXAM OBJECTIVES COVERED IN THIS CHAPTER MAY INCLUDE, BUT ARE NOT LIMITED TO THE FOLLOWING:

Domain 2: Security

✓ **2.2 Define AWS Cloud security and compliance concepts**

✓ **2.4 Identify resources for security support**

Domain 3: Technology

✓ **3.1 Define methods of deploying and operating in the AWS Cloud**

✓ **3.3 Identify the core AWS services**

Domain 4: Billing and Pricing

✓ **4.4 Identify resources available for billing support**

Introduction

In this chapter, you'll learn the key tools that enable you to configure and monitor your AWS resources. Although each AWS service has its own unique aspects when it comes to configuration, AWS offers two common tools to interact with all of them.

The primary way you'll interact with AWS services is through the AWS Management Console, a web-based application you can use from any compatible web browser. Until you get intimately familiar with the core AWS services, you'll likely use the AWS Management Console almost exclusively. The AWS Management Console gives you a user friendly, point-and-click way to navigate your AWS resources, and you'll start by learning your way around it. You'll also learn about the AWS Console Mobile Application, which allows you to view and manage some of your AWS resources from an Android or iOS mobile device.

After that, you'll learn how to use the AWS Command Line Interface (AWS CLI) to perform configurations and view information about your AWS resources from the command line of your favorite desktop operating system. The AWS CLI lets you work with AWS services at the application programming interface (API) level.

Next, you'll learn about the different software development kits (SDKs) that AWS offers to help developers write applications that seamlessly integrate with AWS services. Although you won't need to know how to use SDKs personally, it's important to understand their capabilities and use cases.

You'll then learn how to use CloudWatch to monitor the performance of your resources, create alarms that notify you when things aren't working right, and collect, view, and search logs from your applications and AWS services.

After that, you'll learn how CloudTrail works to keep a detailed log of every action that anyone or anything performs against your AWS resources. CloudTrail is a key security service that's essential for validating that your AWS account is secure and that services are configured and working properly.

Lastly, you'll learn how to use Cost Explorer to understand what your AWS services are costing you, spot usage and billing trends over time, and get recommendations to help you save money.

The AWS Management Console

The *AWS Management Console*, also known as the AWS Console or the AWS Web Console, is a web interface you can use to manage all of your AWS cloud resources using a web browser, including compute, storage, and networking.

The AWS Management Console is what you'll choose if you want to do things using a point-and-click interface. Each AWS service has its own service console. Some services such as CloudWatch and AWS Billing and Cost Management offer visual reports that you can view and download.

Most settings for your AWS resources can be configured using the console, although there are a few options that require the AWS CLI. Most of these are advanced options that you won't need to know about unless you pursue the AWS Certified Solutions Architect Associate or similarly advanced certification.

The AWS Management Console is compatible with the following web browsers:

- Apple Safari
- Google Chrome
- Microsoft Edge
- Microsoft Internet Explorer
- Mozilla Firefox

Accessing the AWS Management Console

To access the AWS Management Console, browse to `https://console.aws.amazon.com` in your web browser. There are two ways to sign in: as the root user or as an Identity and Access Management (IAM) user.

Logging In as a Root User

To log in as the root user for your account, enter the email address and password associated with your AWS account, as shown in Figure 6.1. If you haven't created an AWS account yet, go back to Chapter 1, "The Cloud," and complete Exercise 1.1.

FIGURE 6.1   Logging in as a root user

Logging In as an IAM User

To log in as an IAM user, enter your account ID or account alias and choose Next. Refer to Figure 6.2 for an illustration.

FIGURE 6.2   Entering the account alias to log in as an IAM User

The AWS Management Console will take you to another page where you should enter your IAM username and password, as shown in Figure 6.3. If you don't have an IAM user, create one by following Exercise 5.2 in Chapter 5, "Securing Your AWS Resources."

FIGURE 6.3   Logging in as an IAM user

Once you're logged in, your session will remain active for 12 hours. After that, it'll expire and log you out to protect your account. No worries, though—as you can log right back in.

Opening a Service Console

Each AWS service has its own service console where you can manage resources that are part of that service. Choosing the Services link at the top of the AWS Management Console will let you search for a service by name in the search box, or you can browse services grouped by type, such as compute, storage, and database, as shown in Figure 6.4. Choosing a service name will bring you to the service console for that service.

FIGURE 6.4   Browsing available service consoles

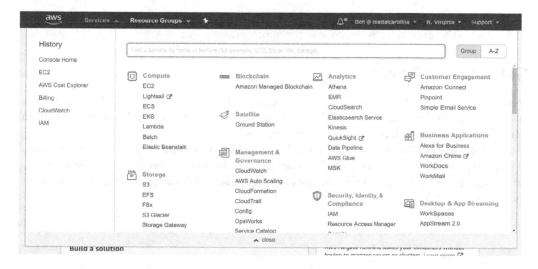

When a new service is launched, it's always available in the console within 180 days but is usually available immediately.

Working with Shortcuts

For services that you frequently use, you can pin shortcuts to the navigation bar. Just choose the pushpin icon and drag the service to the navigation bar, as shown in Figure 6.5.

FIGURE 6.5   Pinning a shortcut to the navigation bar

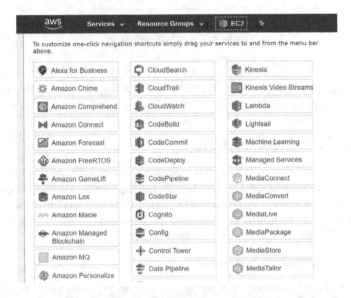

To access the service console, choose the shortcut.

Selecting a Region

Most AWS services are region-specific. For example, the EC2 service in the US East region is separate from the EC2 service in the US West region. Select a region from the navigation bar using the region selector, as shown in Figure 6.6.

As discussed in Chapter 4, "Understanding the AWS Environment," some services such as IAM, Route 53, and S3 are global. Consequently, the service consoles for these global services don't use the region selector. Instead, they display Global in the region selector, as shown in Figure 6.7.

FIGURE 6.6   Selecting a region

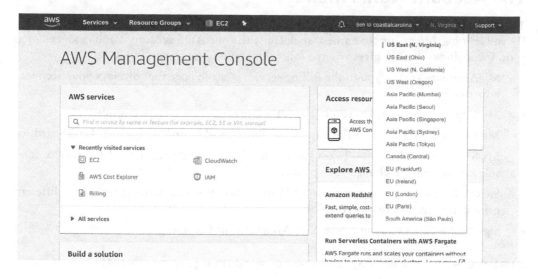

FIGURE 6.7   Some global services don't require selecting a region

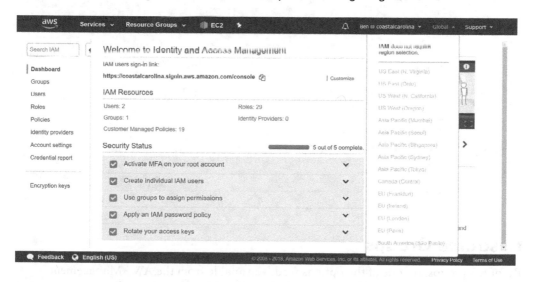

If you seem to be missing resources, make sure you have the correct region selected.

The Account Name Menu

The account name menu in the navigation bar displays the IAM user and account alias or ID you're logged in as, or the name associated with your AWS account if you're logged in as root. Choosing the menu gives you the following options, as shown in Figure 6.8:

- My Account—Takes you to the Billing service console page that displays your account information

- My Organization—Takes you to the AWS Organizations service console

- My Billing Dashboard—Takes you to the Billing and Cost Management Dashboard

- My Security Credentials—Takes you to the My Password page in the IAM service console where you can change your password

- Switch Role—Lets you assume an IAM role where you can perform tasks as a different principal with different permissions

- Sign Out—Signs you out of the AWS Management Console

FIGURE 6.8   The account name menu when you're logged in as an IAM user

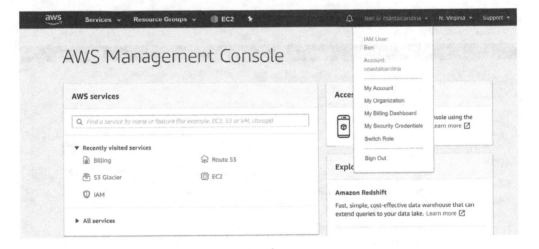

Resource Groups

Resource groups are one of the options readily available from the AWS Management Console. Choosing the Resource Groups link in the navigation bar, as shown in Figure 6.9, will reveal options to create new resource groups and view existing ones.

Resource groups let you view, manage, and automate tasks on multiple AWS resources at a time. They are ideal for grouping AWS resources that all compose a particular application. Rather than having to remember which resources belong to which application, you can add those resources to a resource group and let AWS remember for you! You can then perform bulk actions against those resources.

FIGURE 6.9 The Resource Groups menu

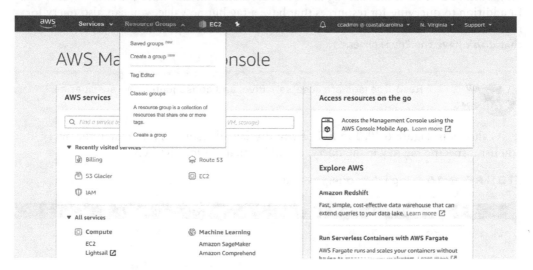

A resource group is a collection of AWS resources in the same region that match the results of a query. You can create a resource group from a query based on resource tags or from a CloudFormation Stack.

Resource tags   *Resource tags* are optional metadata that you can assign to AWS resources. A tag must contain a label called a *key* and may optionally contain a value. For example, you may tag your production resources using a key named Environment and a value named Production. Tag keys and values can include letters, numbers, spaces, and these characters: + - = . _ : / @. You can assign multiple tags to a resource, up to 50. Tag keys and values are case-sensitive. To create a resource group using tags, you can query based on a tag key only or both a tag key and its value.

AWS CloudFormation stacks   CloudFormation, which you'll learn about in Chapter 11, "Automating Your AWS Workloads," lets you programmatically deploy and manage multiple AWS resources as a single unit called a *stack*. You can create resource groups that contain some or all of the resources in a CloudFormation stack. You can choose all resources in the stack or filter by resource type, such as EC2 instance, EC2 security group, or S3 bucket.

Tag Editor

If you want to create a resource group based on tags, you'll first need to tag the resources you want to include in the group. Thankfully the AWS Management Console makes this easy. Choose the Resource Groups link in the navigation bar of the AWS Management Console, and then choose Tag Editor, as shown in Figure 6.9.

To get started with Tag Editor, create a query to find the resources you want to tag. At a minimum, you must select at least one region and one or more resource types, such as EC2 instances, EC2 volumes, VPCs, or S3 buckets. You can select all resources if you want. Optionally, you can list resources that already have an existing tag. For example, you may want to add an additional tag to all resources that already have the Environment tag. In addition to querying for resources that have a tag but no value, you can also query for resources that don't have a specific tag. For example, you may want to exclude resources that *don't* have the Environment tag.

WARNING   Resource tags are case-sensitive, and consequently, so are queries.

As shown in Figure 6.10, Tag Editor will display all resources that match the query. If you list a specific tag key in the query, it will list that tag for each resource.

FIGURE 6.10   Tag Editor query results

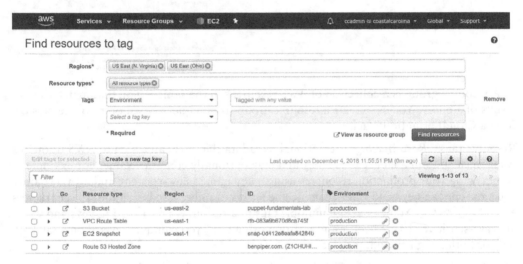

If you don't specify a tag key in the query, it will list the Name tag key for any resources that have it. You can customize the view of columns by choosing the cog icon. You can edit existing tags individually or in bulk. You can also create new tags.

Tagging Strategies

How you use tags is up to your preference and your organization's requirements. But if you're not sure where to start, you can use tags to organize resources along the following broad categories: technical, automation, business, and security. Keep in mind that you can use multiple strategies together or come up with your own tagging scheme.

Technical

One tagging strategy is to tag according to technical properties of a resource. You can use the Name tag to assign a name to an individual resource. For example, you may tag an EC2 instance hosting a web server with the Name tag and a value of webserver01. Many AWS service consoles recognize the Name tag and display it alongside resources such as EC2 instances, EBS volumes, and VPC security groups. Be careful, though. Tags don't have to be unique, so it's possible to inadvertently give different resources a Name tag with the same value.

You can use the Environment tag to specify whether the resource is part of your production, test, or development infrastructure. For instance, you may apply an Environment tag with a value of Development to a VPC that hosts development workloads.

You may also want to create an Application role tag to classify the type of role a resource performs. For example, you may tag an EC2 instance with a value of web server or database server, depending on its function.

Automation

Automation tags can be used to define the resources that should be part of an automation process. Some automation processes may include updating security patches on an instance, taking backups, deleting old snapshots, or turning off development servers after hours.

You might specify Date or Time tags to specify when automation tasks should occur on a resource. You may also specify Opt in or Opt out tags as flags to enable or disable automation on particular resources.

Business

In an organization where AWS is being used for multiple projects or by different departments, it can be helpful to group resources into categories that the business can use for billing, management, and analysis. Some example tags you might choose to create for business purposes include the following:

- Owner to identify the person or group responsible for the resource
- Business Unit or Cost Center to indicate who's responsible for paying for the resource
- Project to identify the name of the program or project the resource is a part of
- Customer to identify resources that are dedicated to a particular customer

Security

Conditions in IAM policies can look at resource tags to determine whether to allow a particular action. For example, you can specify a condition that permits an EC2 instance to access a production database only if the instance has the Environment tag with the value Production. Other instances tagged with a different value or no Environment tag at all would be denied access to the database.

In environments with strict security requirements, you may need to tag resources according to the confidentiality level of data they process or their compliance requirements.

Confidentiality   If your resources process or store data that has varying confidentiality requirements, you may use resource tags to designate that. For example, resources that are part of a medical records application that processes protected health information (PHI) may be tagged with the Confidentiality key name and the key value PHI.

Compliance   If any of your resources must adhere to specific compliance requirements such as the Health Insurance Portability and Accountability Act (HIPAA) or the Payment Card Industry Data Security Standard (PCI DSS), you can tag those resources accordingly.

The AWS Console Mobile Application

The *AWS Console Mobile Application* is a smartphone application that lets you manage your AWS account and resources on the go. The application features a dashboard showing key information about your AWS account and resources, including the following:

- Service Health—View any current health issues with AWS services across different regions.

- CloudWatch Alarms—View alarm graphs and current alarm status.

- Billing—View your current billing balance and a graph of usage charges.

Take a look at Figure 6.11 for an example of what kind of information the dashboard can show you.

FIGURE 6.11   The AWS Console Mobile Application dashboard

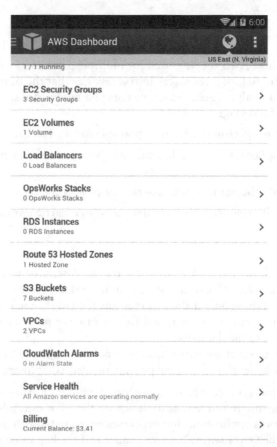

You can use the application to make limited changes to some AWS resources, including CloudWatch Alarms, EC2 security groups, EC2 instances, and CloudFormation stacks. For example, you can view or modify a CloudWatch alarm, as shown in Figure 6.12.

FIGURE 6.12   Viewing a CloudWatch alarm from the AWS Console Mobile Application

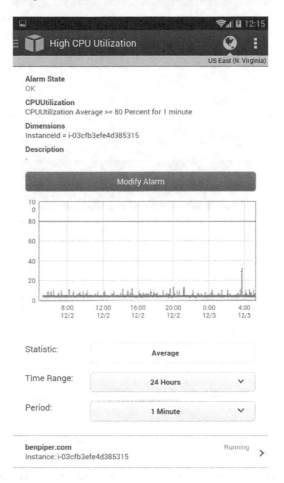

Or you can stop or reboot an EC2 instance, as shown in Figure 6.13.

FIGURE 6.13   Viewing an EC2 Instance from the AWS Console Mobile Application

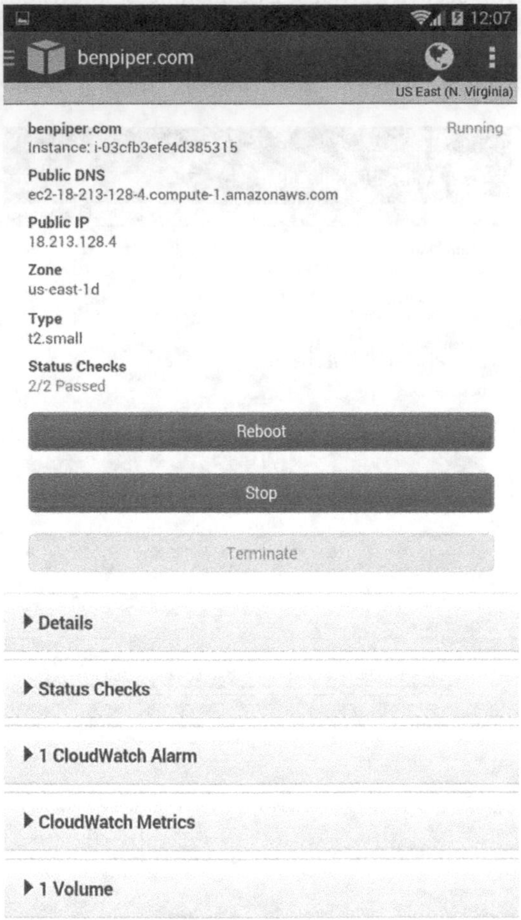

Supported Services

The application doesn't support all AWS services and resources. Services it does support include the following:

- AWS Billing and Cost Management
- AWS CloudFormation
- Amazon CloudWatch
- Amazon DynamoDB
- Amazon EC2
- AWS Elastic Beanstalk

- Elastic Load Balancing
- AWS OpsWorks
- AWS Personal Health Dashboard
- Amazon Relational Database Service (Amazon RDS)
- Amazon Route 53
- Amazon Simple Storage Service (Amazon S3)
- Amazon Virtual Private Cloud (Amazon VPC)

Requirements

The AWS Console Mobile Application supports Apple iOS 7.0+ and Android 4.0+. You can download it from the Amazon Appstore, Google Play, or iTunes.

When you first launch the application, it'll prompt you to authenticate to an existing AWS account by adding an identity, as shown in Figure 6.14.

FIGURE 6.14 Adding an identity to the AWS Console Mobile Application

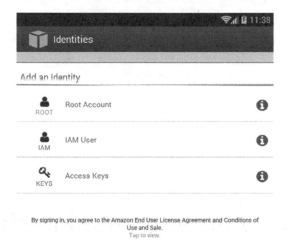

You can add multiple identities, which is handy if you need to keep an eye on multiple AWS accounts. You can authenticate in any of the following ways:

- Root account credentials (remember that it's a best practice to avoid using the root account)
- An IAM username and password
- An access key ID and secret key

The application is especially convenient for looking up important information on the go. For instance, you can quickly see how an S3 bucket policy is configured, as shown in Figure 6.15.

FIGURE 6.15   S3 bucket policy configuration, as shown in the AWS Console Mobile Application

The AWS Command Line Interface

The *AWS Command Line Interface* (AWS CLI) is a unified command-line tool to manage your AWS resources.

AWS gives access to the public application programming interfaces for all AWS services within 180 days of service launch. Anything you can do in the AWS Management Console, you can do from your terminal using the AWS CLI.

The AWS CLI is useful for performing repetitive tasks, such as launching EC2 instances, taking EBS snapshots, or attaching policies to IAM users. You can enter AWS CLI commands manually for convenience, or you can incorporate them into a script for automation. For example, you can write a reporting script that shows you your S3 buckets or all running EC2 instances. The AWS CLI is a versatile tool that can save you a lot of time versus the AWS Management Console.

Requirements

The AWS CLI is compatible with Windows, macOS, and Linux. To connect to AWS using the CLI, your network should allow outbound access to the internet on TCP port 443. You'll also need an IAM access key ID and secret key to authenticate to AWS using the CLI. Refer to Chapter 5 for details on creating an IAM access key ID and secret key.

Installation

The AWS CLI comes preinstalled on Amazon Linux AMIs, so if you want to run it from an EC2 instance running an Amazon Linux AMI, there's no need to install it. Otherwise, the installation procedure for the AWS CLI varies by operating system.

Installation Using Python and Pip

On any supported operating system, you can install the AWS CLI using the Python pip package manager. This is the method AWS recommends as it allows you to easily upgrade to new versions of the CLI. You'll need the following to install the AWS CLI using Python and pip:

- Python 2 version 2.6.5+ or Python 3 version 3.3+ (www.python.org)—If you have a choice, go with Python 3.
- The pip package installer—This comes with Python 2 version 2.7.9+ and Python 3 version 3.4 downloaded from python.org. If you're running an earlier version of Python or if your version came from somewhere else, you can install pip by following the instructions at https://pip.pypa.io/en/stable/installing.
- Internet access during installation.

Installation Using the Stand-Alone Installer

Alternatively, you can install the AWS CLI using a stand-alone installer that doesn't require internet access during installation. This is useful for offline and automated installations. AWS offers one stand-alone installer for Linux and macOS and another for Windows.

The stand-alone installer for Linux and macOS is a bundled installer that includes the AWS CLI, dependencies, and a script to install it. You need Python already installed, but not the pip package manager. Follow the instructions at https://docs.aws.amazon.com/cli/latest/userguide/awscli-install-bundle.html to install using the bundled installer.

For Windows, use the MSI installer that includes setup packages for Windows 64-bit and 32-bit architectures. You can download the setup MSI at https://s3.amazonaws.com/aws-cli/AWSCLISetup.exe. Note that the MSI installer doesn't work with Windows Server 2008. You'll have to use pip to install it.

Follow the steps in Exercise 6.1 to install the AWS CLI.

EXERCISE 6.1

Install the AWS Command Line Interface

In this exercise, you'll install the AWS CLI for your operating system.

If you're using Windows, download the MSI from https://s3.amazonaws.com/aws-cli/ AWSCLISetup.exe, and install it.

If you're using Linux, you can try to use your distribution's package manager to install it as follows:

- If you're running Ubuntu, run **sudo apt-get install awscli** from a terminal.

- If you're using CentOS or Red Hat try **sudo yum install awscli**.

If you can't or don't want to install the AWS CLI using your distribution's package manager (as its packages may be out of date), complete the steps at https://docs.aws.amazon.com/cli/latest/userguide/installing.html to install the AWS CLI for your operating system.

Once you've installed the AWS CLI, you'll need to configure it. Follow these steps:

1. Test that the AWS CLI works by issuing the **aws --version** command. You should see something like this:

   aws-cli/1.16.69 Python/2.7.10 Darwin/18.2.0 botocore/1.12.59

2. In the AWS Management Console, generate an access key ID and secret key for an IAM user.

3. In your terminal, run the command **aws configure** and enter the access key ID and secret key from step 2 when prompted.

4. Enter the AWS Region you want the AWS CLI to default to, such as **us-east-1**.

5. Enter the default output format, which can be **json**, **text**, or **table**. Note that this is case-sensitive.

Once you're done configuring the CLI, your terminal should look something like this:

```
~ ben$ aws configure
AWS Access Key ID [None]: AKIAIVAV4K7QVNLKIYIA
AWS Secret Access Key [None]: Ot9FQBftY1A59Hh2U/mrWSb8l6BOXeeyjVikcEjf
Default region name [None]: us-east-1
Default output format [None]: json
```

Try testing the CLI by issuing the following command to display a list of IAM access keys: **aws iam list-access-keys**. You should see some JSON-formatted output similar to the following:

```
~ ben$ aws iam list-access-keys
{
    "AccessKeyMetadata": [
        {
            "UserName": "Ben",
            "Status": "Active",
            "CreateDate": "2018-12-05T21:12:24Z",
            "AccessKeyId": "AKIAIVAV4K7QVNLKIYIA"
        }
    ]
}
```

Software Development Kits

AWS software development kits simplify the use of AWS services in custom applications. Application developers can use an SDK to integrate their applications with AWS services easily and reliably. SDKs save application developers from having to write low-level code to interact directly with the AWS service API endpoints. Instead, the developer just uses the SDK's well-documented methods to learn how to incorporate it into their application.

AWS offers SDKs for the following popular programming languages:

- Java
- .NET
- Node.js
- PHP
- Python
- Ruby
- JavaScript
- Go
- C++

Mobile Software Development Kits

AWS also offers mobile SDKs for the development of applications for smartphones and tablets. Available mobile SDKs include the following:

- AWS Mobile SDK for Android.
- AWS Mobile SDK for iOS.

- AWS Mobile SDK for Unity, a popular engine for creating games that can run on both iOS and Android.

- AWS Mobile SDK for .NET and Xamarin, which are cross-platform application development frameworks that can you can use to develop applications for iOS and Android.

- AWS Amplify, which is an open source framework to build mobile and web applications on AWS. It lets you both build an application backend on AWS and integrate it with your Android, iOS, and web applications. AWS Amplify uses AWS services to offer cloud-based authentication, notification, offline data sync, analytics, and more. You can use it to integrate mobile applications with AWS services without having to write a lot of custom code. AWS Amplify includes a JavaScript library with support for React Native, a framework for building mobile cross-platform mobile applications using JavaScript.

Internet of Things Device Software Development Kits

You can use the AWS IoT SDKs to create applications that run on Internet of Things (IoT) devices, such as sensors, microcontrollers, smart appliances, smart lightbulbs, and AWS IoT buttons.

AWS IoT is a collection of services that allow IoT devices to interact with AWS services, other applications, and even other devices. The AWS IoT platform lets you centrally onboard, manage, and monitor IoT devices.

Using the AWS IoT SDKs and the AWS IoT platform, applications running on these devices can integrate with other AWS services, including the following:

- Amazon S3

- Amazon DynamoDB

- Amazon Kinesis

- AWS Lambda

- Amazon Simple Notification Service

- Amazon Simple Queue Service

The AWS IoT SDKs allow developers to optimize memory, network, and power usage; reduce the size of applications; and ensure secure, fast communication with AWS.

IoT device SDKs are available for the following languages and platforms:

- Embedded C

- JavaScript

- Arduino Yún

- Python

- Java

- C++

CloudWatch

Amazon CloudWatch is a key service that helps you plan, monitor, and fine-tune your AWS infrastructure and applications. It lets you collect, search, and visualize data from your applications and AWS resources in the form of logs, metrics, and events. Common CloudWatch use cases include the following:

Infrastructure monitoring and troubleshooting   Visualize performance metrics to discover trends over time and spot outliers that might indicate a problem. Correlate metrics and logs across your application and infrastructure stacks to understand the root cause of failures and performance issues.

Resource optimization   Save money and help with resource planning by identifying overused or underused resources. Ensure performance and availability by using AWS Auto Scaling to automatically provision new EC2 instances to meet demand.

Application monitoring   Create CloudWatch alarms to alert you and take corrective action when a resource's utilization, performance, or health falls outside of a threshold that you define.

Log analytics   Search, visualize, and correlate logs from multiple sources to help with troubleshooting and identify areas for improvement.

CloudWatch Metrics

CloudWatch Metrics is a feature that collects numeric performance metrics from both AWS and non-AWS resources such as on-premises servers. A *metric* is a variable that contains a time-ordered set of data points. Each data point contains a timestamp, a value, and optionally a unit of measure. For example, a data point for the CPU Utilization metric for an EC2 instance may contain a timestamp of December 25, 2018 13:37, a value of 75, and Percent as the unit of measure.

All AWS resources automatically send their metrics to CloudWatch. These metrics include things such as EC2 instance CPU utilization, S3 bucket sizes, and DynamoDB consumed read and write capacity units. CloudWatch stores metrics for up to 15 months. You can graph metrics to view trends and how they change over time, as illustrated in Figure 6.16.

FIGURE 6.16   Using CloudWatch to graph the CPU Utilization metric for an EC2 Instance

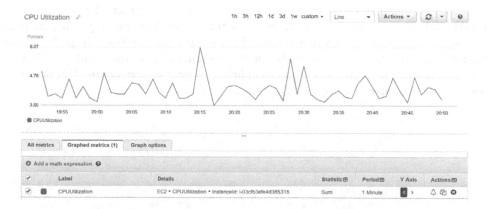

CloudWatch Alarms

A CloudWatch alarm watches over the value of a single metric. If the metric crosses a threshold that you specify (and stays there), the alarm will take an action. For example, you might configure an alarm to take an action when the average CPU utilization for an instance exceeds 80% for five minutes. The action can be one of the following:

Notification using Simple Notification Service   The *Simple Notification Service* (SNS) allows applications, users, and devices to send and receive notifications from AWS. SNS uses a publisher-subscriber model, wherein a publisher such as an AWS service generates a notification and a subscriber such as an end user receives it. The communication channel that SNS uses to map publishers and subscribers is called a *topic*. SNS can send notifications to subscribers via a variety of protocols including the following:

- HTTP(S)
- Simple Queue Service (SQS)
- Lambda
- Mobile push notification
- Email
- Email-JSON
- Short Message Service (SMS) text messages

Auto Scaling action   By specifying an EC2 Auto Scaling action, the EC2 Auto Scaling service can add or remove EC2 instances in response to changing demand. For example, if a metric indicates that instances are overburdened, you can have EC2 Auto Scaling respond by adding more instances.

EC2 action   If you're monitoring a specific instance that's having a problem, you can use an EC2 action to stop, terminate, or recover the instance. Recovering an instance migrates the instance to a new EC2 host, something you may need to do if there's a physical hardware problem on the hardware hosting the instance.

CloudWatch Dashboards

CloudWatch dashboards are your one-stop shop for keeping an eye on all of your important metrics. You can create multiple dashboards and add to them metric graphs, the latest values for a metric, and CloudWatch alarms. You can save your dashboards for future use and share them with others. Dashboards can also visualize metrics from multiple AWS Regions, so you can keep an eye on the global health of your infrastructure. Check out Figure 6.17 for a sample CloudWatch dashboard.

FIGURE 6.17   A CloudWatch dashboard

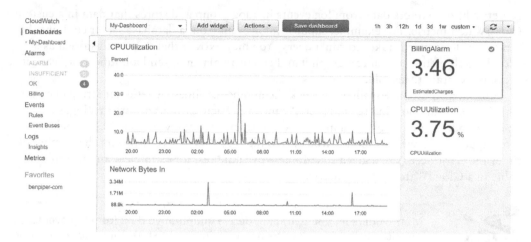

CloudWatch Logs

CloudWatch Logs collects and stores log files from AWS and non-AWS sources and makes it easy to view, search, and extract custom metrics from them.

Log Events, Streams, and Groups

You configure your applications and AWS services to send log events to CloudWatch Logs. A log event is analogous to a line in a log file and always contains a timestamp and an event message. Many AWS services produce their own logs called *vended logs* that you can stream to CloudWatch Logs. Such logs include Route 53 DNS query logs, VPC flow logs, and CloudTrail logs. CloudWatch Logs can also receive custom logs from your applications, such as web server access logs.

CloudWatch Logs organizes log events by log streams by storing log events from the same source in a single log stream. For example, web server access logs from a specific EC2 instance would be stored in one log stream, while Route 53 DNS query logs would be stored in a separate log stream.

CloudWatch further organizes log streams into log groups. To organize related log streams, you can place them into the same log group. For instance, if you have several log streams that are collecting web server log events from multiple web servers, you can group all of those log streams into a single log group.

CloudWatch Logs stores log events indefinitely by default, but you can configure a log group's retention settings to delete events automatically. Retention settings range from 1 day to 10 years. You can also archive your logs by exporting them to an S3 bucket.

Metric Filters

A metric filter extracts data from log events in a log group and stores that data in a custom CloudWatch metric. For example, suppose a log event from a database server contains the time in milliseconds it takes to run a query. You may extract that value and store it as a CloudWatch metric so you can graph it and create an alarm to send a notification when it exceeds a certain threshold.

You can also use metric filters to track the number of times a particular string occurs. This is useful for counting the number of times a particular event occurs in a log, such as an error code. For example, you might want to track how many times a 403 Forbidden error appears in a web server log. You can configure a metric filter to count the number of times the error occurs in a given timeframe—five minutes, for example—and record that value in a CloudWatch custom metric.

> Metric filters let you extract or derive quantitative data from log events, so metric values will always be numeric. You can't store a non-numeric string such as an IP address in a metric.

CloudWatch Events

The CloudWatch Events feature lets you continuously monitor for specific events that represent a change in your AWS resources—particularly write-only API operations—and take an action when they occur. For example, an EC2 instance going from the running state to the stopped state would be an event. An IAM user logging into the AWS Management Console would also be an event. CloudWatch Events can then automatically and immediately take actions in response to those events.

You start by creating a rule to define the events to monitor, as well as the actions you want to take in response to those events. You define the action to take by selecting a target, which is an AWS resource. Some targets you can choose from include the following:

- Lambda functions
- EC2 instances
- SQS queues
- SNS topics
- ECS tasks

CloudWatch responds to events as they occur, in real time. Unlike CloudWatch alarms, which take action when a metric crosses and remains crossing a numeric threshold, CloudWatch events trigger immediately. For example, you can create a CloudWatch event to send an SNS notification whenever an EC2 instance terminates. Or you could trigger a Lambda function to process an image file as soon as it hits an S3 bucket.

Alternatively, you can create a schedule to automatically perform actions at regular intervals. For example, to save money you might create a schedule to shut down development instances every day at 7 p.m., after the developers have ideally stopped working!

CloudTrail

CloudTrail keeps detailed event logs of every action that occurs against your AWS resources. Each event that CloudTrail logs includes the following parameters:

- The service. Specifically, this is the address of the service's global endpoint, such as `iam.amazonaws.com` for IAM.

- The name of the API action performed, such as `RunInstances`, `CreateUser`, or `PutObject`.

- The region the resource is located in. For global services, this is always us-east-1.

- Response elements. In the case of an API operation that changes or creates a resource, this contains information about the results of the action. For example, the response elements for a `RunInstances` action to launch an EC2 instance would yield information such as the instance ID and private IP address.

- The principal that made the request. This may include the type of principal (IAM user or role), its Amazon resource name (ARN), and the name.

- The date and time of the request, given in coordinated universal time (UTC).

- The IP address of the requester.

API and Non-API Events

The events CloudTrail logs consist of two different actions: API and non-API actions. API actions include things such as launching an instance, creating an S3 bucket, creating a new IAM user, or taking an EBS snapshot. Note that the term *API action* has nothing to do with how the action was performed. For example, terminating an EC2 instance is an API event whether you do it via the AWS Management Console, the AWS command-line interface, or an AWS software development kit. Non-API actions include everything else, such as logging into the management console.

Management and Data Events

CloudTrail also classifies events along two other dimensions: management events and data events.

Management events—also known as *control plane operations*—are operations that a principal (such as a user or service) attempts to execute against an AWS resource. Management events include write-only events—API operations that modify or might modify resources, and read-only events that read resource information but don't make any changes. For example, the RunInstances API operation can create an EC2 instance, so it would be a write-only event. On the other hand, the DescribeInstances API operation returns a list of EC2 instances but doesn't make any changes, so it's a read-only operation.

Data events consist of S3 object-level activity and Lambda function executions, both of which tend to be high volume. As such, CloudTrail treats data events as separate from management events. And when it comes to S3 object-level operations, CloudTrail draws a distinction between read-only events like GetObject and write-only events such as PutObject and DeleteObject.

    CloudTrail logs API operations regardless of whether they're successful.

Event History

When you open an AWS account, CloudTrail begins logging all of your management events automatically. It stores 90 days of management events in the event history, which you can view, search, and download at any time. The event history log doesn't record data events.

For each region, CloudTrail maintains a separate event history log containing the events that occurred in that region. But events generated by global services including IAM and Route 53 are included in the event history for every region.

Trails

If you want to customize the types of events CloudTrail logs—such as specific management or data events—or if you need to store more than 90 days of event history, you need to create a trail. A *trail* is a configuration that directs CloudTrail to record specified events in log files and deliver them to an S3 bucket. A trail can log events from either a single region or all regions. You can choose to log management events, data events, or both. You can also choose whether to log read-only or write-only events, or both.

CloudTrail doesn't provide a way to search trail logs, which are written in JavaScript Object Notation (JSON) format. But you can download the log files directly from S3. You can also configure CloudTrail to send a trail log to CloudWatch Logs, making them available for storage, searching, and metric filtering.

Log File Integrity Validation

Log file integrity validation is an optional feature that provides assurance that no CloudTrail log files are surreptitiously modified or deleted. Here's how it works: every time CloudTrail writes a log file to the trail's S3 bucket, it calculates and stores a cryptographic hash of the file, which is a unique value based on the contents of the log file itself. If anyone modifies the file, even by one bit, the hash of the modified file will be completely different than the original hash. This can tell you whether anyone has tampered with the log file, but it can't tell you exactly how it's been modified.

Log files can be encrypted using server-side encryption with Amazon S3-managed encryption keys (SSE-S3) or server-side encryption with AWS KMS-managed keys (SSE-KMS).

Cost Explorer

As you recall from Chapter 2, "Understanding Your AWS Account," AWS Cost Explorer is a feature of AWS Billing and Cost Management that offers configurable reports and graphs to help you understand how each of your AWS services impacts your monthly bill.

AWS Cost Explorer offers the following three categories of reports:

- Cost and usage reports
- Reservation reports
- Reserved instance recommendations

Cost and Usage

You can generate cost and usage reports to give you a graphical view of your daily and monthly costs and usage over time. Cost Explorer can also show you the forecast for the current month, 3 months out, and 12 months out, helping you plan ahead. Figure 6.18 shows the monthly costs for the last 12 months and a forecast for the current month.

FIGURE 6.18   Cost and usage report showing monthly costs

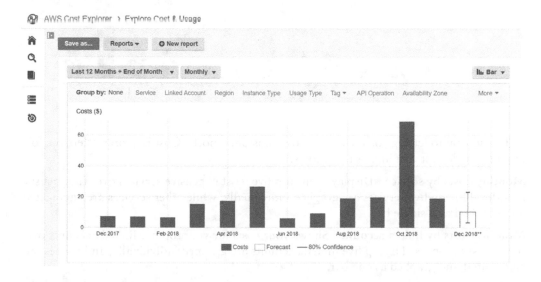

You can go back as far as one year and filter or group by several parameters including but not limited to the following:

- Service
- Availability Zone
- Region
- Instance type
- Usage type
- Tag
- API operation
- Charge type
- Platform

This can help you quickly see which services are incurring the greatest costs and how those services costs are trending over time. Figure 6.19 shows the monthly costs for the last 12 months grouped by service.

FIGURE 6.19   Cost and usage report showing monthly costs grouped by service

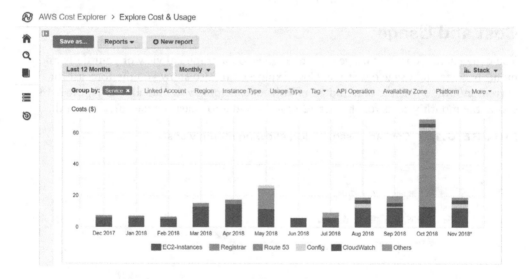

In addition to letting you create your own custom reports, Cost Explorer offers the following five default cost and usage reports:

Monthly costs by service   Displays your top five most expensive services over the past six months. The top five services are graphed individually, while other services are aggregated and graphed as a single bar.

Monthly costs by linked account   Shows your costs for your top five linked accounts over the past six months. The top five linked accounts are grouped individually, and the rest are aggregated and graphed as one bar.

Monthly EC2 running hours costs and usage   Displays two monthly graphs showing the costs and running hours for your EC2 instances.

Daily costs   Shows your monthly spend for the last six months and a forecast for the current month.

AWS marketplace   As you'll learn in Chapter 7, "The Core Compute Services," the AWS Marketplace allows vendors to make their products and services available to you via AWS. License, subscription, and usage costs are bundled together and billed through AWS. This report shows you how much you've spent on AWS Marketplace solutions.

Reservation Reports

Cost Explorer offers the following two built-in reservation reports to give you insight on how much you are saving—or could have saved—with instance reservations. Instance reservations allow you to save money by prepaying for compute instances including those used by Amazon EC2, Amazon Elasticsearch Service, Amazon ElastiCache, Amazon RDS, and Amazon Redshift. You'll learn more about reserved instances in Chapter 7.

Reserved Instances Utilization

The Reserved Instances (RI) Utilization report shows you the percentage of your reserved instances you've used and how much money you've saved or overspent by using reserved instances. The RI Utilization report also shows you your net savings from reserved instances, giving you insight into whether you've had too few or too many reserved instances. Figure 6.20 shows a sample reservation utilization for a six-month time range.

FIGURE 6.20   RI Utilization report

Reserved Instances Coverage

The Reserved Instances Coverage report tells you how many of your running instance hours are covered by instance reservations, how much you've spent for on-demand instances, and how much you could have saved by purchasing reserved instances. Figure 6.21 shows a graph of reservation coverage for the past 12 months, as well as the average coverage percentage and the total on-demand costs.

FIGURE 6.21   RI Coverage report

Reserved Instance Recommendations

Cost Explorer can provide reserved instance recommendations to help reduce your costs. Here's how recommendations work: Cost Explorer analyzes your on-demand instance usage over the past 7, 30, or 60 days. It then searches for all available reserved instances that would cover that usage. Finally, it selects the most cost-effective reserved instances and recommends them.

Costs Explorer makes recommendations separately for each service such as EC2 or RDS. You can also customize the recommendations by selecting a reserved instance term and payment option.

Keep in mind that for the purposes of making reserved instance recommendations, Cost Explorer ignores any usage that's already covered by a reservation. So, if your instances are already fully covered by instance reservations, Cost Explorer will not make any recommendations.

NOTE   Cost Explorer updates report data at least once every 24 hours.

Summary

Starting out, you'll spend most of your time interacting with AWS using the AWS Management Console. It's always changing, but even when it does, AWS takes great care to let you know what changed. Sometimes AWS will even let you preview new console features before they go live, giving you the chance to adjust to the change before it's rolled out permanently.

As you find yourself working with AWS more and getting more familiar with the services, you'll begin to use the AWS Command Line Interface for many common tasks. The AWS Command Line Interface is a must for scripting AWS tasks and collecting information from your AWS resources in bulk.

CloudWatch collects metrics from AWS services. You can create alarms to take some action, such as a notification, when a metric crosses a threshold. CloudWatch receives and stores logs from AWS and non-AWS services and even extracts metrics from those logs using metric filters.

CloudTrail records events that occur against your AWS account. By default, the CloudTrail event history log captures the last 90 days of management events in each region. If you want to log more than this or customize the events that it logs, you must create a trail to cause CloudTrail to store events in an S3 bucket. You can also configure a trail to stream logs to CloudWatch Logs for storage, viewing, and searching.

Exam Essentials

Understand when to use the AWS Management Console versus the AWS CLI. The Management Console is required if you want to use the point-and-click interface and want to view visual elements such as CloudWatch graphs or Cost Explorer graphs. You can log into the Management Console using an email address and password for the root account. If you're logging in as an IAM user, you'll need the account alias or number, IAM username, and password. If MFA is set up, you'll be prompted for an MFA one-time passcode. The AWS CLI is what you'll use to manage your AWS resources manually from the command line or using scripts. It's good for repetitive or bulk tasks that would take a long time using the Web. To use the CLI, you need an access key ID and secret key.

Know how to use resource tags and resource groups. Resource tags are keys associated with your AWS resources. A key can optionally contain a value. You can use tags to label your resources according to whatever you like, be it owner, business unit, or environment. You can group resources into a resource group according to resource tags or CloudFormation stacks.

Be able to identify use cases for CloudWatch.   CloudWatch can collect logs and metrics from AWS and non-AWS services. Many AWS services such as EC2 automatically send metric data to CloudWatch. You can create alarms to trigger when a metric falls above or below a threshold. In response to an alarm, you can send a notification using SNS, or you can take an action using an Auto Scaling action or EC2 action. You can also graph metrics to view trends visually. CloudWatch Logs lets you aggregate and search log files. Some services, such as VPC and Route 53, can be configured to stream vended logs to CloudWatch logs. You can extract metrics from these logs using metric filters. CloudWatch events let you take actions in response to specific events that occur with your AWS resources, such as launching an EC2 instance or creating an S3 bucket. Unlike alarms that are triggered by metrics crossing a threshold, CloudWatch Events acts in response to specific API operations.

Know the options for developing applications that integrate with AWS.   AWS offers SDKs for a variety of programming languages and platforms. You can use the SDKs to quickly develop desktop, server, web-based, or mobile apps that use AWS services. Although many AWS services offer the HTTPS-based AWS Query API that you can interface with directly, the SDKs handle the heavy lifting of request authentication, serialization, and connection management, freeing you up to write your application without having to learn the nitty-gritty API details of every AWS service you want to use.

Understand what CloudTrail does and how it differs from and integrates with CloudWatch.   CloudTrail logs management and data operations on your account. By default, it logs 90 days of management events per region. If you want to log more than this or customize which events it logs, you can create a trail to log those events and store them in an S3 bucket. You can optionally stream CloudTrail logs to CloudWatch for storage, searching, and analysis.

Review Questions

1. Which of the following credentials can you use to log into the AWS Management Console?
   A. Access key ID
   B. Account alias
   C. Account ID
   D. Identity and Access Management (IAM) username

2. How long will your session with the AWS Management Console remain active?
   A. 6 hours
   B. 12 hours
   C. 8 hours
   D. 24 hours
   E. 15 minutes

3. While looking at the EC2 service console in the AWS Management Console while logged in as the root user, you notice all of your instances are missing. What could be the reason?
   A. You've selected the wrong region in the navigation bar.
   B. You don't have view access.
   C. You've selected the wrong Availability Zone in the navigation bar.
   D. You don't have an access key.

4. Which of the following is true regarding a resource tag?
   A. It must be unique within an account.
   B. It's case insensitive.
   C. It must have a key.
   D. It must have a value.

5. Which of the following is required to use the AWS Command Line Interface (CLI)?
   A. A secret key
   B. An IAM user
   C. Outbound network access to TCP port 80
   D. Linux

6. Which of the following are options for installing the AWS CLI on Windows 10? (Select TWO.)
   A. The MSI installer
   B. An AWS software development kit (SDK)
   C. The Yum or Aptitude package manager
   D. Using Python and pip

7. After installing the AWS Command Line Interface, what should you do before using it to securely manage your AWS resources?

A. Issue the `aws --version` command.

B. Issue the `aws configure` command.

C. Reboot.

D. Generate a new access key ID and secret access key for the root user.

8. Which output format does the AWS CLI support?

A. Tab-separated values (TSV)

B. Comma-separated values (CSV)

C. JavaScript object notation (JSON)

D. None of these

9. Which of the following programming languages are AWS software development kits available for? (Select THREE.)

A. Fortran

B. JavaScript

C. JSON

D. Java

E. PHP

10. Which of the following software development kits (SDKs) enable developers to write mobile applications that run on both Apple and Android devices? (Select TWO.)

A. AWS Mobile SDK for Unity

B. AWS Mobile SDK for .NET and Xamarin

C. AWS SDK for Go

D. AWS Mobile SDK for iOS

11. Which of the following programming languages are AWS Internet of Things (IoT) device software development kits available for? (Select TWO.)

A. JavaScript

B. C++

C. Swift

D. Ruby

12. What's the difference between the AWS Command Line Interface (CLI) and the AWS software development kits (SDK)? (Select TWO.)

A. The AWS SDKs allow you to use popular programming languages to write applications that interact with AWS services.

B. The AWS CLI allows you to interact with AWS services from a terminal.

C. The AWS SDKs allow you to interact with AWS services from a terminal.

D. The AWS CLI allows you to use popular programming languages to write applications that interact with AWS services.

13. Which of the following CloudWatch features store performance data from AWS services?

    A. Logs

    B. Metrics

    C. Events

    D. Metric filters

    E. Alarms

14. For which of the following scenarios can you create a CloudWatch alarm to send a notification?

    A. A metric that doesn't change for 24 hours

    B. Termination of an EC2 instance

    C. The presence of a specific IP address in a web server log

    D. A metric that exceeds a given threshold

15. Which of the following Simple Notification Service (SNS) protocols can you use to send a notification? (Select TWO.)

    A. Short Message Service (SMS) text message

    B. CloudWatch Events

    C. Simple Queue Service (SQS)

    D. Mobile pull notification

16. Which of the following are true regarding CloudWatch Events? (Select TWO.)

    A. It can reboot an EC2 instance when an error appears in a log file.

    B. It can send an SNS notification when an EC2 instance's CPU utilization exceeds 90%.

    C. It can send an SNS notification when an IAM user logs in to the AWS Management Console.

    D. It can shut down an EC2 instance at a specific time.

17. Which of the following trigger an API action? (Select TWO.)

    A. Configuring the AWS Command Line Interface (CLI)

    B. Viewing an S3 bucket from the AWS Management Console

    C. Logging into the AWS Management Console

    D. Listing IAM users from the AWS Command Line Interface (CLI)

18. What's the most cost-effective way to view and search only the last 60 days of management API events on your AWS account?

    A. Use CloudTrail event history.

    B. Create a trail.

    C. Stream CloudTrail logs to CloudWatch.

    D. Use CloudWatch Events.

19. You want to log every object downloaded from an S3 bucket in a specific region. You want to retain these logs indefinitely and search them easily. What's the most cost-effective way to do this? (Select TWO.)

    A. Stream CloudTrail logs to CloudWatch Logs.

    B. Use CloudTrail event history.

    C. Enable CloudTrail logging of global service events.

    D. Create a trail to log S3 data events.

20. What is a benefit of using CloudTrail log file integrity validation?

    A. It lets you assert that no CloudTrail log files have been deleted from CloudWatch.

    B. It lets you assert that no CloudTrail log files have been deleted from S3.

    C. It prevents unauthorized users from deleting CloudTrail log files.

    D. It tells you how a CloudTrail log file has been tampered with.

21. Which of the following Cost Explorer report types can show you the monthly costs for your reserved EC2 instances?

    A. Reserved instance recommendations

    B. Reserved Instances (RI) Coverage reports

    C. Reserved Instances (RI) Utilization reports

    D. Costs and usage reports

22. Which of the following services allow you to purchase reserved instances to save money?

    A. Amazon Relational Database Service (RDS)

    B. Lambda

    C. S3

    D. AWS Fargate

23. Which Cost Explorer report shows the amount of money you've saved using reserved instances?

    A. Daily costs

    B. Reservation Utilization

    C. Reservation Coverage

    D. Monthly EC2 running hours costs and usage

24. You've been running several Elasticsearch instances continuously for the past three months. You check the reserved instance recommendations in Cost Explorer but see no recommendations. What could be a reason for this?

    A. The recommendation parameters are based on the past seven days.

    B. You haven't selected the Elastic Compute Cloud (EC2) service.

    C. Cost Explorer doesn't make reservation recommendations for Elasticsearch.

    D. Your instances are already covered by reservations.

    E. You haven't selected the ElastiCache service.

Chapter

7

The Core Compute Services

THE AWS CERTIFIED CLOUD PRACTITIONER EXAM OBJECTIVES COVERED IN THIS CHAPTER MAY INCLUDE, BUT ARE NOT LIMITED TO, THE FOLLOWING:

Domain 3: Technology

✓ **3.1** Define methods of deploying and operating in the AWS Cloud

✓ **3.3** Identify the core AWS services

Domain 4: Billing and Pricing

✓ **4.1** Compare and contrast the various pricing models for AWS

✓ **4.2** Recognize the various account structures in relation to AWS billing and pricing

Introduction

While Elastic Compute Cloud (EC2) wasn't quite the first service announced by AWS, once it did show up in 2006, it became the obvious cornerstone tool for many cloud deployments. EC2 faithfully mirrors the functionality of traditional on-premises data centers: you provision and launch virtual servers (known as *instances*) to run the same kinds of application workloads that would once have kept legacy servers busy. The fact that EC2 instances are more resilient and scalable and, often, cheaper than their on-premises cousins was just a happy bonus.

In the years since EC2 appeared, Amazon has introduced other compute tools aimed at providing the same end-user experience but through a simplified or abstracted interface. In this chapter, you'll learn about how it all happens using EC2 and its more lightweight counterparts like Elastic Beanstalk, Lightsail, Docker (including via the Kubernetes orchestrator), and Lambda.

Deploying Amazon Elastic Compute Cloud Servers

To get your virtual machine (VM) instance running, you'll first define the elements one at a time. Rather than installing an operating system and a software stack from scratch the traditional way, you'll select an Amazon Machine Image (AMI). Instead of choosing the right CPU, memory modules, and network adapters and adding them to your physical motherboard, you'll choose the instance type matching your application needs. And rather than purchasing storage drives and sliding them into your server chassis, you'll define virtual storage volumes available through the Elastic Block Store (EBS).

Let's see how all that works.

Amazon Machine Images

An *image* is a software bundle that was built from a template definition and made available within a single AWS Region. The bundle can be copied to a freshly created storage volume that, once the image is extracted, will become a bootable drive that'll turn the VM it's attached to into a fully operational server.

The nice thing about AMIs is that they're available in so many flavors. You can select AMIs that will give you clean, cloud-optimized operating systems like official versions of Red Hat Enterprise Linux (RHEL), Ubuntu, Windows Server, or Amazon's own Amazon Linux. But you can also find the OS you need preloaded with one of hundreds of popular software stacks like OpenVPN (secure remote connectivity), TensorFlow (neural networks), or a Juniper firewall already installed and ready to go.

AMIs are organized into four collections: the Quick Start set, any custom AMIs you might have created, the AWS Marketplace, and Community AMIs.

Using Quick Start AMIs

AWS makes the three dozen or so most popular AMIs easily available through the Quick Start tab on the Choose An Amazon Machine Image page—the first page you'll face when you choose the Launch Instance button in the EC2 Dashboard. For the most part, they're Free Tier–eligible. This means that launching them on a lightweight instance type within an account's first year will, as you saw in Chapter 2, "Understanding Your AWS Account," incur no costs.

The available Linux distributions you'll find here are mostly categorized as *long-term support* (LTS) releases, meaning that they'll be eligible for security and functional updates for at least five years from their original release date. This can be an important consideration for deployment planning since you will often prefer not to have to rebuild your production servers any more than absolutely necessary.

Even outside of the Free Tier, the use of the open source operating systems like Ubuntu and CentOS will always be free. But other choices—like Windows Server and RHEL—will carry the normal *licensing charges*. Once you launch an instance running one of those images, the charges will be billed through your AWS account.

Besides the general-purpose OS choices available through Quick Start, you can also find images optimized for deep learning, container hosting, .NET Core, and Microsoft SQL Server. Figure 7.1 shows two listings in the Quick Start menu. Note how the OS, release number, volume type (solid-state drive—SSD—in this case), AMI ID, and preferred hardware architecture—64-bit (x86) is selected in this case—are displayed.

FIGURE 7.1 A couple of EC2 AMI listings displaying features and options

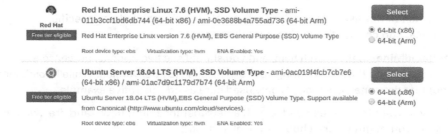

Using AWS Marketplace and Community AMIs

AWS Marketplace is a software store managed by Amazon where vendors make their products available to AWS customers as ready-to-run AMIs (or, alternatively, in additional formats like CloudFormation stacks and containers). Companies like SAP, Oracle, and NVIDIA will package their software solutions into AMIs, often running on one or another Linux distribution.

When you select a Marketplace AMI, you'll be shown its total billing cost, broken down into separate software license and EC2 infrastructure amounts. The Barracuda CloudGen Firewall AMI, for example, would, at the time of writing, cost $1.68 USD each hour for the software and $0.192 for an M5 Extra Large EC2 instance type, for a total hourly charge of $1.872. Running the same AMI on a much larger M5 Quadruple Extra Large instance type would cost you $5.72 for the software and $0.768 for the instance.

Marketplace AMIs will often offer a limited-time free trial for their software and reduced annual subscription rates. You can also view and search through Marketplace offerings outside of the EC2 Launch Instance interface through the Marketplace site: https://aws.amazon.com/marketplace.

Looking for a more specialized image built with a software stack that's not available in the Quick Start or Marketplace tab? There are more than 100,000 AMIs to choose from in the Community AMIs tab. Some are supported by recognized vendors such as Canonical, but others are provided as is, often by end users like you. Given the informal sources of some Community AMIs, you must take responsibility for the security and reliability of AMIs you launch. Why not take a quick look at the process by working through Exercise 7.1?

EXERCISE 7.1

Select an EC2 AMI

1. From the EC2 Dashboard, choose the Launch Instance button.

2. With the Quick Start tab selected, scroll through the available options, noting the various operating systems (Amazon Linux, SUSE Linux, Windows, etc.).

3. Try to identify each one's OS and release number (Ubuntu 18.04, for example), volume type (SSD), AMI ID (for instance, ami-0ac019f4fcb7cb7e6), and the choice of hardware architecture (in most cases, it'll be either 64-bit x86 or 64-bit ARM).

4. Now switch to the AWS Marketplace tab, scroll down to the links to specific categories, and choose the Business Intelligence link.

5. Enter **RapidMiner** in the search field, and you should see two options: purchase a license along with the AMI, or bring your own license (BYOL) version. While RapidMiner is a popular data analytics tool, it's only used here as an illustrative example.

6. Unless you want to go ahead and launch a new instance right now—and are aware of any costs you might incur—choose Cancel and Exit.

Creating Your Own AMIs

It's possible to convert any EC2 instance into an AMI by creating a snapshot from the EBS volume used with an instance and then creating an image from the snapshot. The resulting image will be available as an AMI either in the AMIs menu on the EC2 Dashboard or on the My AMIs tab in the Choose An Amazon Machine Image page of the instance launch process.

But why bother? Well, suppose you've spent a full week carefully configuring an instance as your company's application server. In fact, you did such a good job that you'd now like to be able to deploy exact copies of the instance to meet growing demand for your application. One way to make that both possible and painless is to create an AMI from your instance and select the AMI whenever another instance is needed.

Understanding EC2 Instance Types

An EC2 instance type is simply a description of the kind of hardware resources your instance will be using. The t2.micro instance type, for instance, comes with 1 GB of memory, low-to-moderate data transfer rates to network connections, and one *virtual CPU* (vCPU) running on a 2.5 GHz Intel Xeon processor. A c5d.18xlarge instance type, on the other hand, gives you 72 vCPUs on a 3 GHz Intel Xeon Platinum 8124M processor, and 144 GB of memory. You'll use the instance type definitions to figure out the best match for your application.

A vCPU, by the way, is an arbitrary—and somewhat mysterious—metric used by AWS to describe the compute power you'll get from a given instance. It's meant to make you think in terms of the multiprocessor CPUs on consumer and server motherboards, where more is generally better. But it's notoriously difficult to accurately map the value of a single vCPU against any one real-world device.

While, in general, the more vCPUs and memory you get, the better your instance will perform, that's definitely not the whole story. EC2 offers instance type families that are optimized for very different computing tasks. The T2, T3, and M5 types are included in the general-purpose family because of their ability to perform well for a wide range of uses. Besides *general-purpose*, EC2 also offers *compute-optimized*, *memory-optimized*, *accelerated-computing*, and *storage-optimized* families of instance types. Table 7.1 lists the families and types available at the time of writing. Although you should be aware that this will constantly change, the most up-to-date list will always be available here: https://aws .amazon.com/ec2/instance-types.

TABLE 7.1   EC2 Instance Type Families (At the Time of This Writing)

Family	Instance types
General purpose	A1 T3 T2 M5 M5a M4 T3a
Compute optimized	C5 C5n C4
Memory optimized	R5 R5a R4 X1e X1 High Memory z1d
Accelerated computing	P3 P2 G3 F1
Storage optimized	H1 I3 D2

The bottom line is that choosing the right instance type family will sometimes let you get away with fewer vCPUs and less memory—and a lower cost.

If regulatory restrictions or company policy requires you to use only physically isolated instances, you can request either a *dedicated instance* or a *dedicated host*. What's the difference? A dedicated instance is a regular EC2 instance that, instead of sharing a physical host with other AWS customers, runs on an isolated host that's set aside exclusively for your account. A dedicated host also gives you instance isolation but, in addition, allows a higher level of control over how your instances will be placed and run within the host environment. Dedicated hosts can also simplify and reduce the costs of running licensed software. Both levels involve extra per-hour pricing and are available using on-demand, reserved, or spot models (which we'll discuss a bit later in this chapter).

Server Storage: Elastic Block Store and Instance Store Volumes

Like everything else in the cloud, the storage volumes holding your instance's OS and data are going to be virtual. In most cases, that'll mean the 20 or 30 (or 2,000) GB drive holding your application is really just a 20 or 30 GB partition cleverly disguised to look like a stand-alone device. In fact, however, it was actually carved out of a much larger drive. What's going on with the rest of the drive space? It's probably being used for instances run by other AWS customers.

Some instance types support only volumes from the Elastic Block Store (EBS), others get their storage from instance store volumes, and some can happily handle both.

Amazon Elastic Block Store

The physical drive where an EBS volume actually exists may live quite a distance from the physical server that's giving your instance life. Rather than connecting directly to the motherboard via, say, a SATA cable the way a physical drive plugs into a physical computer, EBS volumes speak with your instance over a super low-latency network connection spanning the data center.

As fast as the EBS-EC2 responses are, they're still not quite as good as the experience you'll get from EC2 instance store volumes. So, what does EBS offer to compensate?

- Unlike the instance store that's ephemeral, the data stored on EBS volumes will survive shutdowns and system crashes. That can be a factor for workloads where data persistence is necessary.

- EBS volumes can be encrypted, which, when you're working with sensitive data, can make a big difference.

- EBS volumes can be moved around, mounted on other instances, and, as you've seen, converted to AMIs.

Amazon EC2 Instance Store Volumes

Unlike EBS, those instance types compatible with instance store volumes can enjoy the benefits of having their data on physical drives attached directly to the physical instance server. The downsides of instance store volumes (ephemeral data, no encryption, and lack of flexibility) are offset by faster data reads and writes. This can be useful for processing and analyzing fast-moving data streams where the data itself doesn't need to be persistent.

Understanding EC2 Pricing Models

What you'll pay for your EC2 instances will depend on the way you consume the service. Here's where you'll learn about the consumption options EC2 offers.

On-Demand Instances

The most expensive pricing tier is on-demand, where you pay for every hour the instance is running regardless of whether you're actually using it. Depending on the instance type you're using and the AWS Region where it's running, you could pay as little as $0.0058 per hour (that's around half a U.S. penny) for a t2.nano or as much as $24.48 per hour for a p3.16xlarge.

On-demand is great for workloads that need to run for a limited time without interruption. You could, for instance, schedule an on-demand instance in anticipation of increased requests against your application—perhaps your ecommerce site is offering a one-day, 50% off sale. But running an on-demand instance 24/7 for months at a time when you need it for only a couple of hours a day is going to cost you far more than it's worth. Instead, for such cases you should consider an alternative pricing model.

Reserved Instances

If your application needs to run uninterrupted for more than a month at a time, then you'll usually be better off purchasing a reserved instance. Practically, however, you're unlikely to find an available reservation with a term shorter than 12 months. One- and three-year terms are always available.

As it turns out, when you go shopping for a reservation, you're not actually purchasing an instance of any sort. Instead, you're paying AWS—or other AWS customers who are selling reservations they're no longer using—for the *right* to run an EC2 instance at a specified cost during the reservation term. Once you have your reservation, it will automatically be applied against any instance you launch in the specified AWS Region that matches the reservation instance type.

Reserved instances are paid for using an *All Upfront*, *Partial Upfront*, or *No Upfront* payment option. Predictably, the more you pay up front, the less it'll cost you overall.

Spot Instances

For workloads that don't need to run constantly and can survive unexpected shutdowns, your cheapest option will probably involve requesting instances on the EC2 spot market. AWS makes unused compute capacity available at steep discounts—as much as 90% off the on-demand cost. The catch is that the capacity can, on two minutes' notice, be reclaimed by shutting down your instance.

This wouldn't be an option for many typical use cases that require persistence and predictability. But it can be perfect for certain classes of containerized big data workloads or test and development environments.

Spot deployments can also be automated by defining your capacity and pricing needs as part of a *spot fleet*. The use of spot instances can, in addition, be incorporated into sophisticated, multitier operations that are deeply integrated with other automation and deployment orchestration tools. The https://aws.amazon.com/ec2/spot page provides helpful background and links.

Why not follow the steps in Exercise 7.2 to configure and launch an actual EC2 on-demand instance from start to finish?

EXERCISE 7.2

Launch an Apache Web Server on an EC2 Instance

1. From the EC2 Dashboard, choose the Launch Instance button. With the Quick Start tab selected, choose the Select button next to one of the Amazon Linux instance types.

2. On the Choose An Instance Type page, make sure the box next to the t2.micro entry is selected, and choose Next: Configure Instance Details.

3. Accept the default settings, but expand the Advanced Details section at the bottom of the page. You're going to copy the following text and paste it into the User Data field so it'll be run as a script when the instance boots. The first line tells Linux that the lines that follow should be executed as commands. The first command will install the Apache web server package, and the next one will fire up the Apache process:

   ```
   !/bin/bash
   yum install httpd -y
   systemctl start httpd
   ```

4. Choose the Next: Add Storage button and, when you're satisfied with the default (8 GB) storage volume you're shown, choose Next: Add Tags. You won't need to add any tags for this demo, so choose the Next: Configure Security Group button.

5. Since the plan is to configure your instance as a web server, you'll need to choose Add Rule to add a new security group rule to permit HTTP traffic into your instance. Choose the Type drop-down button in your new rule, and select HTTP (not HTTPS—encrypted access won't be necessary for this demo). Note how the Port Range setting is automatically populated with 80—the default port used for HTTP browser access. Note also how the value of Source is 0.0.0.0/0, ::/0. Those will permit access to your web server from any location using either Internet Protocol: IPv4 or IPv6.

6. Once you've reviewed your settings and chose the Launch button, you'll be prompted to select an existing authentication key pair. You can create a new pair and download it to your local computer if you like, but you won't need to access the instance

through the Secure Shell (SSH) protocol for this demo. Otherwise, acknowledge the consequences of launching an instance without a key pair (something that would normally be a bit crazy), and go ahead with the launch.

7. The blue View Instances button at the bottom of the confirmation screen will take you to the EC2 Instances Dashboard where you should see your instance status. When the Instance State indicator turns green and the word *running* appears next to it, your web server should be live.

8. Making sure this instance is selected, find the IPv4 Public IP entry on the Description tab in the bottom half of the screen. Hover your mouse over the IP address that's listed there, and choose the Copy To Clipboard icon to its right. Open a new tab in your browser, and paste the IP address into the URL field. You should see the default Apache test page.

9. When you're done admiring your handiwork, you can shut down the instance from the Actions menu at the top of the Instances page. With your instance selected, choose Action, then Instance State, and finally Terminate. When you confirm the action, your instance will be shut down, and you won't be billed any further. If your account is still in its first year and you haven't been running similar instances for more than 750 hours this month, this Free Tier instance won't have cost you anything anyway.

Simplified Deployments Through Managed Services

Building and administrating software applications can be complex wherever you deploy them. Whether they're on-premises or in the cloud, you'll face a lot of moving parts existing in a universe where they all have to play nicely together or the whole thing can collapse. To help lower the bar for entry into the cloud, some AWS services will handle much of the underlying infrastructure for you, allowing you to focus on your application needs. The benefits of a managed service are sometimes offset by premium pricing. But it's often well worth it.

One important example of such a managed service is the Relational Database Service (RDS). RDS, as you'll see in Chapter 9, "The Core Database Services," lets you set the basic configuration parameters for the database engine of your choice, gives you an endpoint address through which your applications can connect to the database, and takes care of all the details invisibly. Besides being responsible for making top-level configuration decisions, you won't need to worry about maintaining the database instance hosting the database, software updates, or data replication.

One step beyond a managed service—which handles only *one part* of your deployment stack for you—is a managed *deployment*, where the *whole stack* is taken care of behind the scenes. All you'll need to make things work with one of these services is your application code or, if it's a website you're after, your content. Until Amazon figures out how to secretly listen in on your organization's planning meetings and then automatically convert your ideas to code without you knowing, things are unlikely to get any simpler than this.

Two AWS services created with managed deployments in mind are Amazon Lightsail and AWS Elastic Beanstalk.

Amazon Lightsail

Lightsail is promoted as a low-stress way to enter the Amazon cloud world. It offers *blueprints* that, when launched, will automatically provision all the compute, storage, database, and network resources needed to make your deployment work. You set the pricing level you're after (currently that'll cost you somewhere between $3.50 and $160 USD each month) and add an optional script that will be run on your instance at startup, and AWS will take over. For context, $3.50 will get you 512 MB of memory, 1 vCPU, a 20 GB solid-state drive (SSD) storage volume, and 1 TB of transfers.

Lightsail uses all the same tools—such as the AMIs and instances you saw earlier in the chapter—to convert your plans to reality. Since it's all AWS from top to bottom, you're also covered should you later decide to move your stack directly to EC2, where you'll have all the added access and flexibility standard to that platform.

Because things are packaged in blueprints, you won't have the unlimited range of tools for your deployments that you'd get from EC2 itself. But, as you can see from these lists, there's still a nice selection:

- **Operating systems:** Amazon Linux, Ubuntu, Debian, FreeBSD, OpenSUSE, and Windows Server

- **Applications:** WordPress, Magento, Drupal, Joomla, Redmine, and Plesk

- **Stacks:** Node.js, GitLab, LAMP, MEAN, and Nginx

In case you're curious, a LAMP stack is a web server built on Linux, Apache, MySQL (or MariaDB), and PHP (or Python). By contrast, MEAN is a JavaScript stack for dynamic websites consisting of MongoDB, Express.js, AngularJS (or Angular), and Node.js.

AWS Elastic Beanstalk

If anything, Elastic Beanstalk is even simpler than Lightsail. All that's expected from you is to define the application platform and then upload your code. That's it. You can choose between preconfigured environments (including Go, .NET, Java Node.js, and PHP) and a number of Docker container environments. The "code" for Docker applications is defined with specially formatted `Dockerrun.aws.json` files.

One key difference between the two services is that while Lightsail bills at a flat rate (between $3.50 and $160 per month, as you saw), Beanstalk generates costs according to how resources are consumed. You don't get to choose how many vCPUs or how much memory you will use. Instead, your application will scale its resource consumption according to demand. Should, say, your WordPress site go viral and attract millions of viewers one day, AWS will invisibly ramp up the infrastructure to meet demand. As demand falls, your infrastructure will similarly drop. Keep this in mind, as such variations in demand will determine how much you'll be billed each month.

Deploying Container and Serverless Workloads

Even virtualized servers like EC2 instances tend to be resource-hungry. They do, after all, act like discrete, stand-alone machines running on top of a full-stack operating system. That means that having 5 or 10 of those virtual servers on a single physical host involves some serious duplication because each one will require its own OS kernel and device drivers.

Containers

Container technologies such as Docker avoid a lot of that overhead by allowing individual containers to share the Linux kernel with the physical host. They're also able to share common elements (called *layers*) with other containers running on a single host. This makes Docker containers fast to load and execute and also lets you pack many more container workloads on a single hardware platform.

You're always free to fire up one or more EC2 instances, install Docker, and use them to run as many containers as you'd like. But keeping all the bits and pieces talking to each other can get complicated. Instead, you can use either *Amazon Elastic Container Service* (ECS) or *Amazon Elastic Container Service for Kubernetes* (EKS) to orchestrate swarms of Docker containers on AWS using EC2 resources. Both of those services manage the underlying infrastructure for you, allowing you to ignore the messy details and concentrate on administrating Docker itself.

What's the difference between ECS and EKS? Broadly speaking, they both have the same big-picture goals. But EKS gets there by using the popular open source Kubernetes orchestration tool. They are different paths to the same place.

Serverless Functions

The serverless computing model uses a resource footprint that's even smaller than the one left by containers. Not only do *serverless functions* not require their own OS kernel, but they tend to spring into existence, perform some task, and then just as quickly die within minutes, if not seconds.

On the surface, Amazon's serverless service—AWS Lambda—looks a bit like Elastic Beanstalk. You define your function by setting a runtime environment (like Node.js, .NET, or Python) and uploading the code you want the function to run. But, unlike Beanstalk,

Lambda functions run only when triggered by a preset event. It could be a call from your mobile application, a change to a separate AWS resources (like an S3 bucket), or a log-based alert.

If an hour or a week passes without a trigger, Lambda won't launch a function (and you won't be billed anything). If there are a thousand concurrent executions, Lambda will scale automatically to meet the demand. Lambda functions are short-lived: they'll time out after 15 minutes.

Summary

Configuring EC2 instances is designed to mirror the process of provisioning and launching on-premises servers. Instances are defined by your choice of AMIs, instance type, storage volumes, and pricing model.

AMIs are organized into four categories: Quick Start, custom (My AMIs), AWS Marketplace, and Community. You can create your own AMI from a snapshot based on the EBS volume of an EC2 instance.

EC2 instance types are designed to fit specific application demands, and individual optimizations are generally available in varying sizes.

EBS storage volumes can be encrypted and are more like physical hard drives in the flexibility of their usage. Instance store volumes are located on the same physical server hosting your instance and will, therefore, deliver faster performance.

EC2 on-demand pricing is best for short-term workloads that can't be interrupted. Longer-term workloads—like ecommerce websites—will often be much less expensive when purchased as reserved instances. Spot instances work well for compute-intensive data operations that can survive unexpected shutdowns.

Lightsail, Elastic Beanstalk, Elastic Container Service, Elastic Container Service for Kubernetes, and Lambda are all designed to provide abstracted compute services that simplify, automate, and reduce the cost of compute operations.

Exam Essentials

Understand the elements required to provision an EC2 instance.   An instance requires a base OS (AMI) and—optionally—an application stack, an instance type for its hardware profile, and either an EBS or an instance volume for storage.

Understand the sources, pricing, and availability of EC2 AMIs.   The Quick Start and Marketplace AMIs are supported by Amazon or a recognized third-party vendor, which may not be true of AMIs selected from the Community collection. In any case, you should confirm whether using a particular AMI will incur extra charges beyond the normal EC2 usage.

Understand how EC2 instance types determine the compute power of your instance. Instance types are divided into type *families*, each of which focuses on a functional niche (general purpose, compute optimized, memory optimized, accelerated computing, and storage optimized). Your application needs and budget will determine which instance type you choose.

Understand the differences between EBS and instance store volumes. EBS volumes are versatile (they can, for instance, be converted into AMIs) and will survive an instance shutdown. Instance store volumes, on the other hand, provide faster reads and writes and can be more secure for some purposes. Which storage you use will often depend on the instance type you choose.

Understand the differences between EC2 pricing models. On-demand is the most expensive way to consume EC2 instances, but it's also flexible and reliable (you control when an instance starts or stops). Reserved instances work well for instances that must remain running for longer periods of time. Spot instances are the least expensive but can be shut down with only a two-minute warning.

Be familiar with Amazon's managed deployment services. Amazon Lightsail provides blueprints for simplified flat-rate deployments using EC2 resources under the hood. Lightsail deployments can, if needed, be transferred to regular EC2 infrastructure without service interruption. Elastic Beanstalk manages the underlying infrastructure for your application and automatically scales according to demand.

Understand how container and serverless models work in the cloud. Containers—like Docker—share the OS kernel and device drivers with their host and share common software layers with each other to produce fast and lightweight applications. ECS and EKS are AWS services focused on simplifying Docker orchestration within the EC2 framework. Lambda functions are designed to respond to event triggers to launch short-lived operations.

Review Questions

1. What is the function of an EC2 AMI?
   A. To define the hardware profile used by an EC2 instance
   B. To serve as an instance storage volume for high-volume data processing operations
   C. To serve as a source image from which an instance's primary storage volume is built
   D. To define the way data streams are managed by EC2 instances

2. Where can you find a wide range of verified AMIs from both AWS and third-party vendors?
   A. AWS Marketplace
   B. Quick Start
   C. Community AMIs
   D. My AMIs

3. Which of the following could be included in an EC2 AMI? (Select TWO.)
   A. A networking configuration
   B. A software application stack
   C. An operating system
   D. An instance type definition

4. Which of the following are EC2 instance type families? (Select TWO.)
   A. c5d.18xlarge
   B. Compute optimized
   C. t2.micro
   D. Accelerated computing

5. When describing EC2 instance types, what is the role played by the vCPU metric?
   A. vCPUs represent an instance's potential resilience against external network demands.
   B. vCPUs represent an instance type's system memory compared to the class of memory modules on a physical machine.
   C. vCPUs represent an AMI's processing power compared to the number of processors on a physical machine.
   D. vCPUs represent an instance type's compute power compared to the number of processors on a physical machine.

6. Which of the following describes an EC2 dedicated instance?
   A. An EC2 instance running on a physical host reserved for the exclusive use of a single AWS account
   B. An EC2 instance running on a physical host reserved for and controlled by a single AWS account
   C. An EC2 AMI that can be launched only on an instance within a single AWS account
   D. An EC2 instance optimized for a particular compute role

7. Which of the following describes an EBS volume?

   A. A software stack archive packaged to make it easy to copy and deploy to an EC2 instance

   B. A virtualized partition of a physical storage drive that's directly connected to the EC2 instance it's associated with

   C. A virtualized partition of a physical storage drive that's not directly connected to the EC2 instance it's associated with

   D. A storage volume that's encrypted for greater security

8. Why might you want to use an instance store volume with your EC2 instance rather than a volume from the more common EBS service? (Select TWO.)

   A. Instance store volumes can be encrypted.

   B. Instance store volumes, data will survive an instance shutdown.

   C. Instance store volumes provide faster data read/write performance.

   D. Instance store volumes are connected directly to your EC2 instance.

9. Your web application experiences periodic spikes in demand that require the provisioning of extra instances. Which of the following pricing models would make the most sense for those extra instances?

   A. Spot

   B. On-demand

   C. Reserved

   D. Dedicated

10. Your web application experiences periodic spikes in demand that require the provisioning of extra instances. Which of the following pricing models would make the most sense for the "base" instances that will run constantly?

   A. Spot

   B. On-demand

   C. Spot fleet

   D. Reserved

11. Which of the following best describes what happens when you purchase an EC2 reserved instance?

   A. Charges for any instances you run matching the reserved instance type will be covered by the reservation.

   B. Capacity matching the reserved definition will be guaranteed to be available whenever you request it.

   C. Your account will immediately and automatically be billed for the full reservation amount.

   D. An EC2 instance matching your reservation will automatically be launched in the selected AWS Region.

12. Which of the following use cases are good candidates for spot instances? (Select TWO.)
    A. Big data processing workloads
    B. Ecommerce websites
    C. Continuous integration development environments
    D. Long-term, highly available, content-rich websites

13. Which AWS services simplify the process of bringing web applications to deployment? (Select TWO.)
    A. Elastic Block Store
    B. Elastic Compute Cloud
    C. Elastic Beanstalk
    D. Lightsail

14. Which of the following services bills at a flat rate regardless of how it's consumed?
    A. Lightsail
    B. Elastic Beanstalk
    C. Elastic Compute Cloud
    D. Relational Database Service

15. Which of these stacks are available from Lightsail blueprints? (Select TWO.)
    A. Ubuntu
    B. Gitlab
    C. WordPress
    D. LAMP

16. Which of these AWS services use primarily EC2 resources under the hood? (Select TWO.)
    A. Elastic Block Store
    B. Lightsail
    C. Elastic Beanstalk
    D. Relational Database Service

17. Which of the following AWS services are designed to let you deploy Docker containers? (Select TWO.)
    A. Elastic Container Service
    B. Lightsail
    C. Elastic Beanstalk
    D. Elastic Compute Cloud

18. Which of the following use container technologies? (Select TWO.)
    A. Docker
    B. Kubernetes
    C. Lambda
    D. Lightsail

19. What role can the Python programming language play in AWS Lambda?
    A. Python cannot be used for Lambda.
    B. It is the primary language for API calls to administrate Lambda remotely.
    C. It is used as the underlying code driving the service.
    D. It can be set as the runtime environment for a function.

20. What is the maximum time a Lambda function may run before timing out?
    A. 15 minutes
    B. 5 minutes
    C. 1 minute
    D. 1 hour

Chapter

8

The Core Storage Services

THE AWS CERTIFIED CLOUD PRACTITIONER EXAM OBJECTIVES COVERED IN THIS CHAPTER MAY INCLUDE, BUT ARE NOT LIMITED TO, THE FOLLOWING:

Domain 2: Security

✓ **2.2** Define AWS Cloud security and compliance concepts

✓ **2.3** Identify AWS access management capabilities

Domain 3: Technology

✓ **3.1** Define methods of deploying and operating in the AWS Cloud

✓ **3.3** Identify the core AWS services

Introduction

For many organizations, their most valuable asset is their data. But organizations often have their data split between the cloud and on-premises locations such as offices and data centers. It's therefore critical to understand the different options AWS provides for storing data in the cloud, transferring data between the cloud and on-premises, and doing both in a cost-effective way without sacrificing performance.

In this chapter, you'll learn about the following AWS services that answer these challenges:

- Simple Storage Service (S3)—Amazon's flagship cloud storage service that lets you store and retrieve unlimited amounts of data. Because it's part of the AWS ecosystem, data in S3 is available to other AWS services, including EC2, making it easy to keep storage and compute together for optimal performance.

- S3 Glacier—Offers long-term archiving of infrequently accessed data, such as backups that must be retained for many years.

- AWS Storage Gateway—A virtual appliance that seamlessly moves data back and forth between your on-premises servers and AWS S3. It uses industry-standard storage protocols, making integration seamless.

- AWS Snowball—A hardware storage appliance designed to physically move massive amounts of data to or from S3, particularly when transferring the data over a network would take days or weeks.

Simple Storage Service

Amazon Simple Storage Service (S3) lets you store and retrieve unlimited amounts of data from anywhere in the world at any time. You can use S3 to store any kind of file. Although AWS calls it "storage for the internet," you can implement access controls and encryption to restrict access to your files to specific individuals and IP addresses. S3 opens up a variety of uses, both inside and outside of AWS. Many AWS services use S3 to store logs or retrieve data for processing, such as with analytics. You can even use S3 to host static websites!

Objects and Buckets

S3 differs from Elastic Block Store (EBS), which you learned about in Chapter 7, "The Core Compute Services." Rather than storing blocks of raw data, S3 stores files, or, as AWS calls them, *objects* on disks in AWS data centers. You can store any kind of file, including text, images, videos, database files, and so on. Each object can be up to 5 TB in size.

The filename of an object is called its *key* and can be up to 1,024 bytes long. An object key can consist of alphanumeric characters and some special characters, including the following:

```
! - _ . * ( )
```

S3 stores objects in a container called a *bucket* that's essentially a flat file system. A bucket can store an unlimited number of objects. When you create a bucket, you must assign it a name between 3 and 63 characters long, and the name must be globally unique across AWS. Within a bucket, each object key must be unique. One reason for this is to make it easier to access objects using an S3 endpoint URL. For example, the object text.txt stored in a bucket named benpiper would have a URL of https://benpiper.s3.amazonaws.com/text.txt.

To ensure a globally unique name when creating a bucket, try using a friendly name with a random string appended to the end.

Although bucket names must be globally unique, each bucket—and by extension any objects in that bucket—can exist in only one region. This helps with latency, security, cost, and compliance requirements, as your data is stored only in the region in which you create the bucket. You can use cross-region replication to copy the contents of an object from a bucket in one region to a bucket in another, but the objects are still uniquely separate objects. AWS never moves objects between regions.

Even though S3 functions as a flat file system, you can organize objects into a folder structure by including a forward slash (/) delimiter in the name. For example, you could create an object with the name production/database.sql and another object named development/database.sql in the same bucket. Because the delimiter is part of the name, the objects are unique.

As you might expect, S3 comes with a cost. You're not charged for uploading data to S3, but you may be charged when you download data. For example, in the US East region, you can download up to 1 GB of data per month at no charge. Beyond that, the rate is $0.09 or less per gigabyte. S3 also charges you a monthly fee based on how much data you store and the storage class you use.

S3 Storage Classes

All data is not created equal. Depending on its importance, certain files may require more or less availability or protection against loss than others. Some data you store in S3 is irreplaceable, and losing it would be catastrophic. Examples of this might include digital photos, encryption keys, and medical records.

Durability and Availability

Objects that need to remain intact and free from inadvertent deletion or corruption are said to need high *durability*, which is the percent likelihood that an object will not be lost over the course of a year. The greater the durability of the storage medium, the less likely you are to lose an object.

To understand how durability works, consider the following two examples. First, suppose you store 100,000,000,000 objects on storage with 99.999999999 percent durability. That means you could expect to lose only one (0.000000001 percent) of those objects over the course of a year! Now consider a different example. Suppose you store the same number of objects on storage with only 99.99 percent durability. You'd stand to lose 10,000,000 objects per year!

Different data also has differing availability requirements. *Availability* is the percent of time an object will be available for retrieval. For instance, a patient's medical records may need to be available around the clock, 365 days a year. Such records would need a high degree of both durability and availability.

The level of durability and availability of an object depends on its storage class. S3 offers six different storage classes at different price points. S3 charges you a monthly storage cost based on the amount of data you store and the storage class you use. Table 8.1 gives a complete listing of storage classes.

TABLE 8.1   S3 Storage Classes

Storage Class	Durability	Availability	Availability Zones	Storage Pricing in the US East Region (per GB/ month)
STANDARD	99.999999999%	99.99%	>2	$0.023
STANDARD_IA	99.999999999%	99.9%	>2	$0.0125
INTELLIGENT_TIERING	99.999999999%	99.9%	>2	Frequent access tier: $0.023 Infrequent access tier: $0.0125
ONEZONE_IA	99.999999999%	99.5%	1	$0.01
GLACIER	99.999999999%	Varies	>2	$0.004
REDUCED_REDUNDANCY (RRS)	99.99%	99.99%	>2	$0.024

With one exception that we'll cover in the following section, you'll want the highest degree of durability available. Your choice of storage class then hinges upon your desired level of availability, which depends on how frequently you'll need to access your files. You may find it helpful to categorize your files in terms of the following three access patterns:

- Frequently accessed objects

- Infrequently accessed objects

- A mixture of frequently and infrequently accessed objects

Storage Classes for Frequently Accessed Objects

If you need to access objects frequently and with minimal latency, the following two storage classes fit the bill:

STANDARD   This is the default storage class. It offers the highest levels of durability and availability, and your objects are always replicated across at least three Availability Zones in a region.

REDUCED_REDUNDANCY   The REDUCED_REDUNDANCY (RRS) storage class is meant for data that can be easily replaced, if it needs to be replaced at all. It has the lowest durability of all the classes, but it has the same availability as STANDARD. AWS recommends against using this storage class but keeps it available for people who have processes that still depend on it. If you see anyone using it, do them a favor and tell them to move to a storage class with higher durability!

Storage Classes for Infrequently Accessed Objects

Two of the storage classes designed for infrequently accessed objects are suffixed with the "IA" initialism for "infrequent access." These IA classes offer millisecond-latency access and high durability but the lowest availability of all the classes. They're designed for objects that are at least 128 KB in size. You can store smaller objects, but each will be billed as if it were 128 KB:

STANDARD_IA   This class is designed for important data that can't be re-created. Objects are stored in multiple Availability Zones and have an availability of 99.9 percent.

ONEZONE_IA   Objects stored using this storage class are kept in only one Availability Zone and consequently have the lowest availability of all the classes: only 99.5 percent. An outage of one Availability Zone could affect availability of objects stored in that zone. Although unlikely, the destruction of an Availability Zone could result in the loss of objects stored in that zone. Use this class only for data that you can re-create or have replicated elsewhere.

GLACIER   The GLACIER class is designed for long-term archiving of objects that rarely need to be retrieved. Objects in this storage class are stored using the S3 Glacier service, which you'll read about later in this chapter. Unlike the other storage classes, you can't retrieve an object in real time. Instead, you must initiate a restore request for the object and wait until the restore is complete. The time it takes to complete a restore depends on the retrieval option you choose and can range from 1 minute to 12 hours. Consequently, the availability of data stored in Glacier varies. Refer to the "S3 Glacier" section later in this chapter for information on retrieval options.

Storage Class for Both Frequently and Infrequently Accessed Objects

S3 currently offers only one storage class designed for both frequently and infrequently accessed objects:

INTELLIGENT_TIERING   This storage class automatically moves objects to the most cost-effective storage tier based on past access patterns. An object that hasn't been accessed for 30 consecutive days is moved to the lower-cost infrequent access tier. Once the object is accessed, it's moved back to the frequent access tier. Note that objects less than 128 KB are always charged at the higher-cost frequent access tier rate. In addition to storage pricing, you're charged a monthly monitoring and automation fee.

Access Permissions

S3 is storage for the internet, but that doesn't mean everyone on the internet can read your data. By default, objects you put in S3 are inaccessible to anyone outside of your AWS account.

S3 offers the following three methods of controlling who may read, write, or delete objects stored in your S3 buckets:

- Bucket policies
- User policies
- Bucket and object access control lists

Bucket Policies

A bucket policy is a resource-based policy that you apply to a bucket. You can use bucket policies to grant access to all objects within a bucket or just specific objects. You can also control which principals and accounts can read, write, or delete objects. You can also grant anonymous read access to make an object, such as a webpage or image, available to everyone on the internet.

User Policies

In Chapter 5, "Securing Your AWS Resources," you learned about Identity and Access Management (IAM) user policies. You can use these policies to grant IAM principals access to S3 objects. Unlike bucket policies that you apply to a bucket, you can apply user policies only to an IAM principal. Keep in mind that you can't use user policies to grant public (anonymous) access to an object.

Bucket and Object Access Control Lists

Bucket and object access control lists (ACLs) are legacy access control methods that have mostly been superseded by bucket and user policies. Nevertheless, you can still use bucket and object ACLs to grant other AWS accounts and anonymous users access to your S3 resources. You can't use ACLs to grant access to specific IAM principals. Due in part to this limitation, AWS recommends using bucket and user policies instead of ACLs whenever possible.

 You can use any combination of bucket policies, user policies, and access control lists. They're not mutually exclusive.

Encryption

S3 doesn't change the contents of an object when you upload it. That means if you upload a document containing personal information, that document is stored unencrypted. Using appropriate access permissions can protect your data from unauthorized access, but to add an additional layer of security, you have the option of encrypting objects before storing them in S3. This is called *encryption at rest*. S3 gives you the following two options for encrypting objects at rest:

- Server-side encryption—When you create an object, S3 encrypts the object and saves only the encrypted content. When you retrieve the object, S3 decrypts it and delivers the unencrypted object. Server-side encryption is the easiest to implement and doesn't require you to keep track of encryption keys. Amazon manages the keys and therefore has access to your objects.

- Client-side encryption—You encrypt the data prior to uploading it to S3. You must decrypt the object when you retrieve it from S3. This option is more complicated, as you're responsible for encryption and decryption. If you lose the key used to encrypt an object, you won't be able to decrypt it. Organizations with strict security requirements may choose this option to ensure Amazon doesn't have the ability to read their encrypted objects.

Versioning

To further protect against accidentally deleting or overwriting the contents of your important files, you can use versioning. To understand how versioning works, consider this example. Without versioning, if you upload an object with the same name as an existing object in the same bucket, the contents of the original object will get overwritten. But if you enable versioning on the bucket and then upload an object with the same name as an existing object, S3 will simply create a new version of that object. The original version will remain intact and available.

If you delete an object in a bucket on which versioning is disabled, the contents of the object aren't deleted. Instead, S3 adds a delete marker to the object and hides it from the S3 service console view.

Versioning is disabled by default when you create a bucket. You must explicitly enable versioning on a bucket to use it, and it applies to all objects in the bucket. There's no limit to the number of versions of an object you can store. You can delete versions manually or automatically using object life cycle configurations.

WARNING   Deleting a bucket will also delete all objects contained in it. Be careful!

Object Life Cycle Configurations

Because S3 can store practically unlimited amounts of data, it's possible to run up quite a bill if you continually upload objects but never delete any. This could happen if you have an application that frequently uploads log files to a bucket. You may also spend more than necessary by keeping objects in a more expensive storage class when a cheaper one would meet your needs. Object life cycle configurations can help you control costs by automatically moving objects to different storage classes or deleting them after a time.

Object life cycle configuration rules are applied to a bucket and consist of one or both of the following types of actions:

Transition actions   Transition actions move objects to a different storage class once they've reached a certain age. For example, you can create a rule to move objects from the STANDARD storage class to the STANDARD_IA storage class 90 days after creation.

Expiration actions   These can automatically delete objects after they reach a certain age. For example, you can create a rule to delete an object older than 365 days. If you have versioning enabled on a bucket, you can create expiration actions to delete object versions of a certain age. This allows you to take advantage of versioning without having to store endless versions of an object.

It's common to use both types of actions together. For example, if you're storing web server log files in a bucket, you may want to initially keep each log file in STANDARD storage. Once the file reaches 90 days, you can have S3 transition it to STANDARD_IA storage. Then, after 365 days in STANDARD_IA storage, the file is deleted.

Follow the steps in Exercise 8.1 to create your own S3 bucket.

EXERCISE 8.1

Create an S3 Bucket

To create an S3 bucket with versioning enabled

1.   In the S3 service console, choose the Create Bucket button.

2.   Enter a bucket name. Remember that this must be globally unique, so try to pick something that nobody else is likely to have used.

3.   Select a region of your choice, and then choose the Next button.

4.   Enable versioning by checking the Versioning check box, and then choose the Next button.

5.   Choose the Next button again to stick with the default settings. By default, objects in an S3 bucket are not publicly accessible.

---

6.   Choose the Create Bucket button.

7.   You should see the bucket you just created. Choose the bucket name.

From here, you can upload a file, create a folder, and view and delete object versions. It costs nothing to keep an empty bucket around, but when you're done with your bucket, feel free to delete it.

S3 Glacier

S3 Glacier offers long-term archiving of infrequently accessed data at an incredibly low cost. You upload large amounts of data for long-term, durable storage in the hopes that you'll never need it, but with the expectation that it will be there in the unlikely event that you do. Glacier guarantees 99.999999999 percent durability over a given year. Not coincidentally, this is the same durability level as the GLACIER storage class in S3.

Archives and Vaults

With Glacier, you store one or more files in an archive, which is a block of information. Although you can store a single file in an archive, the more common approach is to combine multiple files into a .zip or .tar file and upload that as an archive. An archive can be anywhere from 1 byte to 40 TB. Glacier stores archives in a vault, which is a region-specific container (much like an S3 bucket) that stores archives. Vault names must be unique within a region but don't have to be globally unique.

You can create and delete vaults using the Glacier service console. But to upload, download, or delete archives, you must use the AWS command line interface (CLI) or write your own code to interact with Glacier using an AWS software development kit (SDK). There are also third-party programs that let you interact with Glacier, such as CloudBerry Backup (https://www.cloudberrylab.com/backup.aspx), FastGlacier (https://fastglacier.com), and Arq Backup (https://www.arqbackup.com).

Retrieval Options

Because Glacier is designed for long-term archiving, it doesn't provide real-time access to archives. Downloading an archive from Glacier is a two-step process that requires initiating a retrieval job and then downloading your data once the job is complete. The length of time it takes to complete a job depends on the retrieval option you choose. There are three retrieval options:

Expedited   Except during times of unusually high demand, expedited retrievals usually complete within 1 to 5 minutes, although archives larger than 250 MB may take longer. In the US East region, the cost is $0.03 per gigabyte. You can optionally purchase provisioned capacity to ensure expedited retrievals complete in a timely fashion.

Standard   Standard retrievals typically complete within 3 to 5 hours. This is the default option. The cost of this option is $0.01 per gigabyte in the US East region.

Bulk   Bulk retrievals are the lowest-cost option, at $0.0025 per gigabyte in the US East region, and they typically complete within 5 to 12 hours.

AWS Storage Gateway

AWS Storage Gateway makes it easy to connect your existing on-premises servers to storage in the AWS cloud. Because it uses industry-standard storage protocols, there's no need to install special software on your existing servers. Instead, you just provision an AWS Storage Gateway virtual machine on-premises and connect your servers to it. Storage Gateway handles the data transfer between your servers and the AWS storage infrastructure. The virtual machine can run on a VMware ESXi or Microsoft Hyper-V hypervisor.

AWS Storage Gateway offers the following three virtual machine types for different use cases:

- File gateways
- Volume gateways
- Tape gateways

File Gateways

A file gateway lets you use the Network File System (NFS) and Server Message Block (SMB) protocols to store data in Amazon S3. Although data is stored on S3, it's cached locally, allowing for low-latency access. A file gateway can function as a normal on-premises file server. Because data is stored in S3, you can take advantage of all S3 features including versioning, bucket policies, life cycle management, encryption, and cross-region replication.

Volume Gateways

Volume gateways offer S3-backed storage volumes that your on-premises servers can use via the Internet Small Computer System Interface (iSCSI) protocol. Volume gateways support the following two configurations:

Stored volumes   With a stored volume, Storage Gateway stores all data locally and asynchronously backs it up to S3 as Elastic Block Store (EBS) snapshots. Stored volumes are a good option if you need uninterrupted access to your data. A stored volume can be from 1 GB to 16 TB in size.

Cached volumes   The volume gateway stores all your data on S3, and only a frequently used subset of that data is cached locally. A cached volume can range from 1 GB to 32 TB in size. This is a good option if you have a limited amount of local storage. A cached volume can range from 1 GB to 32 TB in size. Because only a subset of data is cached locally, it's possible that any interruption in connectivity to AWS could make some data inaccessible. If this isn't acceptable, you should use stored volumes instead.

Both configurations allow you to take manual or scheduled EBS snapshots of your volumes. EBS snapshots are always stored in S3. You can restore an EBS snapshot to an on-premises gateway storage volume or an EBS volume that you can attach to an EC2 instance.

Tape Gateways

A tape gateway mimics traditional tape backup infrastructure. It works with common backup applications such as Veritas Backup Exec and NetBackup, Commvault, and Microsoft System Center Data Protection Manager. You simply configure your backup application to connect to the tape gateway via iSCSI. On the tape gateway, you create virtual tapes that can store between 100 GB and 2.5 TB each.

A tape gateway stores virtual tapes in a virtual tape library (VTL) backed by S3. Here's how it works: when your backup software writes data to a virtual tape, the tape gateway asynchronously uploads that data to S3. Because backups can be quite large and take a long time to upload, the tape gateway keeps the data in cache storage until the upload is complete. If you need to recover data from a virtual tape, the tape gateway will download the data from the S3-backed VTL and store it in its cache.

For cost-effective, long-term storage, you can archive virtual tapes by moving them out of a VTL and into a virtual tape shelf backed by Glacier. To restore an archived virtual tape, you must initiate a retrieve request, which can take 3 to 5 hours. Once the retrieval is complete, the virtual tape will be available in your S3-backed VTL and will be available to transfer to the tape gateway.

AWS Snowball

AWS Snowball is a hardware appliance designed to move massive amounts of data between your site and the AWS cloud in a short time. Some common use cases for Snowball include the following:

- Migrating data from an office or data center to the AWS cloud
- Quickly transferring a large amount of data to or from S3 for backup or recovery purposes
- Distributing large volumes of content to customers and partners

The idea behind Snowball is that it's quicker to physically ship a large amount of data than it is to transfer it over a network. For instance, suppose you want to migrate a 40 TB database to AWS. Such a transfer even over a blazing-fast 1 Gbps connection would still take more than 4 days!

But instead, for a nominal fee, AWS will send you a Snowball device. You simply transfer your files to it and ship it back. When AWS receives it, AWS transfers the files from Snowball to one or more S3 buckets. You're not charged any transfer fees for importing files into S3, and once there, they're immediately available for use by other AWS services.

Hardware Specifications

The largest 80 TB Snowball device costs $250 to use and can store up to 72 TB. If you don't need to transfer that much, you can opt for the slightly smaller 50 TB Snowball, which costs $200 and stores up to 42 TB. Snowball's RJ45 and SFP+ network interfaces support speeds up to 10 Gbps, making it possible to transfer 72 TB of data to the device in about 2.5 days! (Although a 10 Gbps connection can transfer this amount of data in less than a day, the write speeds of the solid-state drives [SSDs] in Snowball limit the effective transfer rate to around 3 Gbps.)

Once you receive your Snowball, you can keep it for 10 days without incurring any additional costs. If you hold onto it longer than that, you'll be charged an extra $15 per day. You're allowed to keep Snowball for up to 90 days, which is more than enough time to fill it up.

You can use Snowball to export data from S3, but you'll be charged outbound S3 transfer rates, which range from $0.03 to $0.05 per gigabyte, depending on the region.

Security

Snowball is contained in a rugged, tamper-resistant enclosure. It includes a trusted platform module (TPM) chip that detects unauthorized modifications to the hardware, software, or firmware. After each use, AWS verifies that the TPM did not detect any tampering. If any tampering is detected by the TPM chip or if the device appears damaged, AWS does not transfer any data from it.

Snowball uses two layers of encryption. First, when you transfer data to or from Snowball, the data is encrypted in transit using SSL. Second, the data you put on a Snowball is always encrypted at rest. Snowball enforces data encryption by requiring you to transfer data to it using only either the Snowball Client or the more advanced S3 SDK Adapter for Snowball. The former doesn't require any coding knowledge. Both run on Linux, macOS, and Windows operating systems.

Data is encrypted using AES 256-bit encryption that's enforced by the Snowball Client or S3 SDK Adapter for Snowball, ensuring that the device never stores your data unencrypted. As an added security measure, AWS erases your data from Snowball before sending it to another customer, following the media sanitization standards published by the National Institutes for Standards and Technology (NIST) in Special Publication 800-88.

Snowball Edge

Snowball Edge is like Snowball but offers a wider variety of features. Snowball Edge offers the same network connectivity options as Snowball but adds a QSFP+ port, allowing you to achieve faster network speeds than Snowball. Also, Snowball is designed to transfer large amounts of data only between your local environment and S3. Snowball Edge offers the same functionality plus the following:

- Local storage for S3 buckets
- Compute power for EC2 instances and Lambda functions locally
- File server functionality using the Network File System (NFS) version 3 and 4 protocols

There are three different device options to choose from, each optimized for a different application:

Storage Optimized   This option provides up to 80 TB of usable storage, 24 vCPUs, and 32 GB of memory for compute applications. The QSFP+ network interface supports up to 40 Gbps.

Compute Optimized   This offers the most compute power, giving you 52 vCPUs and 208 GB of memory. It has 39.5 TB of usable storage, plus 7.68 TB dedicated to compute instances.

Compute Optimized with GPU   This is identical to the Compute Optimized option, except it includes an NVIDIA V100 Tensor Core graphical processing unit (GPU), making it ideal for machine learning and high-performance computing applications. Both Compute Optimized device options feature a QSFP+ network interface capable of speeds up to 100 Gbps.

You can cluster 5 to 10 Snowball Edge devices together to build a local, highly available compute or storage cluster. This is useful if you have a large amount of data that you need to process locally.

Snowball Edge doesn't support virtual private clouds (VPCs). You can't place an EC2 instance running on Snowball Edge in a VPC. Instead, you assign the instance an IP addresses on your local network.

Table 8.2 highlights some key similarities and differences between Snowball and Snowball Edge.

TABLE 8.2   Comparison of Snowball and Snowball Edge

Feature	Snowball	Snowball Edge
Transfer data to and from S3	Yes	Yes
Local EC2 instances	No	Yes
Local compute with Lambda	No	Yes
File server functionality using NFS	No	Yes
Local S3 buckets	No	Yes

Summary

S3 is the primary storage service in AWS. Although S3 integrates with all other AWS services, it enjoys an especially close relationship with S3 Glacier and the AWS compute services: EC2, and Lambda.

For durable, highly available cloud storage, use S3. You can use bucket policies to make your files as private or as public as you want. If you need long-term storage of infrequently accessed data at a lower cost, S3 Glacier is your best bet.

When it comes to local storage, AWS Storage Gateway lets you access your data by going through a virtual machine that automatically synchronizes your data with S3.

For getting your files to or from S3, most often you'll just transfer your files over the internet, a virtual private network (VPN), or Direct Connect link. But for large amounts of data this is impractical, and a hardware solution makes more sense. Snowball is a rugged, tamper-resistant device that AWS ships to you. You drop your files onto it, send it back, and AWS transfers the files to S3.

Another hardware option is Snowball Edge. It has the same functionality as Snowball but can also function as a durable local file server using the NFSv3 and NFSv4 protocols. Additionally, you can use it to run EC2 instances or Lambda functions locally.

Exam Essentials

Understand the difference between durability and availability in S3.   Durability is the likelihood that an object won't be lost over the course of a year. Availability is the percentage of time an object will be accessible during the year.

Be able to select the best S3 storage class given cost, compliance, and availability requirements. S3 offers six storage classes. STANDARD has the highest availability at 99.99 percent, replicates objects across at least three zones, and is the most expensive in terms of monthly storage cost per gigabyte. ONEZONE_IA has the lowest availability at 99.5 percent and stores objects in only one zone, and its monthly per-gigabyte storage cost is less than half that of the STANDARD storage class.

Know the different options for getting data into and out of S3. You can upload or download an object by using the S3 service console, by using the AWS CLI, or by directly accessing the object's URL. AWS Storage Gateway lets your on-premises servers use industry-standard storage protocols such as iSCSI, NFS, and SMB to transfer data to and from S3. AWS Snowball and Snowball Edge allow secure physical transport of data to and from S3.

Understand when to use bucket policies, user policies, and access control lists in S3. Use bucket policies or ACLs to grant anonymous access to objects, such as webpages or images you want made public. Use user policies to grant specific IAM principals in your account access to objects.

Be able to explain the differences between S3 and Glacier. S3 offers highly available, real-time retrieval of objects. Retrieving data from Glacier is a two-step process that requires first requesting an archive using the Expedited, Standard, or Bulk retrieval option and then downloading the archive once the retrieval is complete.

Know how to use encryption, versioning, and object life cycle configurations in S3. S3 offers server-side and client-side encryption to protect objects at rest from unauthorized access. Versioning helps protect against object overwrites and deletions. Object life cycle configurations let you delete objects or move them to different storage classes after they reach a certain age.

Understand the three virtual machine types offered by AWS Storage Gateway. File gateways offer access to S3 via the NFS and SMB storage protocols. Volume gateways and tape gateways offer access via the iSCSI block storage protocol, but tape gateways are specifically designed to work with common backup applications.

Review Questions

1. When trying to create an S3 bucket named documents, AWS informs you that the bucket name is already in use. What should you do in order to create a bucket?
   A. Use a different region.
   B. Use a globally unique bucket name.
   C. Use a different storage class.
   D. Use a longer name.
   E. Use a shorter name.

2. Which S3 storage classes are most cost-effective for infrequently accessed data that can't be easily replaced? (Select TWO.)
   A. STANDARD_IA
   B. ONEZONE_IA
   C. GLACIER
   D. STANDARD
   E. INTELLIGENT_TIERING

3. What are the major differences between Simple Storage Service (S3) and Elastic Block Store (EBS)? (Select TWO.)
   A. EBS stores volumes.
   B. EBS stores snapshots.
   C. S3 stores volumes.
   D. S3 stores objects.
   E. EBS stores objects.

4. Which tasks can S3 object life cycle configurations perform automatically? (Select THREE.)
   A. Deleting old object versions
   B. Moving objects to Glacier
   C. Deleting old buckets
   D. Deleting old objects
   E. Moving objects to an EBS volume

5. What methods can be used to grant anonymous access to an object in S3? (Select TWO.)
   A. Bucket policies
   B. Access control lists
   C. User policies
   D. Security groups

6. Your budget-conscious organization has a 5 TB database file it needs to retain off-site for at least 5 years. In the event the organization needs to access the database, it must be accessible within 8 hours. Which cloud storage option should you recommend, and why? (Select TWO.)

    A. S3 has the most durable storage.

    B. S3.

    C. S3 Glacier.

    D. Glacier is the most cost effective.

    E. S3 has the fastest retrieval times.

    F. S3 doesn't support object sizes greater than 4 TB.

7. Which of the following actions can you perform from the S3 Glacier service console?

    A. Delete an archive

    B. Create a vault

    C. Create an archive

    D. Delete a bucket

    E. Retrieve an archive

8. Which Glacier retrieval option generally takes 3 to 5 hours to complete?

    A. Provisioned

    B. Expedited

    C. Bulk

    D. Standard

9. What's the minimum size for a Glacier archive?

    A. 1 byte

    B. 40 TB

    C. 5 TB

    D. 0 bytes

10. Which types of AWS Storage Gateway let you connect your servers to block storage using the iSCSI protocol? (Select TWO.)

    A. Cached gateway

    B. Tape gateway

    C. File gateway

    D. Volume gateway

11. Where does AWS Storage Gateway primarily store data?

    A. Glacier vaults

    B. S3 buckets

    C. EBS volumes

    D. EBS snapshots

12. You need an easy way to transfer files from a server in your data center to S3 without having to install any third-party software. Which of the following services and storage protocols could you use? (Select FOUR.)

   A. AWS Storage Gateway—file gateway

   B. iSCSI

   C. AWS Snowball

   D. SMB

   E. AWS Storage Gateway—volume gateway

   F. The AWS CLI

13. Which of the following are true regarding the AWS Storage Gateway—volume gateway configuration? (Select THREE.)

   A. Stored volumes asynchronously back up data to S3 as EBS snapshots.

   B. Stored volumes can be up to 32 TB in size.

   C. Cached volumes locally store only a frequently used subset of data.

   D. Cached volumes asynchronously back up data to S3 as EBS snapshots.

   E. Cached volumes can be up to 32 TB in size.

14. What's the most data you can store on a single Snowball device?

   A. 42 TB

   B. 50 TB

   C. 72 TB

   D. 80 TB

15. Which of the following are security features of AWS Snowball? (Select TWO.)

   A. It enforces encryption at rest.

   B. It uses a Trusted Platform Module (TPM) chip.

   C. It enforces NFS encryption.

   D. It has tamper-resistant network ports.

16. Which of the following might AWS do after receiving a damaged Snowball device from a customer?

   A. Copy the customer's data to Glacier

   B. Replace the Trusted Platform Module (TPM) chip

   C. Securely erase the customer's data from the device

   D. Copy the customer's data to S3

17. Which of the following can you use to transfer data to AWS Snowball from a Windows machine without writing any code?

A. NFS

B. The Snowball Client

C. iSCSI

D. SMB

E. The S3 SDK Adapter for Snowball

18. How do the AWS Snowball and Snowball Edge devices differ? (Select TWO.)

A. Snowball Edge supports copying files using NFS.

B. Snowball devices can be clustered together for storage.

C. Snowball's QSFP+ network interface supports speeds up to 40 Gbps.

D. Snowball Edge can run EC2 instances.

19. Which of the following Snowball Edge device options is the best for running machine learning applications?

A. Compute Optimized

B. Compute Optimized with GPU

C. Storage Optimized

D. Network Optimized

20. Which of the following hardware devices offers a network interface speed that supports up to 100 Gbps?

A. Snowball Edge with the Storage Optimized configuration

B. Snowball Edge with the Compute Optimized configuration

C. Storage Gateway

D. 80 TB Snowball

Chapter

9

The Core Database Services

THE AWS CERTIFIED CLOUD PRACTITIONER EXAM OBJECTIVES COVERED IN THIS CHAPTER MAY INCLUDE, BUT ARE NOT LIMITED TO, THE FOLLOWING:

Domain 3: Technology

✓ **3.1** Define methods of deploying and operating in the AWS Cloud

✓ **3.3** Identify the core AWS services

Introduction

Many applications use databases to store, retrieve, and organize data, so the type of database you choose and how you configure it have a big impact on the performance and availability of such a database-backed application.

In traditional infrastructure, organizations typically installed and configured their own database servers. For example, a business might use a Microsoft SQL Server or Oracle database to store customer information. It's possible to build and run your own database servers in the cloud, but AWS offers another—and for many, better—option: managed database services.

With a managed database service, you use the AWS Management Console or AWS command line interface (CLI) to provision a database. AWS handles the installation and maintenance of the database software, as well as database backups and replication.

In this chapter, you'll learn about the following three different managed database services provided by AWS:

- Relational database service (RDS)
- DynamoDB
- Redshift

Database Models

A database can use a relational or nonrelational model. The model you choose depends on how your application needs to store, organize, and retrieve data. It's important to understand that the needs of the application determine the database model you choose, not the other way around.

Most of the technical differences between relational and nonrelational databases are beyond the scope of this book, but in this chapter, you'll learn the major differences between the two.

Relational Databases

Relational databases have been around a long time, and even if you've never created or maintained one, you're already familiar with its fundamental concepts. A relational database is analogous to a spreadsheet that contains columns and rows. In a relational database, columns are called *attributes*, and rows are called *records*. Both are stored in a *table*, and a database can contain multiple tables. Table 9.1 shows what a simple relational database table might look like.

TABLE 9.1   The Customers Table

Customer ID	Last Name	First Name	Last Purchase
1670	Isaacson	Callan	08/29/18
1680	Ashland	Chessa	12/15/16
1690	Colson	Charlie	02/20/12
1700	Charlotte	Linda	05/09/17

Like a spreadsheet, a relational database table has a defined number of columns. Where spreadsheets and relational databases differ is that each row in a relational database table must be unique. One way of ensuring uniqueness of rows is by defining a primary key—a column that must be unique and present in each record. In Table 9.1, the primary key would be the Customer ID column.

 A primary key can consist of multiple columns.

Another way that spreadsheets and relational databases differ is that you must predefine the type of data that can be stored in each column. For example, a column for storing a person's birthdate would be restricted to storing only numbers. Because of these requirements, relational databases are ideal for storing structured data that follows a predictable, well-defined format.

An advantage of storing structured data in a relational database is that you can quickly search an entire database for specific values. You can also retrieve data from different tables and combine that data into virtually any format you can imagine. For example, you can search for all customers with the last name Smith who have made a purchase in the last 90 days. This sort of query power is why many application developers choose relational databases. Relational databases are ideal for performing complex analytics and generating reports against large data sets. Such uses require multiple complex queries, and this is where relational databases excel.

As a rule, the larger the database and the more complex the query, the longer it takes to retrieve the data you're looking for. Database administrators frequently tune or optimize databases to ensure the best possible performance. Longer query times and increased maintenance are the price you pay for flexible queries.

Structured Query Language

Relational databases use the *Structured Query Language* (SQL). You can use SQL statements to create databases and tables, as well as to read and write data. You can also perform tuning and maintenance tasks using SQL. Not surprisingly, relational databases are often called *SQL databases* for short.

Although you don't need to know how to use SQL, you should be familiar with the following two SQL statements, which come up frequently in conversations around relational databases. If you're interested in learning more about SQL, the SQL tutorial at https://www.w3schools.com/sql is a great place to start.

The SELECT Statement

The SELECT statement reads data from the database and controls how it's formatted. To combine data from different tables, you add a JOIN clause to the SELECT statement. An application that uses a relational database will execute at least one SELECT statement every time it retrieves data from a database.

The INSERT Statement

The INSERT statement writes data to a table. You can think of this as programmatically adding data to individual cells in a spreadsheet. When an application writes data to a database, it uses the INSERT statement to do so.

Nonrelational (No-SQL) Databases

Relational databases are wildly popular, but because of their restrictions, they're also overly complex for applications that don't need to store structured data. Also, relational databases often perform poorly when put under the strain of handling thousands of reads or writes per second.

Nonrelational databases were developed to provide a fast alternative for applications that need to perform tens of thousands of reads or writes per second. In addition to being able to handle these high transaction rates, nonrelational databases let you store data that doesn't have a well-defined, predictable structure. Such data is often called *unstructured data*, in contrast to the structure imposed on data by a relational database. Because of their unstructured nature, nonrelational or no-SQL databases are said to be *schemaless*.

Nonrelational databases also store information in tables; tables are sometimes called *collections*, and each row or record is called an *item*. Nonrelational databases don't require you to specify in advance all the types of data you'll store. The only thing you have to define in advance is a primary key to uniquely identify each item. For example, to store customer data in a table, you might use a unique customer ID number as the primary key.

In exchange for the flexibility of storing unstructured data, the types of queries you can perform against that data are more limited. Nonrelational databases are designed to let you query items based on the primary key. Because the rest of the data doesn't follow a predictable structure, a particular piece of data could be anywhere in the database. Hence, trying to query against any other data requires searching through every item in the entire table—a process that gets slower as the table grows. Nonrelational databases are best suited for applications that need to perform just a few well-defined queries.

Amazon Relational Database Service

The Amazon Relational Database Service (RDS) is Amazon's managed relational database service. RDS lets you provision a number of popular relational database management systems (RDBMSs) including Microsoft SQL Server, Oracle, MySQL, and PostgreSQL.

You can always install and configure your own database server on an EC2 instance. But RDS offers several advantages over this. When you create an RDS database instance, Amazon sets up one or more compute instances and takes care of installing and configuring the RDBMS of your choice. These compute instances are not EC2 instances that you can secure shell (SSH) into, but they are connected to a virtual private cloud (VPC) of your choice, allowing your applications running on AWS or on-premises to take full advantage of an RDS-hosted database. Like EC2 instances, RDS instances use Elastic Block Service (EBS) volumes for storage.

To achieve the level of performance and availability you need, you can choose a multi-Availability Zone (multi-AZ) deployment to have database instances in multiple Availability Zones. RDS can also perform manual or automatic EBS snapshots that you can easily restore to new RDS instances. RDS can also handle the hard work of installing patches and upgrades during scheduled maintenance windows.

Database Engines

When you create an RDS instance, you must choose a database engine, which is the specific RDBMS that will be installed on your instance. You can have only one database engine per instance, but you can provision multiple instances if need be. Amazon RDS supports the following six database engines:

- MySQL
- MariaDB
- Oracle
- PostgreSQL
- Microsoft SQL Server
- Amazon Aurora

With the exception of Amazon Aurora, these database engines are either open source or commercially available products found in many data center environments. Amazon Aurora is a proprietary database designed for RDS, but it's compatible with existing MySQL and PostgreSQL databases. Being able to use RDS to deploy an RDBMS that you're already familiar with makes migrating such databases from on-premises to RDS much easier.

Licensing

Depending on the database engine you choose, you must choose one of two licensing options: *license included* or *bring your own license* (BYOL):

License included   The license is included in the pricing for each RDS instance. The Microsoft SQL Server and Oracle database engine options offer this license model. The free database engines—MariaDB, MySQL, and PostgreSQL—exclusively use the license included model.

Bring your own license   In this model, you must provide your own license to operate the database engine you choose. Unlike the license-included option, licensing costs are not built into RDS pricing. This model is currently available only for Oracle databases.

Instance Classes

Implementing a relational database—even one backed by RDS—requires some capacity planning to ensure the database gives you the level of availability and performance your application needs.

When you deploy an RDS instance, you must choose a database instance class that defines the number of virtual CPUs (vCPU), the amount of memory, and the maximum network and storage throughput the instance can support. There are three instances classes you can choose from: Standard, Memory Optimized, and Burstable Performance.

Standard

The Standard instance class will meet the requirements of most applications. The latest-generation Standard instance class offers the following specs:

- Between 2 and 96 vCPU
- 8–384 GB memory

Memory Optimized

The Memory Optimized instance class is for applications with the most demanding database requirements. This class offers the most disk throughput and network bandwidth. The latest-generation instance class provides the following:

- Between 4 and 128 vCPU
- 122–3,904 GB memory

Database instances use EBS storage. Both the Standard and Memory Optimized instance class types are EBS-optimized, meaning they provide dedicated bandwidth for transfers to and from EBS storage.

Burstable Performance

The Burstable Performance instance class is for nonproduction databases that have minimal performance requirements, such as those for test and development purposes. The latest-generation Burstable Performance instance class has the lowest network bandwidth and disk throughput and offers the following:

- Between 2 and 8 vCPU
- 1–32 GB memory

It can be difficult to predict exactly how many RDS instances you need and how much compute power, memory, and network and storage throughput each of those instances needs. Thankfully, RDS makes it easy to right-size your database deployments in two ways: scaling vertically and scaling horizontally.

Scaling Vertically

Scaling vertically refers to changing the way resources are allocated to a specific instance. After creating an instance, you can scale up to a more powerful instance class to add more memory or improve computing or networking performance. Or you can scale down to a less powerful class to save on costs.

Storage

The level of performance an RDS instance can achieve depends not only on the instance class you choose but also on the type of storage. New RDS instances use EBS volumes, and the maximum throughput a volume can achieve is a function of both the instance class and the number of *input/output operations per second* (IOPS) the EBS volume supports. IOPS measure how fast you can read from and write to a volume. Higher IOPS generally means faster reads and writes. RDS offers three types of storage: general-purpose SSD, provisioned IOPS SSD, and magnetic.

General-Purpose SSD

General-purpose SSD storage is good enough for most databases. You can allocate a volume of between 20 GB and 32 TB. The number of IOPS per volume depends on how much storage you allocate. The more storage you allocate, the better your read and write performance will be.

If you're not sure how much storage to provision, don't worry. General-purpose SSD volumes can temporarily achieve a higher number of IOPS through a process called *bursting*. During spikes of heavy read or write activity, bursting will kick in automatically and give your volume an added performance boost. This way, you don't have to allocate an excessive amount of storage just to get enough IOPS to meet peak demand.

Provisioned IOPS SSD

Provisioned IOPS SSD storage allows you to specify the exact number of IOPS (in thousands) that you want to allocate per volume. Like general-purpose SSD storage, you can allocate up to 32 TB. But unlike general-purpose SSD storage, provisioned IOPS SSD storage doesn't offer bursting, so it's necessary to decide beforehand the maximum number of IOPS you'll need. However, even if your needs change, you can always adjust the number of IOPS later.

Magnetic

Magnetic storage is available for backward compatibility with legacy RDS instances. Unlike the other storage options, it doesn't use EBS, and you can't change the size of a magnetic volume after you create it. Magnetic volumes are limited to 4 TB in size and 1,000 IOPS.

You can increase the size of an EBS volume after creating it without causing an outage or degrading performance. You can't, however, decrease the amount of storage allocated, so be careful not to go overboard.

You can also migrate from one storage type to another, but doing so can result in a short outage of typically a few minutes. But when migrating from magnetic to EBS storage, the process can take up to several days. During this time, the instance is still usable but may not perform optimally.

Scaling Horizontally with Read Replicas

In addition to scaling up by choosing a more powerful instance type or selecting high-IOPS storage, you can improve the performance of a database-backed application by adding additional RDS instances that perform only reads from the database. These instances are called *read replicas*.

In a relational database, only the master database instance can write to the database. A read replica helps with performance by removing the burden of read-only queries from the master instance, freeing it up to focus on writes. Hence, read replicas provide the biggest benefit for applications that need to perform a high number of reads. Read replicas are also useful for running computationally intensive queries, such as monthly or quarterly reports that require reading and processing large amounts of data from the database.

High Availability with Multi-AZ

Even if you use read replicas, only the master database instance can perform writes against your database. If that instance goes down, your database-backed application won't be able to write data until it comes back online. To ensure that you always have a master database instance up and running, you can configure high availability by enabling the multi-AZ feature on your RDS instance.

With multi-AZ enabled, RDS creates an additional instance called a *standby database instance* that runs in a different Availability Zone than your primary database instance. The primary instance instantly or synchronously replicates data to the secondary instance, ensuring that every time your application writes to the database, that data exists in multiple Availability Zones.

If the primary fails, RDS will automatically fail over to the secondary. The failover can result in an outage of up to two minutes, so your application will experience some interruption, but you won't lose any data.

With multi-AZ enabled, you can expect your database to achieve a monthly availability of 99.95 percent. It's important to understand that an instance outage may occur for reasons other than an Availability Zone outage. Routine maintenance tasks such as patching or upgrading the instance can result in a short outage and trigger a failover.

If you use the Amazon Aurora database engine—Amazon's proprietary database engine designed for and available exclusively with RDS—you can take advantage of additional benefits when using multi-AZ. When you use Aurora, your RDS instances are part of an Aurora cluster. All instances in the cluster use a shared storage volume that's synchronously replicated across three different Availability Zones. Also, if your storage needs increase, the cluster volume will automatically expand up to 64 TB.

Backup and Recovery

Whether or not you use multi-AZ, RDS can take manual or automatic EBS snapshots of your instances. Snapshots are stored across multiple Availability Zones. If you ever need to restore from a snapshot, RDS will restore it to a new instance. This makes snapshots useful not only for backups but also for creating copies of a database for testing or development purposes.

You can take a manual snapshot at any time. You can configure automatic snapshots to occur daily during a 30-minute backup window. RDS will retain automatic snapshots between 1 day and 35 days, with a default of 7 days. Manual snapshots are retained until you delete them.

Enabling automatic snapshots also enables point-in-time recovery, a feature that saves your database change logs every 5 minutes. Combined with automated snapshots, this gives you the ability to restore a failed instance to within 5 minutes before the failure—losing no more than 5 minutes of data.

Determining Your Recovery Point Objective

Do you need snapshots *and* multi-AZ? It's important to understand that although both snapshots and multi-AZ protect your databases, they serve slightly different purposes. Snapshots are good for letting you restore an entire database instance. If your database encounters corruption, such as malicious deletion of records, snapshots let you recover that data, even if the corruption occurred days ago (provided you're retaining the snapshots). Multi-AZ is designed to keep your database up and running in the event of an instance failure. To achieve this, data is synchronously replicated to a secondary instance.

How much data loss you can sustain in the event of a failure is called the *recovery point objective* (RPO). If you can tolerate losing an hour's worth of data, then your RPO would be 1 hour. To achieve such an RPO, simply using automatic snapshots with point-in-time recovery is sufficient. For an RPO of less than 5 minutes, you would also want to use multi-AZ to synchronously replicate your data to a secondary instance.

DynamoDB

DynamoDB is Amazon's managed nonrelational database service. It's designed for highly transactional applications that need to read from or write to a database tens of thousands of times a second.

Items and Tables

The basic unit of organization in DynamoDB is an item, which is analogous to a row or record in a relational database. DynamoDB stores items in tables. Each DynamoDB table is stored across one or more partitions. Each partition is backed by solid-state drives, and partitions are replicated across multiple Availability Zones in a region, giving you a monthly availability of 99.99 percent.

Each item must have a unique value for the primary key. An item can also consist of other key-value pairs called *attributes*. Each item can store up to 400 KB of data, more than enough to fill a book! To understand this better, consider the sample shown in Table 9.2.

TABLE 9.2   A Sample DynamoDB Table

Username (Primary Key)	LastName	FirstName	FavoriteColor
hburger	Burger	Hamilton	
dstreet	Street	Della	Fuchsia
pdrake	Drake	Paul	Silver
perry		Perry	

Username, LastName, FirstName, and FavoriteColor are all attributes. In this table, the Username attribute is the primary key. Each item must have a value for the primary key, and it must be unique within the table. Good candidates for primary keys are things that tend to be unique, such as randomly generated identifiers, usernames, and email addresses.

Other than the primary key, an item doesn't have to have any particular attributes. Hence, some items may contain several attributes, while others may contain only one or two. This flexibility makes DynamoDB the database of choice for applications that need to store a wide variety of data without having to know the nature of that data in advance. However, every attribute must have a defined data type, which can be one of the following:

Scalar   A *scalar data type* has only one value and can be a string, a number, binary data, or a Boolean value.

Set   A *set data type* can have multiple scalar values, but each value must be unique within the set.

Document   *The document data type* is subdivided into two subtypes: list and map. Document data types can store values of any type. List documents are ordered, whereas map documents are not. Document data types are useful for storing structured data, such as an IAM policy document stored in JavaScript Object Notation (JSON) format. DynamoDB can recognize and extract specific values nested within a document, allowing you to retrieve only the data you're interested in without having to retrieve the entire document.

Scaling Horizontally

DynamoDB uses the primary key to distribute items across multiple partitions. Distributing the data horizontally in this fashion makes it possible for DynamoDB to consistently achieve low-latency reads and writes regardless of how many items are in a table. The number of partitions DynamoDB allocates to your table depends on the number of write capacity units (WCU) and read capacity units (RCU) you allocate to your table. The higher the transaction volume and the more data you're reading or writing, the higher your RCU or WCU values should be. Higher values cause DynamoDB to distribute your data across more partitions, increasing performance and decreasing latency. As demand on your DynamoDB tables changes, you can change the number of RCU and WCU accordingly. Alternatively, you can configure DynamoDB Auto Scaling to dynamically adjust the number of WCU and RCU based on demand. This automatic horizontal scaling ensures consistent performance, even during times of peak load.

Queries and Scans

Recall that nonrelational databases let you quickly retrieve items from a table based on the value of the primary key. For example, if the primary key of a table is Username, you can perform a query for the user named **pdrake**. If an item exists with that primary key value, DynamoDB will return the item instantly.

Searching for a value in an attribute other than the primary key is possible, but slower. To locate all items with a Username that starts with the letter *p*, you'd have to perform a scan operation to list all items in the table. This is a read-intensive task that requires scanning every item in every partition your table is stored in. Even if you know all the attributes of an item except for the primary key, you'd still have to perform a scan operation to retrieve the item.

Complete Exercise 9.1 to get an idea of how DynamoDB tables work.

EXERCISE 9.1

Create a DynamoDB Table

To create a DynamoDB table and add an item to it

1. In the AWS Management Console, browse to the DynamoDB Service Console.

2. Choose the Create Table button.

3. In the Table Name field, give your table the name **Foods**.

4. In the Primary Key field, enter the word **FoodName**.

5. From the drop-down menu, select String. This defines the primary key for the table.

6. Under the Table Settings section, uncheck Use Default Settings.

7. In the Read/write Capacity Mode section, select the radio button next to On-Demand.

8. Choose the Create button. It will take several seconds to create the table.

9. Choose the Items tab.

10. Choose the Create Item button.

11. In the field next to FoodName String, enter **Asparagus**.

12. Choose the Save button. You should see a new item with Asparagus as the value for the primary key.

13. Choose the Delete Table button.

14. Choose the Delete button.

Amazon Redshift

Amazon Redshift is a specialized type of managed relational database called a *data warehouse*. A data warehouse stores large amounts of structured data from other relational databases and allows you to perform complex queries and analysis against that data. For example, Redshift can combine data from financial, sales, and inventory databases into a single data warehouse and then analyze or generate reports on that data.

Because data warehouses can grow quite large, they require a lot of storage. To use Redshift, you create a cluster consisting of at least one compute node and up to 128 nodes. Using *dense compute* nodes, you can store up to 326 TB of data on magnetic disks, and with *dense storage* nodes you can store up to 2 PB of data on SSDs.

Redshift's usefulness isn't limited to pulling in data from relational databases. Redshift Spectrum is a feature of Redshift that lets you analyze data stored in S3. The data must be structured, and you must define the structure so that Redshift can understand it.

Summary

In most cases, the decision about whether to use a relational or nonrelational database has already been made for you. If you're migrating a database-backed application from your data center to AWS, chances are the application is already using a SQL database. In that case, your migration options are to either use RDS or build and maintain your own SQL server on one or more EC2 instances.

When it comes to developing a new database-backed application, whether to use a relational or nonrelational database is not an easy decision, nor is it always a clear-cut one. Both have their unique advantages and disadvantages, as shown in Table 9.3.

TABLE 9.3   Comparison of Relational and Nonrelational Databases

Relational	Nonrelational
Designed for complex or arbitrary queries	Designed for a few well-defined queries
Requires structured data	Can store structured or unstructured data
Ideal for reporting and analysis	Ideal for highly transactional applications

Note that the trade-off for being able to store unstructured data in a nonrelational database is being more limited in your queries. On the flip side, the reward for structuring your data and keeping it in a relational database is the flexibility to perform a wide variety of queries. Relational databases allow you to construct almost any query you can imagine. You can search based on any attribute, and even search for ranges, such as values starting with any letter between *H* and *N*. Nonrelational databases don't offer this kind of query flexibility.

Nonrelational databases such as DynamoDB are designed to scale horizontally by spreading your data across more partitions, allowing for thousands of reads and writes per second. Relational databases such as RDS can be scaled horizontally to support a high number of reads by adding read replicas. However, because only one database instance can write to the database, it's not feasible to support higher write rates by scaling horizontally. Instead, you can scale the instance vertically by upgrading to a more powerful instance class.

Exam Essentials

Understand the major differences between relational and nonrelational databases. Relational databases are designed for structured data that contains a defined number of attributes per record. They let you perform complex queries against a variety of dimensions, making them ideal for reporting and analytics. Nonrelational databases are designed for data that doesn't follow a predictable structure. Each item in a nonrelational database must have a primary key, and you can query based on that key.

Know the vertical and horizontal scaling options for RDS. You can scale an RDS instance vertically by upgrading to a larger instance class to give it more processing power, memory, or disk or network throughput. You can also select provisioned IOPS SSD storage to ensure your instance always achieves the storage performance it needs. For horizontal scaling of reads, your only option is to use read replicas.

Be able to describe the components of RDS. An RDS deployment consists of at least one instance. You must select an instance class that defines the vCPUs and memory for the instance. You must also select a database engine. For storage, you must select general-purpose or provisioned IOPS SSD. Magnetic storage is a legacy option that's not available for new deployments. You can also add read replicas to scale horizontally to improve read performance. In a multi-AZ deployment, you can add additional secondary instances that the primary synchronously replicates data to.

Know the backup and recovery options for RDS. You can schedule automatic snapshots for your RDS instance to occur daily during a 30-minute backup window of your choice. Backups are retained between 1 day and 35 days. Enabling automatic backups also enables point-in-time recovery, allowing the restoration of a failed database up to 5 minutes prior to failure. Restoring from a snapshot entails creating a new instance from the snapshot. You can also take a manual snapshot at any time.

Understand how DynamoDB stores data. DynamoDB stores data as items in tables. Each item must have primary key whose values are unique within the table. This is how DynamoDB uniquely identifies an item. The primary key's name and data type must be defined when the table is created. When you create an item, you can also add other attributes in addition to the primary key. DynamoDB uses the primary key to distribute items across different partitions. The number of partitions allocated to a table depends on the number of WCU and RCU you configure.

Be able to identify scenarios for using Redshift. Redshift is a data-warehousing service for storing and analyzing structured data from multiple sources, including relational databases and S3. Redshift can store much more data than RDS, up to 2 PB!

Review Questions

1. Which type of database stores data in columns and rows?

    A. Nonrelational

    B. Relational

    C. Key-value store

    D. Document

2. Which of the following Structured Query Language (SQL) statements can you use to write data to a relational database table?

    A. CREATE

    B. INSERT

    C. QUERY

    D. WRITE

3. Which of the following statements is true regarding nonrelational databases?

    A. You can create only one table.

    B. No primary key is required.

    C. You can't store data with a fixed structure.

    D. You don't have to define all the types of data that a table can store before adding data to it.

4. What is a no-SQL database?

    A. A nonrelational database without primary keys

    B. A schemaless relational database

    C. A schemaless nonrelational database

    D. A relational database with primary keys

5. What do new Relational Database Service (RDS) instances use for database storage?

    A. Instance volumes

    B. Elastic Block Store (EBS) volumes

    C. Snapshots

    D. Magnetic storage

6. Which of the following are database engine options for Amazon Relational Database Service (RDS)? (Select TWO.)

    A. IBM dBase

    B. PostgreSQL

    C. DynamoDB

    D. Amazon Aurora

    E. Redis

7. What two databases is Amazon Aurora compatible with? (Select TWO.)

    A. MySQL

    B. PostgreSQL

    C. MariaDB

    D. Oracle

    E. Microsoft SQL Server

8. Which of the following features of Relational Database Service (RDS) can prevent data loss in the event of an Availability Zone failure? (Select TWO.)

    A. Read replicas

    B. Multi-AZ

    C. Snapshots

    D. IOPS

    E. Vertical scaling

9. Which RDS database engine offers automatically expanding database storage up to 64 TB?

    A. Microsoft SQL Server

    B. Amazon Aurora

    C. Oracle

    D. Amazon Athena

10. Which of the following Relational Database Service (RDS) features can help you achieve a monthly availability of 99.95 percent?

    A. Multi-AZ

    B. Read replicas

    C. Point-in-time recovery

    D. Horizontal scaling

11. What is true regarding a DynamoDB partition? (Select TWO.)

    A. It's stored within a table.

    B. It's backed by solid-state drives.

    C. It's a way to uniquely identify an item in a table.

    D. It's replicated across multiple Availability Zones.

12. What is the minimum monthly availability for DynamoDB in a single region?

    A. 99.99 percent

    B. 99.95 percent

    C. 99.9 percent

    D. 99.0 percent

13. Which of the following statements is true regarding a DynamoDB table?

    A. It can store only one data type.

    B. When you create a table, you must define the maximum number of items that it can store.

    C. Items in a table can have duplicate values for the primary key.

    D. Items in a table don't have to have all the same attributes.

14. Which configuration parameters can you adjust to improve write performance against a DynamoDB table? (Select TWO.)

    A. Decrease read capacity units (RCU)

    B. Increase read capacity units

    C. Increase write capacity units (WCU)

    D. Decrease write capacity units

    E. Enable DynamoDB Auto Scaling

15. Which DynamoDB operation is the most read-intensive?

    A. Write

    B. Query

    C. Scan

    D. Update

16. Which of the following would be appropriate to use for a primary key in a DynamoDB table that stores a customer list?

    A. The customer's full name

    B. The customer's phone number

    C. The customer's city

    D. A randomly generated customer ID number

17. Which type of Redshift node uses magnetic storage?

    A. Cost-optimized

    B. Dense compute

    C. Dense storage

    D. Dense memory

18. Which Redshift feature can analyze structured data stored in S3?

    A. Redshift Spectrum

    B. Redshift S3

    C. Amazon Athena

    D. Amazon RDS

19. What is the term for a relational database that stores large amounts of structured data from a variety of sources for reporting and analysis?

   A. Data storehouse

   B. Data warehouse

   C. Report cluster

   D. Dense storage node

20. What's the maximum amount of data you can store in a Redshift cluster when using dense storage nodes?

   A. 2 PB

   B. 326 TB

   C. 2 TB

   D. 326 PB

   E. 236 TB

Chapter

10

The Core Networking Services

THE AWS CERTIFIED CLOUD PRACTITIONER
EXAM OBJECTIVES COVERED IN THIS
CHAPTER MAY INCLUDE, BUT ARE NOT
LIMITED TO, THE FOLLOWING:

Domain 3: Technology

✓ **3.1   Define methods of deploying and operating in the AWS Cloud**

✓ **3.2   Define the AWS global infrastructure**

✓ **3.3   Identify the core AWS services**

Introduction

Networking is ultimately about transporting data to and from your AWS resources. How you achieve this depends on many factors, including the type of data, the speed of data transport, your security requirements, who or what will be accessing that data, and how they'll be accessing it. In this chapter, you'll learn about the following three core networking services AWS offers:

- Virtual Private Cloud
- Route 53
- CloudFront

Virtual Private Cloud

The Amazon Virtual Private Cloud (VPC) service provides the network backbone for many AWS services. A virtual private cloud is a virtual network in the AWS cloud that's logically isolated from other networks. The most well-known use of VPCs is connecting EC2 instances together and to other AWS services and networks, including the internet.

When you create an AWS account, Amazon automatically creates a default VPC in each region. The default VPC is configured to allow instances within the VPC to access the internet. This way you don't have to create and configure your own VPC just to use EC2.

You can create your own nondefault VPCs. Nondefault VPCs are fully isolated from every other network and AWS resource, including other VPCs. This means you'll have to configure them explicitly if you want them to have access to other networks and AWS resources outside of the VPC.

VPC CIDR Blocks

Each VPC requires a Classless Inter-Domain Routing (*CIDR*) block to define the range of IP version 4 (IPv4) addresses that resources within the VPC can use. Default VPCs have a CIDR of 172.31.0.0/16, which includes all addresses from 172.31.0.0 to 172.31.255.255. The /16 refers to the size of the CIDR. You must choose a CIDR size between /16 and /28, but otherwise, any CIDR you could assign to a traditional network can also be assigned to a VPC. The smaller the CIDR size, the greater the number of IP addresses available to the VPC. The following are a few examples of CIDR blocks that you could assign to a VPC:

- 10.0.0.0/16 (10.0.0.0–10.0.255.255)
- 192.168.0.0/24 (192.168.0.0–192.168.0.255)
- 172.16.0.0/28 (172.16.0.0–172.16.0.15)

At your request, AWS can also assign an IPv6 CIDR block to your VPC. The IPv6 CIDR will be a global unicast IPv6 address with a size of /56.

    The acronym CIDR is usually pronounced "cider" for brevity.

Subnets

Each VPC requires further division into one or more subnets. A subnet provides logical separation and isolation of resources within the same VPC. For example, you may want to have web servers and application servers in the same VPC, but you want only the web servers to be accessible from the internet.

As with a VPC, you must define a CIDR for each subnet. The subnet CIDR must be a subset of the VPC CIDR, with a size between /16 and /28. For example, if the default VPC CIDR is 172.31.0.0/16, then a subnet CIDR could be 172.31.16.0/20. Each subnet exists only within a single Availability Zone. Refer to Figure 10.1 for a sample VPC topology with two subnets.

FIGURE 10.1   A VPC with two subnets in different Availability Zones.

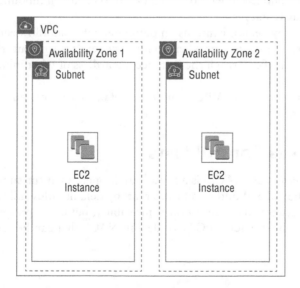

Each EC2 instance exists within a subnet. This is why within each default VPC, Amazon creates a default subnet in each Availability Zone. This way, you can launch EC2 instances without ever having to configure a VPC.

Internet Access

An *internet gateway* is a VPC resource that allows EC2 instances to obtain a public IP address and access the internet.

For instances in a subnet to have internet access, that subnet must contain a default route to the internet gateway that's attached to the VPC. A subnet with a default route to an internet gateway is called a *public subnet*.

Each instance must also have a public IP address. When you launch an instance, you can choose to have AWS automatically assign it one. You can't reassign an automatically assigned public IP address, and when the instance stops or terminates, you lose it. Alternatively, you can allocate an elastic IP address and then assign it to an instance. Elastic IP addresses can be reassigned to different instances and don't change until you deallocate them.

Security Groups

A *security group* is a firewall that determines what network traffic can pass into and out of an instance. Each instance must have least one security group attached.

Security groups consist of inbound and outbound rules that permit network traffic according to IP address and protocol. Inbound rules control what IP addresses can send traffic to the instance, whereas outbound rules control what IP addresses an instance may send traffic to. By default, security groups don't contain inbound rules. This ensures no unsolicited traffic can reach the instance. For example, if you want anyone to be able to reach a web server in a public subnet, you would need to create an inbound rule to allow HTTP traffic from any IP address.

Each security group by default contains an outbound rule that allows access to any IP address. It's important to note that when an instance sends traffic out, the security group will allow reply traffic to reach the instance, regardless of what inbound rules are configured.

Every VPC, not just the default VPC, contains a default security group that you can modify to meet your needs.

Network Access Control Lists

A *network access control list* (NACL) is a firewall that operates at the subnet level. A NACL consists of inbound and outbound rules that, by default, allow all traffic. A NACL can't restrict traffic between instances in the same subnet, but it can prevent traffic from entering or leaving a subnet. Each VPC has a default NACL that can be associated with one or more subnets.

VPC Peering

A *VPC peering connection* is a private, point-to-point connection between only two VPCs. VPC peering allows resources in different VPCs to communicate with each other over the private AWS network instead of the internet. A VPC peering connection allows instances in one VPC to access certain types of resources in another VPC, such as another instance or a network load balancer.

VPC peering connections are fast, reliable, and secure. There's also no need for VPC resources to have internet access in order to use VPC peering. Peered VPCs can be in the same region or in different regions.

Virtual Private Networks

A virtual private network (VPN) allows you to connect a VPC to an external network, such as a data center or office, via a secure connection that traverses the public internet. To set up a VPN connection, you create a virtual private gateway and attach it to a VPC. You then configure your customer gateway—a physical or virtual router or firewall on your network—to connect to the virtual private gateway. AWS has tested a variety of customer gateways from different manufacturers including Cisco, Juniper, Palo Alto Networks, and Check Point.

VPN connections are encrypted using AES 128- or 256-bit encryption. IP routing can be configured statically, or you can use the Border Gateway Protocol (BGP) to share routes between your VPC and external network. A single VPC can have up to 10 VPN connections.

Direct Connect

Direct Connect provides private network connectivity to your VPC and public services such as Amazon S3 and Glacier. There's no need to have a separate internet circuit just to access these services. This means you can bypass the internet altogether when accessing your AWS resources. Keep in mind that Direct Connect doesn't provide internet access, so if you need it, you'll still need a separate internet connection.

Direct Connect links are offered through AWS Partner Network (APN) partners. Direct Connect operates using a dedicated link that operates at 1 or 10 Gbps. Because of this, it's not subject to the high and unpredictable latency of a broadband internet connection. If you need fast, consistent connectivity to AWS, Direct Connect is a good option versus connecting via the internet. It is, however, more expensive.

If you need less than 1 Gbps of bandwidth, you can obtain a hosted Direct Connect connection from an APN partner. A hosted connection comes in speeds of 50 Mbps, 100 Mbps, 200 Mbps, 300 Mbps, 400 Mbps, and 500 Mbps.

Route 53

Route 53 is Amazon's global Domain Name System (DNS) service. The primary purpose of DNS is to translate human-readable domain names (such as example.com) into IP addresses. Here's a simplified version of how it works: when you enter the domain name example.com into your web browser, your computer sends out a query to its configured DNS server asking for the IP address of that domain. The DNS server then sends the query to the domain's authoritative DNS server—the one that's in charge of the example.com domain name. The authoritative DNS server responds with the IP address for example.com. This process of translating a domain name to an IP address is called *name resolution*.

Resource Records

Name resolution goes beyond just mapping domain names to IP addresses. DNS can store mappings for different types of data, including IPv6 addresses, mail servers, and even arbitrary text. When you send an email to someone, DNS provides the lookup mechanism to ensure it gets routed to the correct mail server for that domain.

For DNS to work, someone must first define some resource records for a domain. A resource record consists of several fields, but the most important are the name, type, and value. Refer to Table 10.1 for some example resource records.

TABLE 10.1   Resource Records for the benpiper.com Domain

Name	Type	Value
benpiper.com	A - IPv4 address	93.184.216.34
www.benpiper.com	A - IPv4 address	93.184.216.34
benpiper.com	MX - Mail exchange	10 in1-smtp.messagingengine.com

Domain Name Registration

A public domain name is one that anyone on the internet can resolve. To ensure that no two entities try to use the same domain name, anyone who wants to have a public domain name must register it with a domain registrar. When you register a domain name, you must do so under a top-level domain (TLD) such as .com, .net, or .org. For example, you might register the name example.com or example.org. Route 53 is a domain registrar for hundreds of TLDs.

Registering a domain gives you control of it for the duration of the lease, which can be in yearly increments between 1 year and 10 years. Regardless of how long you initially register a domain for, you can renew it in yearly increments indefinitely. If you have an existing domain name with another registrar, you can transfer it to Route 53. Transferring a domain entails extending the registration by at least one year.

It's important to understand that domain name registration and DNS hosting are two different functions. Registering a domain name gives you control over it for the duration of the lease, including the right to specify the service you want to provide DNS hosting for the domain. This means the domain registrar and DNS hosting provider don't have to be the same company, but they often are. Route 53 is both a registrar and a DNS hosting provider.

Hosted Zones

To have Route 53 host the DNS for a public domain name, you create a public hosted zone and specify the domain name. You can then define the resource records for that domain. If you use Route 53 to register a domain name, it automatically takes care of creating a public hosted zone for the domain.

Route 53 can also provide name resolution for private domain names. A private domain name is one used on a network other than the internet. Route 53 private hosted zones provide DNS resolution for a single domain name within multiple VPCs. This is useful for assigning user-friendly domain names to VPC resources such as EC2 instances or application load balancers. For example, instead of hardcoding a database server's IP in an application, you can define a record in a private hosted zone with the name db.example.com that points to the database server's IP address. Because private domain names aren't accessible from the internet, there are no registrars, so you can pick any domain name you want. Name resolution for private hosted zones is not available outside of the VPC you select.

Routing Policies

In some cases, you just need a domain name to resolve to a particular IP address. But there are other times when you want the value of a resource record to change dynamically to work around failures or ensure users get pointed to the least busy server. Route 53 lets you accomplish this with a variety of routing policies.

Simple   The Simple routing policy is the default for new resource records. It simply lets you map a domain name to a single static value, such as an IP address. It doesn't check whether the resource the record points to is available.

Weighted   A Weighted policy distributes traffic across multiple resources according to a ratio. For example, when introducing a new web server, you may want to route only 10 percent of the traffic to the new server while evenly distributing the load across the rest.

Latency   A Latency policy sends users to resources in the AWS Region that's closest to them. This is useful if, for instance, you want to send European users to the eu-west-1 region while sending users in the United States to the us-east-1 region.

Failover   A Failover policy lets you route traffic to a primary resource unless it's unavailable. In that case, traffic will be redirected to a secondary resource.

Geolocation   A Geolocation policy lets you route users based on their specific continent, country, or state.

Multivalue Answer   A Multivalue Answer policy allows you to evenly distribute traffic across multiple resources. Unlike Weighted policies that return a single record, a Multivalue Answer policy returns all records, sorted in a random order.

Health Checks

All routing policies with the exception of Simple can use health checks to determine whether they should route users to a given resource. A health check can check one of three things: an endpoint, a CloudWatch alarm, or another health check. All health checks occur every 10 seconds or 30 seconds.

Endpoint   Endpoint health checks work by connecting to the endpoint you want to monitor via HTTP, HTTPS, or TCP. Route 53 has health checkers in several AWS Regions, and you can choose which health checkers a health check uses. This lets you ensure that an endpoint is reachable from various locations around the world.

CloudWatch alarm   A Route 53 health check can monitor the status of a CloudWatch alarm. This is useful if you want to consider a resource unhealthy if it's experiencing high latency or is servicing a high number of connections.

Calculated   This type of health check monitors the status of other health checks. For example, if you want to consider the status of both an Endpoint health check and a CloudWatch alarm health check, you can create a Calculated health check to take both into account.

Traffic Flow and Traffic Policies

If you require complex routing scenarios for a public hosted zone, creating multiple resource records with a variety of different routing policies can become an administrative nightmare. As an alternative to manually engineering routing policies, you can use the Route 53 Traffic Flow visual editor to create a diagram to represent the desired routing.

The diagram you create represents a traffic policy that you can save and associate with a domain name by creating a policy record. Route 53 doesn't create the individual resource records but instead hides the routing behind the single policy record. The cost is currently $50 USD per month per policy record.

You can use the same routing policies that are available with normal resource records: Simple, Weighted, Latency, Failover, Geolocation, and Multivalue Answer. But in addition, Traffic Flow offers another routing policy that's not otherwise available: Geoproximity. The Geoproximity routing policy lets you direct users to a resource based on how close they are to a geographic location. This differs from the Geolocation routing policy that routes based on the user's specific continent, country, or state.

CloudFront

Amazon CloudFront is a content delivery network (CDN) that helps deliver static and dynamic web content to users faster than just serving it out of an AWS Region. For example, if you're hosting a website from a single AWS Region, as a general rule, the farther a user is away from that region, the more network latency they'll encounter when accessing it. CloudFront solves this problem by caching your content in a number of data centers called *edge locations*. There are more than 150 edge locations spread out around the world on six continents.

CloudFront works by sending users to the edge location that will give them the best performance. Typically, this is the edge location that's physically closest to them. CloudFront also increases the availability of your content because copies of it are stored in multiple edge locations.

The more edge locations you use, the more redundancy you have and the better performance you can expect. As you might expect, the price of CloudFront increases as you utilize more edge locations. You can't select individual edge locations. Rather, you must choose from the following three options:

- United States, Canada, and Europe
- United States, Canada, Europe, Asia, and Africa
- All edge locations

To make your content available via CloudFront, you must create a distribution. A distribution defines the type of content you want CloudFront to cache, as well as the content's origin—where CloudFront should retrieve the content from. There are two types of distributions: Web and Real-Time Messaging Protocol (RTMP).

Web   A Web distribution is the most common type. It's used for static and dynamic content such as web pages, graphic files, and live or on-demand streaming video. Users can access Web distributions via HTTP or HTTPS. When creating a Web distribution, you must specify an origin to act as the authoritative source for your content. An origin can be a web server or a public S3 bucket. You can't use nonpublic S3 buckets.

RTMP   The Real-Time Messaging Protocol (RTMP) delivers streaming video or audio content to end users. To set up an RTMP distribution, you must provide both a media player and media files to stream, and these must be stored in S3 buckets.

Summary

Virtual Private Cloud (VPC) provides the virtual network infrastructure for many AWS resources, most notably EC2. VPCs can connect to other networks, including the following:

- The internet via an internet gateway
- External, private networks via Direct Connect or a virtual private network (VPN)
- Other VPCs using VPC peering

The Route 53 service provides two distinct but related Domain Name System (DNS) services. Route 53 functions as a registrar for many top-level internet domain names (TLDs). You can register a new domain with Route 53 or transfer an existing one that you control. Route 53 also provides DNS hosting services. To use Route 53 with a public domain, you must create a public hosted zone. To use Route 53 for name resolution within a VPC, you must create a private hosted zone.

CloudFront is Amazon's content delivery network (CDN). It improves delivery of data to end users by storing content in edge locations around the world. When a user connects to a CloudFront distribution to retrieve content, CloudFront serves the content from the edge location that will give them the best performance.

Exam Essentials

Know the components of a VPC.   The key components of a VPC include at least one subnet, security groups, network access control lists (NACLs), and internet gateways.

Understand the different options for connecting to resources in a VPC.   You can connect to resources in a VPC over the internet, a Direct Connect link, a VPC peering connection, or a virtual private network (VPN) connection.

Understand the difference between a Route 53 public hosted zone and a private hosted zone. A public hosted zone allows anyone on the internet to resolve records for the associated domain name. A private hosted zone allows resolution only from resources within the associated VPCs.

Be able to select the best Route 53 routing policy for a given scenario.   All routing policies except the Simple routing policy can use health checks to route around failures. If you want to direct traffic to any available resource, Failover, Weighted, and Multivalue Answer routing policies will suffice. If performance is a concern, choose a Latency routing policy. If you need to direct users based on their specific location, use a Geolocation routing policy.

Know how CloudFront improves the speed of content delivery.   CloudFront caches objects in edge locations around the world and automatically directs users to the edge location that will give them the best performance at any given time.

Be able to identify scenarios where CloudFront would be appropriate.   CloudFront is designed to give users the fastest possible access to content regardless of their physical location. By caching content in edge locations that are distributed around the world, CloudFront helps ensure that your content is always close to your users.

Review Questions

1. Which of the following are true of a default VPC? (Select TWO.)

    A. A default VPC spans multiple regions.

    B. AWS creates a default VPC in each region.

    C. AWS creates a default VPC in each Availability Zone.

    D. By default, each default VPC is available to one AWS account.

2. Which of the following is a valid CIDR for a VPC or subnet?

    A. 10.0.0.0/28

    B. 10.0.0.0/29

    C. 10.0.0.0/8

    D. 10.0.0.0/15

3. Which of the following are true regarding subnets? (Select TWO.)

    A. A VPC must have at least two subnets.

    B. A subnet must have a CIDR that's a subset of the CIDR of the VPC in which it resides.

    C. A subnet spans one Availability Zone.

    D. A subnet spans multiple Availability Zones.

4. Which of the following is true of a new security group?

    A. It contains an inbound rule denying access from public IP addresses.

    B. It contains an outbound rule denying access to public IP addresses.

    C. It contains an outbound rule allowing access to any IP address.

    D. It contains an inbound rule allowing access from any IP address.

    E. It contains an inbound rule denying access from any IP address.

5. What's the difference between a security group and a network access control list (NACL)? (Select TWO.)

    A. A network access control list operates at the instance level.

    B. A security group operates at the instance level.

    C. A security group operates at the subnet level.

    D. A network access control list operates at the subnet level.

6. Which of the following is true of a VPC peering connection?

    A. It's a private connection that connects more than three VPCs.

    B. It's a private connection between two VPCs.

    C. It's a public connection between two VPCs.

    D. It's a virtual private network (VPN) connection between two VPCs.

7. What are two differences between a virtual private network (VPN) connection and a Direct Connect connection? (Select TWO.)

   A. A Direct Connect connection offers predictable latency because it doesn't traverse the internet.

   B. A VPN connection uses the internet for transport.

   C. A Direct Connect connection uses AES 128- or 256-bit encryption.

   D. A VPN connection requires proprietary hardware.

8. Which of the following are true about registering a domain name with Route 53? (Select TWO.)

   A. The registrar you use to register a domain name determines who will host DNS for that domain.

   B. You can register a domain name for a term of up to 10 years.

   C. Route 53 creates a private hosted zone for the domain.

   D. Route 53 creates a public hosted zone for the domain.

9. Which of the following Route 53 routing policies can return set of randomly ordered values?

   A. Simple

   B. Multivalue Answer

   C. Failover

   D. Latency

10. Which of the following Route 53 routing policies doesn't use health checks?

   A. Latency

   B. Multivalue Answer

   C. Simple

   D. Geolocation

11. Which of the following types of Route 53 health checks works by making a test connection to a TCP port?

   A. Simple

   B. CloudWatch alarm

   C. Endpoint

   D. Calculated

12. You have two EC2 instances hosting a web application. You want to distribute 20 percent of traffic to one instance and 80 percent to the other. Which of the following Route 53 routing policies should you use?

   A. Weighted

   B. Failover

   C. Multivalue Answer

   D. Simple

13. Resources in a VPC need to be able to resolve internal IP addresses for other resources in the VPC. No one outside of the VPC should be able to resolve these addresses. Which of the following Route 53 resources can help you achieve this?

    A. A public hosted zone

    B. A private hosted zone

    C. Domain name registration

    D. Health checks

14. You want to provide private name resolution for two VPCs using the domain name company.pri. How many private hosted zones do you need to create?

    A. 1

    B. 2

    C. 3

    D. 4

15. On how many continents are CloudFront edge locations distributed?

    A. 7

    B. 6

    C. 5

    D. 4

16. From where does CloudFront retrieve content to store for caching?

    A. Regions

    B. Origins

    C. Distributions

    D. Edge locations

17. Which CloudFront distribution type requires you to provide a media player?

    A. Streaming

    B. RTMP

    C. Web

    D. Edge

18. You need to deliver content to users in the United States and Canada. Which of the following edge location options will be the most cost effective for your CloudFront distribution?

    A. United States, Canada, and Europe

    B. United States, Canada, Europe, and Asia

    C. United States, Canada, Europe, Asia, and Africa

    D. All edge locations

19. Approximately how many different CloudFront edge locations are there?

   A. About 50

   B. More than 150

   C. More than 300

   D. More than 500

20. Which of the following are valid origins for a CloudFront distribution? (Select TWO.)

   A. EC2 instance

   B. A public S3 bucket

   C. A private S3 bucket that you don't have access to

   D. A private S3 bucket that you own

Chapter

11

Automating Your AWS Workloads

THE AWS CERTIFIED CLOUD PRACTITIONER EXAM OBJECTIVES COVERED IN THIS CHAPTER MAY INCLUDE, BUT ARE NOT LIMITED TO, THE FOLLOWING:

Domain 1: Cloud Concepts

✓ 1.3   List the different cloud architecture design principles

Domain 3: Technology

✓ 3.1   Define methods of deploying and operating in the AWS Cloud

✓ 3.3   Identify the core AWS services

Introduction

Automation is a best practice when it comes to designing architectures in the cloud. Automation allows common tasks to be repeated faster than doing them manually. These tasks can be simple and routine, such as installing the latest security patches on an EC2 instance running Linux. Or they can be complex, perhaps creating an entirely new and pristine AWS environment containing dozens of EC2 instances running a multitier, database-backed web application behind an application load balancer.

Whatever the task, whether simple or complex, automation confers several benefits, including the following:

- Rapid testing and experimentation
- Reducing expenses
- Minimizing human error
- Rolling back changes safely and completely

Some have a misconception of automation as replacing a human with a machine. But the truth is that automation requires a tremendous amount of human intelligence and ongoing effort. Ultimately, automation is about increasing the capacity of the people doing the work so that they can spend more time being productive and less time fixing problems.

Automation is not an all-or-nothing decision. You can deploy automation at different levels of your AWS environment, picking and choosing where it makes the most sense for you. You may find it helpful to approach automation in two different ways: imperative and declarative.

The Imperative Approach

The most common example of automation using an imperative approach is scripting, wherein you use a scripting language such as Bash or PowerShell, or even a tool such as the AWS Command Line Interface (CLI), to provide the explicit steps necessary to carry out a task. For example, you may write a Bash script to install a web server on an instance and then copy HTML files from an S3 bucket to a particular directory on the instance. The imperative approach focuses on the specific step-by-step operations required to carry out a task.

The Declarative Approach

Using a declarative approach, you write code that declares the desired result of the task, rather than how to carry it out. For example, rather than using the AWS CLI to create a new virtual private cloud (VPC) and subnets, you could write declarative code that simply defines the configuration for the VPC and subnets. This approach naturally requires some intelligent software to figure out the operations required to achieve the desired result. CloudFormation, which is covered in the first part of this chapter, is the most well-known AWS service that takes a declarative approach to building and configuring your AWS infrastructure. In short, you write code containing the specifics of the AWS resources you want and present that code to CloudFormation, and it builds and configures those resources on your behalf in a matter of seconds.

Infrastructure as Code

Using code to define your infrastructure and configurations is commonly called the *infrastructure as code* (IaC) approach. Defining IaC is a fundamental element of automation in the cloud. Because automation relies on code being executed by a machine, it reduces the risk of human error inherent in carrying out the same work manually. This in turn reduces rework and other problems down the line.

In this chapter, we cover the following AWS services that enable automation in different ways:

- CloudFormation—Lets you automate the building and configuration of your AWS resources
- The AWS Developer Tools of CodeCommit, CodeBuild, CodeDeploy, and CodePipeline—Automate the testing, building, and deployment of applications to EC2 and on-premises instances
- EC2 Auto Scaling—Automatically launches, configures, and terminates EC2 instances as needed to meet fluctuating demand
- Systems Manager—Automates common operational tasks such as patching instances and backing up Elastic Block Store (EBS) volumes
- OpsWorks—A collection of three different offerings that help automate instance configuration and application deployments using the popular Chef and Puppet configuration management platforms

CloudFormation

CloudFormation automatically creates and configures your AWS infrastructure from code that defines the resources you want it to create and how you want those resources configured.

Templates

The code that defines your resources is stored in text files called *templates*. Templates use the proprietary CloudFormation language, which can be written in JavaScript Object Notation (JSON) or YAML format.

Templates contain a description of the AWS resources you want CloudFormation to create, so they simultaneously function as infrastructure documentation. Because templates are files, you can store them in a version-controlled system such as an S3 bucket or a Git repository, allowing you to track changes over time.

You can use the same template to build AWS infrastructure repeatedly, such as for development or testing. You can also use a single template to build many similar environments. For example, you can use one template to create identical resources for both production and test environments. Both environments can have the same infrastructure—VPCs, subnets, application load balancers, and so on—but they'll be separate environments. CloudFormation uses random identifiers when naming resources to ensure the resources it creates don't conflict with each other.

You can write templates to optionally take parameter inputs, allowing you to customize your resources without modifying the original template. For instance, you can write a template that asks for a custom resource tag to apply to all the resources CloudFormation creates. You can make a parameter optional by specifying a default value, or you can require the user to specify a value in order to use the template.

Stacks

To provision resources from a template, you must specify a stack name that's unique within your account. A *stack* is a container that organizes the resources described in the template.

The purpose of a stack is to collectively manage related resources. If you delete a stack, CloudFormation automatically deletes all of the resources in it. This makes CloudFormation perfect for test and development environments that need to be provisioned as pristine and then thrown away when no longer needed. Deleting a stack helps ensure that all resources are deleted and that no forgotten resources are left lingering, running up charges.

One of the fundamental principles of good cloud design is to make your test environments mirror your production environments as closely as possible. CloudFormation makes this not only possible but almost trivially easy!

Stack Updates

You can have CloudFormation change individual resources in a stack. Just modify the template to delete, modify, or add resources, and then instruct CloudFormation to perform a stack update using the template. CloudFormation will automatically update the resources accordingly. If any other resources are dependent upon a resource that you've updated,

CloudFormation will detect that and make sure those downstream resources are also reconfigured properly.

Alternatively, you can create a change set. Make the desired changes to your template, and then have CloudFormation generate a change set based on the template. CloudFormation will let you review the specific changes it will make, and then you can decide whether to execute those changes or leave everything as is.

CloudFormation makes it easy to update stacks, increasing the possibility that a less skilled user might inadvertently update a stack, making undesired changes to a critical resource. If you're concerned about this possibility, you can create a stack policy to guard against accidental updates. A stack policy is a JSON document, separate from a template, that specifies what resources may be updated. You can use it prevent updates to any or all resources in a stack. If you absolutely need to update a stack, you can temporarily override the policy.

Tracking Stack Changes

Each stack contains a timestamped record of events that occur within the stack, including when resources were created, updated, or deleted. This makes it easy to see all changes made to your stack.

It's important to understand that resources in CloudFormation stacks can be changed manually, and CloudFormation doesn't prevent this. For instance, you can manually delete a VPC that's part of a CloudFormation stack. Drift detection is a feature that monitors your stacks for such changes and alerts you when they occur.

CloudFormation vs. the AWS CLI

You can script AWS CLI commands to create resources fast and automatically, but those resources won't be kept in a stack, so you won't get the same advantages that stacks provide.

When you're using the AWS CLI, you can't update your resources as easily as you can with CloudFormation. With CloudFormation, you simply adjust the template or parameters to change your resources, and CloudFormation figures out how to perform the changes. With the AWS CLI, it's up to you to understand how to change each resource and to ensure that a change you make to one resource doesn't break another.

EXERCISE 11.1

Explore the CloudFormation Designer

In this exercise, you'll use the CloudFormation Designer to look at a sample template that defines a simple environment containing a Linux EC2 instance. In addition to letting you view and edit the template directly, the CloudFormation Designer also visualizes the resources in a template, making it easy to see exactly what CloudFormation will build.

1. Browse to the CloudFormation service console.

2. Choose the Create New Stack button.

3. In the Choose A Template section, choose the Select A Sample Template drop-down, and select LAMP Stack.

4. Choose the View/Edit Template In Designer link.

5. The Designer will show you icons for two resources: an EC2 instance and a security group. Choose the instance icon. The Designer will take you to the section of the template that defines the instance.

AWS Developer Tools

The AWS Developer Tools are a collection of tools designed to help application developers develop, build, test, and deploy their applications onto EC2 and on-premises instances. These tools facilitate and automate the tasks that must take place to get a new application revision released into production.

However, the AWS Developer Tools enable more than just application development. You can use them as part of any IaC approach to automate the deployment and configuration of your AWS infrastructure.

In this section, you'll learn about the following AWS Developer Tools:

- CodeCommit
- CodeBuild
- CodeDeploy
- CodePipeline

CodeCommit

CodeCommit lets you create private Git repositories that easily integrate with other AWS services. Git (https://git-scm.com) is a version control system that you can use to store source code, CloudFormation templates, documents, or any arbitrary files—even binary files such as Amazon Machine Images (AMI) and Docker containers. These files are stored in a repository, colloquially known as a *repo*.

Git uses a process called *versioning*, where all changes or commits to a repository are retained indefinitely, so you can always revert to an old version of a file if you need it.

CodeCommit is useful for teams of people who need to collaborate on the same set of files, such as developers who collaborate on a shared source code base for an application. CodeCommit allows users to check out code by copying or cloning it locally to their machine. They make changes to it locally and then check it back in to the repository.

Git performs differencing to identify the differences between different versions of a file. If a developer makes a code change that breaks the application, differencing lets the developer see exactly what changed. They can then revert to the previous, working version of the file.

Differencing is one of the fundamental differences between a version control system such as Git and a file storage system such as S3.

CodeBuild

CodeBuild is a fully managed build service. A *build* is a set of actions performed on source code to get it ready for deployment. A build could include testing the code for errors or transforming it into a machine-readable language, but the specific build actions depend on the application.

Build Actions

One of the primary purposes of the build process is to run tests against the new code to ensure it works properly. This could include tests to validate that the source code is formatted properly and doesn't contain syntax errors. It may also involve testing the functionality of the code by simulating how a user might use it.

Automated testing is a key part of a software development practice called *continuous integration* (CI). In CI, developers check their new or modified code into a shared repository multiple times a day. A build provider, such as CodeBuild, runs tests against this code. This rapid testing and feedback provides early detection of bugs that the developer can fix immediately.

A build can also consist of compiling source code into a binary such as an executable or a package installer. You can even use CodeBuild to create Docker containers and Amazon Machine Images (AMIs).

You define your specific tasks in a build specification file that must be included with the source code. CodeBuild can get source code from a CodeCommit, GitHub, or Bitbucket repository, or an S3 bucket.

CodeBuild can perform multiple builds simultaneously. Any outputs or artifacts that CodeBuild creates are stored in an S3 bucket, making them accessible to the rest of your AWS environment.

Build Environments

CodeBuild performs builds in an isolated build environment that runs on a compute instance. It creates the build environment before each build and discards it when the build is finished. This isolation ensures a consistent build process that isn't affected by leftovers from previous builds.

The build environment always consists of an operating system and a Docker image that can include a programming language runtime and tools. AWS offers preconfigured build environments for Java, Ruby, Python, Go, Node.js, Android, .NET Core, PHP, and Docker. You can also create your own custom build environment.

You can choose from the following three different compute types for your build environment:

- build.general1.small—3 GB of memory and 2 vCPU
- build.general1.medium—7 GB of memory and 4 vCPU
- build.general1.large—15 GB of memory and 8 vCPU

All of the compute types support Linux, while the medium and large types also support Windows.

CodeDeploy

CodeDeploy can automatically deploy applications to EC2 instances, the Elastic Container Service (ECS), Lambda, and even on-premises servers.

CodeDeploy works by pulling source files from an S3 bucket, or a GitHub or Bitbucket repository. In addition to your application's source files, you must provide an application-specification file that contains information about how to deploy the application.

The CodeDeploy service doesn't offer the option to deploy from a CodeCommit repo. But don't worry, as CodePipeline makes this possible. We'll cover CodePipeline later in the chapter.

Deploying to EC2 or On-Premises Instances

CodeDeploy can deploy applications, scripts, configuration files, and virtually any other file to an EC2 or on-premises instance. To deploy to an instance, you must install the CodeDeploy agent. The agent allows the CodeDeploy service to copy files to the instance and perform deployment tasks on it. The agent has been tested with current versions of the following:

- Amazon Linux
- Ubuntu Server
- Microsoft Windows Server
- Red Hat Enterprise Linux (RHEL)

CodeDeploy gives you many options for how to carry out an application deployment. You can deploy to instances according to specific resource tags, based on Auto Scaling Group membership, or by just manually selecting them. You can also control the cadence of deployment by deploying to instances one at a time, all at once, half at a time, or anywhere in between.

When it comes to upgrade deployments, CodeDeploy supports two different deployment types:

In-place deployment   An in-place deployment deploys the application to existing instances. If your application is running, CodeDeploy can stop it, perform any needed cleanup, deploy the new version, and then restart the application.

Blue/Green deployment   With a blue/green deployment, CodeDeploy deploys your application to a new set of instances that you either create manually or have CodeDeploy create by replicating an existing Auto Scaling group. CodeDeploy then deploys the application to the new instances. It can also optionally decommission the old instances. If you're using an elastic load balancer, CodeDeploy can also automatically redirect traffic to the new instances.

Deploying to ECS

The process for deploying to ECS is almost the same as for deploying to EC2 instances, except instead of deploying application files to an instance, you deploy Docker images that run your application in containers.

If you're doing a deployment upgrade of your application and using an application load balancer, CodeDeploy can shift the traffic from your old containers to your new ones. CodeDeploy works with both EC2 and Fargate ECS launch types.

Deploying to Lambda

Lambda is Amazon's serverless computing platform that runs functions that can be written in a variety of languages.

Because you don't have to even think about servers when using Lambda, deploying a new Lambda application with CodeDeploy simply involves creating a new Lambda function.

If you need to update an existing function, CodeDeploy just creates a new version of that function. You can then choose how CodeDeploy handles the switchover to the new version. You can have CodeDeploy shift traffic slowly from one version to the other, or you can do an immediate, full cutover to the new version.

CodePipeline

CodePipeline helps orchestrate and automate every task required to move software from development to production. It works by taking your source code and processing it through a series of stages, up to and including a deployment stage. In between the required source and deployment stages, you can add other stages also, such as a build stage that runs tests, or an approval stage that requires manual approval before deployment.

CodePipeline enables automation of certain tasks that the respective services don't offer on their own. For example, as noted earlier, CodeDeploy doesn't allow deploying directly from a CodeCommit repository, but it does allow deploying from an S3 bucket. CodePipeline can automatically take an application in the CodeCommit repository and trigger CodeBuild to perform automated testing against it. Once the tests pass, CodePipeline packages up the application files and places them it into an S3 bucket. You can then require manual approval before calling CodeDeploy to deploy the application to production. Deploying software this way is called *continuous delivery.*

Each stage consists of one or more actions, and these actions can occur sequentially or in parallel. There are six types of actions that you can include in a pipeline:

- Source
- Build
- Test
- Approval
- Deploy
- Invoke

With the exception of the Approval action, each action is performed by a provider that depending on the action can be an AWS or third-party service:

Source providers   Source providers include S3, CodeCommit, GitHub, and the Elastic Container registry (ECR) that stores Docker containers for Elastic Container Service.

Build and test providers   CodeBuild and third-party tools such as CloudBees, Jenkins, and TeamCity can provide building and testing services.

Deploy providers   CodePipeline supports a number of deploy providers. The most common ones you're likely to see include the following:

   CloudFormation   CodePipeline can automatically deploy your AWS infrastructure using CloudFormation. For example, developers can create their own template that builds a complete test environment. Whenever they update the template, CodePipeline can automatically deploy it to CloudFormation. This approach allows developers to create their own development infrastructure.

   CodeDeploy   CodeDeploy can only source application files from GitHub or S3. But you can configure CodePipeline to pull files from CodeCommit, package them up, and put them in an S3 bucket for CodeDeploy to pick up and deploy.

   ECS   CodePipeline can deploy Docker containers directly to ECS. By combining this with ECR for the source stage, you can use ECR as a source for images, rather than having to keep your images in an S3 bucket.

   S3   Suppose you have a website hosted in S3. You can keep the HTML and other files for your website in a CodeCommit repo for versioning. If you want to update your website, you make your changes in the repo. CodePipeline detects the change and copies the updates to your S3 bucket.

Other supported deploy providers include Elastic Beanstalk, OpsWorks Stacks, the AWS Service Catalog, and the Alexa Skills Kit.

Invoke   The Invoke action invokes Lambda functions, and it works only with AWS Lambda.

Approval   You can insert manual approvals anywhere in the pipeline after the source stage.

EC2 Auto Scaling

EC2 Auto Scaling automatically launches preconfigured EC2 instances. The goal of Auto Scaling is to ensure you have just enough computing resources to meet user demand without over-provisioning.

Launch Configurations and Launch Templates

Auto Scaling works by spawning instances from either a launch configuration or a launch template. For the purposes of Auto Scaling, both achieve the same basic purpose of defining the instance's characteristics, such as AMI, disk configuration, and instance type. You can also install software and make custom configurations by placing commands into a Userdata script that automatically runs when Auto Scaling launches a new instance.

But there are some differences between launch configurations and launch templates. Launch templates are newer and can be used to spawn EC2 instances manually, even without Auto Scaling. You can also modify them after you create them. Launch configurations, on the other hand, can be used only with Auto Scaling. And once you create a launch configuration, you can't modify it.

Auto Scaling Groups

Instances created by Auto Scaling are organized into an Auto Scaling group. All instances in a group can be automatically registered with an application load balancer target group. The application load balancer distributes traffic to the instances, spreading the demand out evenly among them.

Desired Capacity

When you configure an Auto Scaling group, you define a desired capacity—the number of instances that you want Auto Scaling to create. Auto Scaling creates this many instances and strives to maintain the desired capacity. If you raise or lower the capacity, Auto Scaling launches or terminates instances to match.

Self-Healing

Failed instances are self-healing. If an instance fails or terminates, Auto Scaling re-creates a replacement. This way you always get the number of instances you expect.

Auto Scaling can use EC2 or elastic load balancing (ELB) health checks to determine whether an instance is healthy. EC2 health checks consider the basic health of an instance, whether it's running, and whether it has network connectivity. ELB health checks look at the health of the application running on an instance. An unhealthy instance is treated as a failed instance and is terminated, and Auto Scaling creates another in its place.

Scaling Actions

Scaling actions control when Auto Scaling launches or terminates instances. You control how many instances Auto Scaling launches or terminates by specifying a minimum and maximum group size. Auto Scaling will ensure the number of instances never goes outside of this range. Naturally, the desired capacity must rest within the minimum and maximum bounds.

Dynamic Scaling

With dynamic scaling, Auto Scaling launches new instances in response to increased demand using a process called *scaling out*. It can also scale in, terminating instances when demand ceases. You can scale in or out according to a metric, such as average CPU utilization of your instances, or based on the number of concurrent application users.

Scheduled Scaling

Instead of or in addition to dynamic scaling, Auto Scaling can scale in or out according to a schedule. This is particularly useful if your demand has predictable peaks and valleys.

Predictive scaling is a feature that looks at historic usage patterns and predicts future peaks. It then automatically creates a scheduled scaling action to match. It needs at least one day's worth of traffic data to create a scaling schedule.

EC2 Auto Scaling fulfills one of the core principles of sound cloud architecture design: don't guess your capacity needs. Auto Scaling can save money by reducing your capacity when you don't need it and improve performance by increasing it when you do.

Configuration Management

Configuration management is an approach to ensuring accurate and consistent configuration of your systems. While automation is concerned with carrying out tasks, configuration management is primarily concerned with enforcing and monitoring the internal configuration state of your instances to ensure they're what you expect. Such configuration states primarily include but aren't limited to operating system configurations and what software is installed.

As with automation in general, configuration management tools use either imperative or declarative approaches. AWS offers both approaches using two tools to help you achieve configuration management of your EC2 and on-premises instances: Systems Manager and OpsWorks.

Systems Manager

Systems Manager uses the imperative approach to get your instances and AWS environment into the state that you want.

Command Documents

Command documents are scripts that run once or periodically that get the system into the state you want.

Using Command documents, you can install software on an instance, install the latest security patches, or take inventory of all software on an instance. You can use the same Bash or PowerShell commands you'd use with a Linux or Windows instance. Systems Manager can run these periodically, or on a trigger, such as a new instance launch. Systems Manager requires an agent to be installed on the instances that you want it to manage.

Configuration Compliance

Configuration Compliance is a feature of Systems Manager that can show you whether instances are in compliance with your desired configuration state—whether it's having a certain version of an application installed or being up-to-date on the latest operating system security patches.

Automation Documents

In addition to providing configuration management for instances, Systems Manager lets you perform many administrative AWS operations you would otherwise perform using the AWS Management Console or the AWS CLI. These operations are defined using Automation documents. For example, you can use Systems Manager to automatically create a snapshot of an Elastic Block Store (EBS) volume, launch or terminate an instance, create a CloudFormation stack, or even create an AMI from an existing EBS volume.

Distributor

Using Systems Manager Distributor, you can deploy installable software packages to your instances. You create a .zip archive containing installable or executable software packages that your operating system recognizes, put the archive in an S3 bucket, and tell Distributor where to find it. Distributor takes care of deploying and installing the software. Distributor is especially useful for deploying a standard set of software packages that already come as installers or executables.

OpsWorks

OpsWorks is a set of three different services that let you take a declarative approach to configuration management. As explained earlier in this chapter, using a declarative approach requires some intelligence to translate declarative code into imperative operations. OpsWorks uses two popular configuration management platforms that fulfill this requirement: Chef (https://www.chef.io) and Puppet Enterprise (https://puppet.com).

Puppet and Chef are popular configuration management platforms that can configure operating systems, deploy applications, create databases, and perform just about any configuration task you can dream of, all using code. Both Puppet and Chef are widely used for on-premises deployments, but OpsWorks brings their power to AWS as the OpsWorks managed service.

Just as with automation in general, configuration management is not an all-or-nothing decision. Thankfully, OpsWorks comes in three different flavors to meet any configuration management appetite.

AWS OpsWorks for Puppet Enterprise and AWS OpsWorks for Chef Automate are robust and scalable options that let you run managed Puppet or Chef servers on AWS. This is good if you want to use configuration management across all your instances.

AWS OpsWorks Stacks provides a simple and flexible approach to using configuration management just for deploying applications. Instead of going all-in on configuration management, you can just use it for deploying and configuring applications. OpsWorks Stacks takes care of setting up the supporting infrastructure.

AWS OpsWorks for Puppet Enterprise and AWS OpsWorks for Chef Automate

The high-level architectures of AWS OpsWorks for Puppet Enterprise and Chef Automate are similar. They consist of at least one Puppet master server or Chef server to communicate with your managed nodes—EC2 or on-premises instances—using an installed agent.

You define the configuration state of your instances—such as operating system configurations applications—using Puppet modules or Chef recipes. These contain declarative code, written in the platform's domain-specific language, that specifies the resources to provision. The code is stored in a central location, such as a Git repository like CodeCommit or an S3 bucket.

OpsWorks manages the servers, but you're responsible for understanding and operating the Puppet or Chef software, so you'll need to know how they work and how to manage them. No worries, though, because both Chef and Puppet have large ecosystems brimming with off-the-shelf code that can be used for a variety of common scenarios.

AWS OpsWorks Stacks

If you like the IaC concept for your applications, but you aren't familiar with managing Puppet or Chef servers, you can use AWS OpsWorks Stacks.

OpsWorks Stacks lets you build your application infrastructure in stacks. A *stack* is a collection of all the resources your application needs: EC2 instances, databases, application load balancers, and so on. Each stack contains at least one layer, which is a container for some component of your application.

To understand how you might use OpsWorks Stacks, consider a typical database-backed application that consists of three layers:

- An application layer containing EC2 instances or containers
- A database layer consisting of self-hosted or relational database service (RDS) database instances
- An application load balancer that distributes traffic to the application layer

There are two basic types of layers that OpsWorks uses: OpsWorks layers and service layers.

> Despite the name, an OpsWorks stack is not the same as a CloudFormation stack and doesn't use CloudFormation templates.

OpsWorks layers   An OpsWorks layer is a template for a set of instances. It specifies instance-level settings such as security groups and whether to use public IP addresses. It also includes an auto-healing option that automatically re-creates your instances if they fail. OpsWorks can also perform load-based or time-based auto scaling, adding more EC2 instances as needed to meet demand.

An OpsWorks layer can provision Linux or Windows EC2 instances, or you can add existing Linux EC2 or on-premises instances to a stack. OpsWorks Stacks supports Amazon Linux, Ubuntu Server, CentOS, and Red Hat Enterprise Linux.

To configure your instances and deploy applications, OpsWorks uses the same declarative Chef recipes as the Chef Automate platform, but it doesn't provision a Chef server. Instead, OpsWorks Stacks performs configuration management tasks using the Chef Solo client that it installs on your instances automatically.

Service layers   A stack can also include service layers to extend the functionality of your stack to include other AWS services. Service layers include the following layers:

Relational Database Service (RDS)   Using an RDS service layer, you can integrate your application with an existing RDS instance.

Elastic Load Balancing (ELB)   If you have multiple instances in a stack, you can create an application load balancer to distribute traffic to them and provide high availability.

Elastic Container Service (ECS) Cluster   If you prefer to deploy your application to containers instead of EC2 instances, you can create an ECS cluster layer that connects your OpsWorks stack to an existing ECS cluster.

Summary

If there's one thing that should be clear, it's that AWS provides many different ways to automate the same task. The specific services and approaches you should use are architectural decisions beyond the scope of this book, but you should at least understand how each of the different AWS services covered in this chapter can enable automation.

Fundamentally, automation entails defining a task as code that a system carries out. This code can be written as imperative commands that specify the exact steps to perform the task. The most familiar type of example is the Bash or PowerShell script system administrators write to perform routine tasks. AWS Systems Manager, CodeBuild, and CodeDeploy use an imperative approach. Even the Userdata scripts that you use with EC2 Auto Scaling are imperative.

Code can also be written in a more abstract, declarative form, where you specify the end result of the task. The service providing the automation translates those declarative statements into step-by-step operations that it carries out. CloudFormation, OpsWorks for Puppet Enterprise, OpsWorks for Chef Automate, and OpsWorks Stacks use declarative languages to carry out automation.

At the end of the day, both the imperative and declarative approaches result in nothing more than a set of commands that must be carried out sequentially. It's important to understand that the imperative and declarative approaches are not opposites. Rather, the declarative approach abstracts away from you the step-by-step details in favor of a more results-oriented, user-friendly paradigm. The difference comes down to what approach you prefer and what the service requires.

Configuration management is a form of automation that emphasizes configuration consistency and compliance. Naturally, the focus on achieving and maintaining a certain state lends itself to a declarative approach, so many configuration management platforms such as Puppet and Chef use declarative language. However, AWS Systems Manager also provides configuration management, albeit by using an imperative approach.

Exam Essentials

Know what specific tasks AWS services can automate.   CloudFormation can automatically deploy, change, and even delete AWS resources in one fell swoop.

The AWS Developer Tools—CodeCommit, CodeBuild, CodeDeploy, and CodePipeline—can help automate some or all of the software development, testing, and deployment process.

EC2 Auto Scaling automatically provisions a set number of EC2 instances. You can optionally have it scale in or out according to demand or a schedule.

Systems Manager Command documents let you automate tasks against your instance operating systems, such as patching, installing software, enforcing configuration settings, and collecting inventory. Automation documents let you automate many administrative AWS tasks that would otherwise require using the management console or CLI.

OpsWorks for Puppet Enterprise and OpsWorks for Chef Automate also let you configure your instances and deploy software but do so using the declarative language of Puppet modules or Chef recipes.

OpsWorks Stacks can automate the build and deployment of an application and its supporting infrastructure.

Understand the benefits of automation and infrastructure as code.   Automation allows common, repetitive tasks to be executed faster than doing them manually and reduces the risk of human error. When you automate infrastructure builds using code, the code simultaneously serves as *de facto* documentation. Code can be placed into version control, making it easy to track changes and even roll back when necessary.

Be able to explain the concepts of continuous integration and continuous delivery.   The practice of continuous integration involves developers regularly checking in code as they create or change it. An automated process performs build and test actions against it. This immediate feedback loop allows developers to fix problems quickly and early.

Continuous delivery expands upon continuous integration but includes deploying the application to production after a manual approval. This effectively enables push-button deployment of an application to production.

Review Questions

1. Which of the following is an advantage of using CloudFormation?

    A. It uses the popular Python programming language.

    B. It prevents unauthorized manual changes to resources.

    C. It lets you create multiple separate AWS environments using a single template.

    D. It can create resources outside of AWS.

2. What formats do CloudFormation templates support? (Select TWO.)

    A. XML

    B. YAML

    C. HTML

    D. JSON

3. What's an advantage of using parameters in a CloudFormation template?

    A. Allow customizing a stack without changing the template.

    B. Prevent unauthorized users from using a template.

    C. Prevent stack updates.

    D. Allow multiple stacks to be created from the same template.

4. Why would you use CloudFormation to automatically create resources for a development environment instead of creating them using AWS CLI commands? (Select TWO.)

    A. Resources CloudFormation creates are organized into stacks and can be managed as a single unit.

    B. CloudFormation stack updates help ensure that changes to one resource won't break another.

    C. Resources created by CloudFormation always work as expected.

    D. CloudFormation can provision resources faster than the AWS CLI.

5. What are two features of CodeCommit? (Select TWO.)

    A. Versioning

    B. Automatic deployment

    C. Differencing

    D. Manual deployment

6. In the context of CodeCommit, what can differencing accomplish?

    A. Allowing reverting to an older version of a file

    B. Understanding what code change introduced a bug

    C. Deleting duplicate lines of code

    D. Seeing when an application was last deployed

7. What software development practice regularly tests new code for bugs but doesn't do anything else?
   A. Differencing
   B. Continuous deployment
   C. Continuous delivery
   D. Continuous integration

8. Which CodeBuild build environment compute types support Windows operating systems? (Select TWO.)
   A. build.general2.large
   B. build.general1.medium
   C. build.general1.small
   D. build.general1.large
   E. build.windows1.small

9. What does a CodeBuild environment always contain? (Select TWO.)
   A. An operating system
   B. A Docker image
   C. The Python programming language
   D. .NET Core
   E. The PHP programming language

10. Which of the following can CodeDeploy do? (Select THREE.)
    A. Deploy an application to an on-premises Windows instance.
    B. Deploy a Docker container to the Elastic Container Service.
    C. Upgrade an application on an EC2 instance running Red Hat Enterprise Linux.
    D. Deploy an application to an Android smartphone.
    E. Deploy a website to an S3 bucket.

11. What is the minimum number of actions in a CodePipeline pipeline?
    A. 1
    B. 2
    C. 3
    D. 4
    E. 0

12. You want to predefine the configuration of EC2 instances that you plan to launch manually and using Auto Scaling. What resource must you use?
    A. CloudFormation template
    B. Instance role
    C. Launch configuration
    D. Launch template

13. What Auto Scaling group parameters set the limit for the number of instances that Auto Scaling creates? (Select TWO.)

    A. Maximum

    B. Group size

    C. Desired capacity

    D. Minimum

14. An Auto Scaling group has a desired capacity of 7 and a maximum size of 7. What will Auto Scaling do if someone manually terminates one of these instances?

    A. It will not launch any new instances.

    B. It will launch one new instance.

    C. It will terminate one instance.

    D. It will change the desired capacity to 6.

15. What Auto Scaling feature creates a scaling schedule based on past usage patterns?

    A. Predictive scaling

    B. Scheduled scaling

    C. Dynamic scaling

    D. Pattern scaling

16. What type of AWS Systems Manager document can run Bash or PowerShell scripts on an EC2 instance?

    A. Run document

    B. Command document

    C. Automation document

    D. Script document

17. What type of AWS Systems Manager document can take a snapshot of an EC2 instance?

    A. Command document

    B. Run document

    C. Script document

    D. Automation document

18. Which of the following OpsWorks services uses Chef recipes?

    A. AWS OpsWorks for Puppet Enterprise

    B. AWS OpsWorks Stacks

    C. AWS OpsWorks Layers

    D. AWS OpsWorks for Automation

19. What configuration management platforms does OpsWorks support? (Select TWO.)

   A. SaltStack

   B. Puppet Enterprise

   C. CFEngine

   D. Chef

   E. Ansible

20. Which of the following OpsWorks Stacks layers contains at least one EC2 instance?

   A. EC2 Auto Scaling layer

   B. Elastic Container Service (ECS) cluster layer

   C. OpsWorks layer

   D. Relational Database Service (RDS) layer

   E. Elastic Load Balancing (ELB) layer

Chapter

12

Common Use-Case Scenarios

THE AWS CERTIFIED CLOUD PRACTITIONER EXAM OBJECTIVES COVERED IN THIS CHAPTER MAY INCLUDE, BUT ARE NOT LIMITED TO, THE FOLLOWING:

Domain 1: Cloud Concepts

✓ 1.3   List the different cloud architecture design principles

Domain 3: Technology

✓ 3.1   Define methods of deploying and operating in the AWS Cloud

Introduction

When running an application, you expect it to perform well and be reliable, secure, and cost-efficient. Not only does AWS make it possible to meet these expectations, it also provides a set of guiding principles to help you achieve them. The AWS Well-Architected Framework codifies these principles and organizes them into the following five pillars:

- Reliability
- Performance efficiency
- Security
- Cost optimization
- Operational excellence

In this chapter, you'll learn how these pillars form the foundation of any sound cloud architecture. You'll have the opportunity to perform several exercises that will teach you how to implement the following real-world scenarios:

- A highly available web application using Auto Scaling and elastic load balancing
- Static website hosting using S3

Following all of the exercises will cost a little money, but you can complete some of them within the bounds of the AWS Free Tier. For more information about the AWS Free Tier, refer to the beginning of Chapter 2, "Understanding Your AWS Account."

The Well-Architected Framework

The *Well-Architected Framework* is a set of principles that AWS recommends as a way of evaluating the pros and cons of designing and implementing applications in the cloud. The framework is divided into the following five pillars: reliability, performance efficiency, security, cost optimization, and operational excellence. You can think of these pillars as goals. In this section, we'll briefly describe each of these goals at a high level. Later in the chapter, you'll complete some exercises to experience firsthand how to achieve these goals when dealing with real-world scenarios.

Reliability

Reliability means avoiding the complete failure of your application. Depending on how it's architected, your application may depend on many different types of resources, including compute, storage, database, and networking.

Avoiding the complete failure of your application requires two things. First, you must strive to avoid the failure of the resources your application depends on. A resource can fail due to being misconfigured, overloaded, or shut down, either accidentally or intentionally. Second, when such a failure occurs—which it inevitably will—you must replace the failed resource with a healthy one. Later in the chapter, we'll look at some common examples of how to achieve reliability in the cloud.

 Replacing a failed resource rather than trying to fix it removes the need to come up with different procedures for dealing with failures. For example, if an instance is misconfigured, simply replacing it is quicker and easier than attempting to figure out what's misconfigured. Replacing a failed resource lets you recover from a wide variety of failure scenarios.

Performance Efficiency

Performance efficiency means getting the performance you desire without overprovisioning capacity, but also without sacrificing reliability. You want enough resources to provide redundancy when a resource fails, and you also want to add resources as demand increases. But you need assurance that at any given time, you have the right amount of resources for your given availability and performance requirements, and not a bit more.

Performance and reliability are inextricably related. If a resource is overloaded, it's likely that the application will perform poorly. That resource may eventually fail and bring your application down with it. Hence, monitoring the utilization and performance of your resources and adjusting based on those metrics is a critical aspect of both performance efficiency and reliability.

The performance of an application is determined not only by the power and quantity of your compute and storage resources but also by the performance of the network between your resources and your users. For instance, you may have a web application running in an AWS Region in the United States. Users in the United States get excellent performance, but users in Australia may experience poor performance due to the network latency between themselves and your application. You can improve their performance by creating a CloudFront distribution to place your application's content in edge locations that are closer to your them. By significantly improving performance at minimal cost, you're achieving performance efficiency.

Security

Security is concerned with ensuring the confidentiality, integrity, and availability of data. In short, only those people and systems that need access to data should have it, and that data needs to be protected from unauthorized modification. When it comes to securing the data stored on your AWS resources, you should know the following basic principles:

- Follow the principle of least privilege to create IAM user and resource policies that grant delete or modify access only to those principals that need it.

- Avoid data loss by using backups and replication. Use Elastic Block Store (EBS) snapshots at any time to create recovery points for EC2 instances. Configure S3 object versioning and replication to make it possible to recover modified or destroyed data.

- Enforce confidentiality by using encryption to protect data at rest (such as data stored on EBS volumes and in S3 buckets) as well as data in transit as it moves into and out of your AWS infrastructure.

- Track every activity that occurs on your AWS resources by enabling detailed logging. This can tell you how well your security procedures are working. It can also help you identify security incidents during or after the fact.

 These principles are basic guidelines and not an exhaustive checklist for securing your AWS resources. The AWS Trusted Advisor (which you learned about in Chapter 3, "Getting Support on AWS") can offer you specific recommendations for securing your AWS resources.

Cost Optimization

Cost optimization isn't about getting your costs as close to zero as possible. Rather, you achieve cost optimization when you use the cloud to meet your needs at the lowest possible cost. For instance, if reliability is important to you and you reduce costs in a way that makes your application less reliable, then you're not practicing cost optimization.

The first step to achieving cost optimization is to analyze where your money is going in the cloud. Use AWS Cost Explorer and the Cost and Usage reports to see how much you're spending on AWS services and how those expenditures change over time. Use cost allocation tags to break down resource costs by owner, department, or application. For more information on cost allocation tags, refer to Chapter 2, "Understanding Your AWS Account."

One of the most effective ways to achieve cost optimization is to pay only for the resources you need at any given time. For example, if there are temporary EC2 instances used for testing only a few days out of the month, you can save money by terminating those instances when they're not needed.

You can also save money by purchasing instance reservations or using spot instances to save over on-demand costs. See Chapter 7, "The Core Compute Services," for information on reservations and spot instances.

In addition to looking at the cost of a resource, you should also consider the cost of operating it. For example, the hourly cost of running a MySQL database on a relational database service (RDS) instance will be greater than the hourly cost of running the same database on an EC2 instance that you build and manage yourself. But when you factor in the additional labor and time involved in performing database backups, upgrades, and monitoring, you may find that using RDS to handle these tasks for you would be more cost effective.

Operational Excellence

Operational excellence is fundamentally about automating the processes required to achieve and maintain the other four goals of reliability, performance efficiency, cost optimization, and security. In reality, few organizations automate everything, so operational excellence is more of a journey than a goal. But the idea behind operational excellence is to incrementally improve and automate more activities for the purpose of strengthening the other pillars. Here are some simple examples of how automation can help achieve operational excellence:

Reliability   Use elastic load balancing health checks to monitor the health of an application running on several EC2 instances. When an instance fails, route users away from the failed instance and create a new one.

Performance efficiency   Use EC2 Auto Scaling dynamic scaling policies to scale in and out automatically, ensuring you always have as many instances as you need and no more.

Security   Use CodeBuild to automatically test new application code for security vulnerabilities. When deploying an application, use CloudFormation to automatically deploy fresh, secure infrastructure, rather than following a manual checklist.

Cost optimization   Automatically shut down or decommission unused resources. For example, implement S3 object life cycle configurations to delete unneeded objects. Or if you have EC2 instances that are used for testing only during business hours, you can automatically shut them down at the end of the workday and restart them the following morning.

Keep in mind that these examples are by no means exhaustive. Many opportunities for automation aren't obvious until there's a failure. For instance, if someone deletes an application load balancer that's operating as the front end of a critical web application, recovering from such an event would entail performing some quick manual work-arounds and re-creating the load balancer. Understanding how failures affect your application can help you avoid such failures in the future and automate recovery when they occur.

A Highly Available Web Application Using Auto Scaling and Elastic Load Balancing

The first scenario we'll consider is a highly available web application that you'll implement using the topology shown in Figure 12.1.

FIGURE 12.1 A highly available web application using Auto Scaling and elastic load balancing

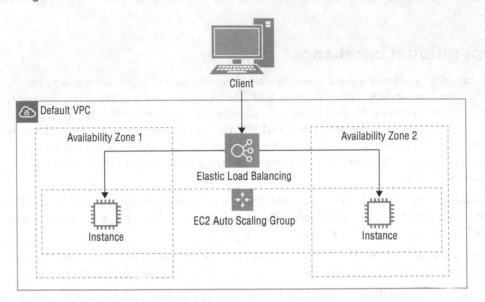

Don't worry if this looks intimidating. We'll start by taking a high-level look at how these components fit together, and then we'll dig into the configuration specifics. EC2 Auto Scaling will initially provision two EC2 instances running in different Availability Zones inside the default VPC. Every default VPC has a default subnet in each Availability Zone, so there's no need to create subnets explicitly. An application load balancer will proxy the connections from clients on the internet and distribute those connections to the instances that are running the popular open-source Apache web server.

We'll implement this scenario in four basic steps:

1. Create an inbound security group rule in the VPC's default security group.

2. Create an application load balancer.

3. Create a launch template.

4. Create an Auto Scaling group.

Creating an Inbound Security Group Rule

Every VPC comes with a default security group. Recall that security groups block traffic that's not explicitly allowed by a rule, so we'll start by adding an inbound rule to the VPC's default security group to allow only inbound HTTP access to the application load balancer and the instances. Complete Exercise 12.1 to create the inbound rule.

EXERCISE 12.1

Create an Inbound Security Group Rule

You'll start by modifying the default security group to allow inbound HTTP access. The application load balancer that you'll create later, as well as the instances that Auto Scaling will create, will use this security group to permit users to connect to the web application.

1. Browse to the EC2 service console. In the navigation pane, choose the Security Groups link.

2. Select the Create Security Group button.

3. Select the default security group for the default VPC.

4. Select the Inbound tab.

5. Select the Edit button.

6. Select the Add Rule button.

7. Under the Type drop-down list, select HTTP. The Management Console automatically populates the Protocol field with TCP and the Port Range field with 80, which together correspond to the HTTP protocol used for web traffic. It also populates the Source field with the IP subnet 0.0.0.0/0 and IPv6 subnet ::0/0, allowing traffic from all sources. You can optionally change the Source field to reflect the subnet of your choice or a specific IP address. For example, to allow only the IP address 198.51.100.100, you'd enter **198.51.100.100/32**. Refer to Figure 12.2 to see what your new inbound rule should look like.

8. Select the Save button.

FIGURE 12.2 Modifying the default security group

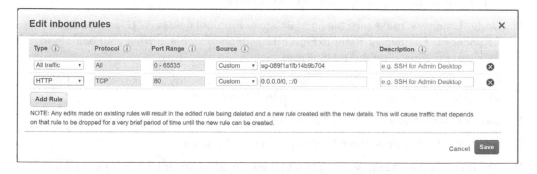

Creating an Application Load Balancer

Next, you need to create an application load balancer that will distribute connections to the instances in the Auto Scaling group that you'll create in a later exercise. The load balancer will route traffic to healthy instances using a round-robin algorithm that distributes traffic evenly to the instances without regard for how busy those instances are.

You'll configure the load balancer to perform a health check to monitor the health of the application on each instance. If the application fails on an instance, the load balancer will route connections away from the failed instance. The Auto Scaling group will also use this health check to determine whether an instance is healthy or needs to be replaced. Follow the steps in Exercise 12.2 to create the application load balancer.

EXERCISE 12.2

Create an Application Load Balancer

Now you'll create an application load balancer to receive incoming connections from users. The application load balancer will distribute those connections to the instances in the Auto Scaling group that you'll create later.

1. While in the EC2 service console, in the navigation pane on the left, choose the Load Balancers link.

2. Select the Create Load Balancer button.

3. Under Application Load Balancer, select the Create button.

4. In the Name field, type **sample-web-app-load-balancer**.

5. For the Scheme, select the radio button next to Internet-facing. This will assign the load balancer a publicly resolvable domain name and allow the load balancer to receive connections from the internet.

6. In the IP Address Type drop-down list, select IPv4.

7. Under Listeners, make sure the Load Balancer Protocol field is HTTP and the Load Balancer Port field is 80. Refer to Figure 12.3 for an example of what your basic load balancer configuration should look like.

8. On the Configure Load Balancer page, under the Availability Zones section, in the VPC drop-down, make sure your default VPC is selected.

9. Select at least two Availability Zones. Refer to Figure 12.4 for an example.

10. Select the button titled Next: Configure Security Settings.

11. You may see a message warning you that your load balancer isn't using a secure listener. Select the button titled Next: Configure Security Groups.

12. Select the default security group for the VPC.

FIGURE 12.3   Application load balancer basic configuration

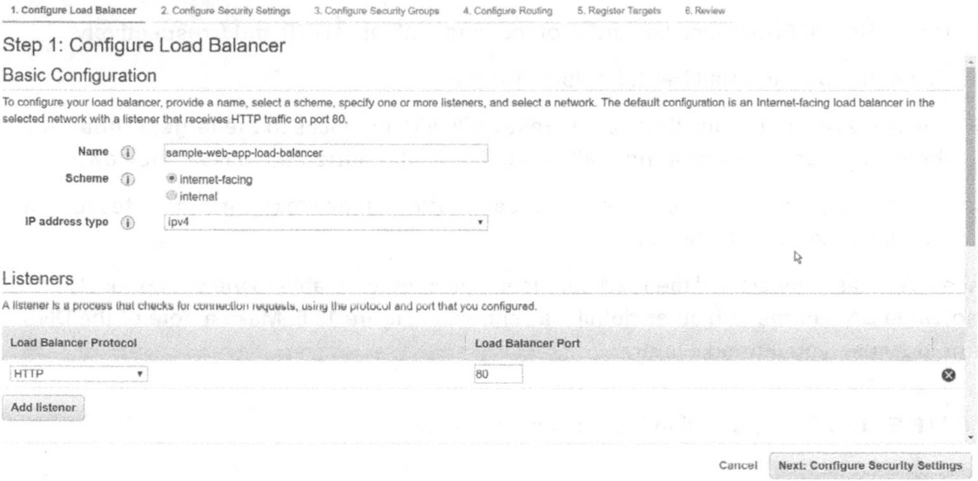

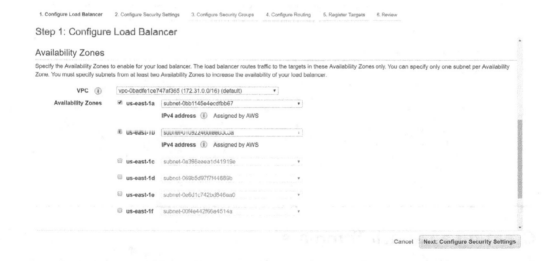

FIGURE 12.4   Application load balancer Availability Zones configuration

13. Select the button titled Next: Configure Routing.

14. Under Target Group, in the Target Group drop-down list, select New Target Group.

15. In the Name field, type **sample-web-app-target-group**.

16. Next to Target Type, select the Instance radio button.

17. For Protocol and Port, select HTTP and 80, respectively.

18. Under Health Checks, make sure Protocol and Path are HTTP and /, respectively.

19. Select the button titled Next: Register Targets.

20. The Auto Scaling group that you'll create will add instances to the target group, so there's no need to do that manually here. Select the button titled Next: Review.

21. Review your settings, and select the Create button. It may take a few minutes for your load balancer to become active.

Once AWS has provisioned the load balancer, you should be able to view its publicly resolvable DNS name and other details, as shown in Figure 12.5. Make a note of the DNS name because you'll need it later.

FIGURE 12.5 Application load balancer details

Creating a Launch Template

Before creating the Auto Scaling group, you need to create a launch template that Auto Scaling will use to launch the instances and install and configure the Apache web server software on them when they're launched. Because creating the launch template by hand would be cumbersome, you'll instead let CloudFormation create it by deploying the CloudFormation template at https://s3.amazonaws.com/aws-ccp/launch-template.yaml. The launch template that CloudFormation will create will install Apache on each instance that Auto Scaling provisions. You can also create a custom launch template for your own application. Complete Exercise 12.3 to get some practice with CloudFormation and create the launch template.

EXERCISE 12.3

Create a Launch Template

In this exercise, you'll use CloudFormation to deploy an EC2 launch template that Auto Scaling will use to launch new instances.

1. Browse to the CloudFormation service console. Make sure you're in the AWS Region where you want your instances created.

2. Select the Create Stack button.

3. Under Choose A Template, select the radio button titled Specify An Amazon S3 Template URL.

4. In the text field, enter **https://s3.amazonaws.com/aws-ccp/launch-template.yaml**.

5. Select the Next button.

6. In the Stack Name field, enter **sample-app-launch-template**.

7. From the drop-down list, select the instance type you want to use, or stick with the default t2.micro instance type.

8. Select the Next button.

9. On the Options screen, stick with the defaults and select the Next button.

10. Review your settings, and select the Create button.

CloudFormation will take you to the Stacks view screen. Once the stack is created, the status of the sample-app-launch-template stack will show as CREATE_COMPLETE, indicating that the EC2 launch template has been created successfully.

Creating an Auto Scaling Group

EC2 Auto Scaling is responsible for provisioning and maintaining a certain number of healthy instances. By default, Auto Scaling provides reliability by automatically replacing instances that fail their EC2 health check. You'll reconfigure Auto Scaling to monitor the ELB health check and replace any instances on which the application has failed.

To achieve performance efficiency and make this configuration cost-effective, you'll create a dynamic scaling policy that will scale the size of the Auto Scaling group in or out between one and three instances, depending on the average aggregate CPU utilization of the instances. If the CPU utilization is greater than 50 percent, it indicates a heavier load, and Auto Scaling will scale out by adding another instance. On the other hand, if the utilization drops below 50 percent, it indicates that you have more instances than you need, so Auto Scaling will scale in. This is called a *target tracking policy*.

EC2 reports these metrics to CloudWatch, where you can graph them to analyze your usage patterns over time. CloudWatch stores metrics for up to 15 months.

This may sound like a lot to do, but the wizard makes it easy. Complete Exercise 12.4 to create and configure the Auto Scaling group.

EXERCISE 12.4

Create an Auto Scaling Group

In this exercise, you'll create an Auto Scaling group that will provision your web server instances using the launch template.

1. Browse to the EC2 service console.

2. In the navigation pane, choose the Launch Templates link.

3. Select the launch template.

4. Select the Action button, and choose Create Auto Scaling Group.

5. In the Group Name field, enter **sample-web-app**.

6. In the Group Size field, enter **2**.

7. In the Network drop-down list, select the default VPC.

8. In the Subnet drop-down list, select at least two subnets. Refer to Figure 12.6 to get an idea of what the basic configuration should look like.

FIGURE 12.6   Auto Scaling group basic configuration

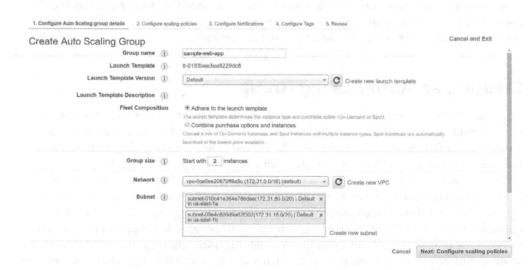

9. Expand the Advanced Details section.

10. Select the check box next to Receive Traffic From One Or More Load Balancers.

11. In the Target Groups field, select sample-web-app-target-group.

12. Next to Health Check Type, select the ELB radio button.

13. Select the button titled Next: Configure Scaling Policies.

14. Under Create Auto Scaling Group, select the Use Scaling Policies To Adjust The Capacity Of This Group radio button. This will create a dynamic scaling policy that will automatically scale in or out based on the average aggregate CPU utilization of the instances in the Auto Scaling group.

15. Adjust the minimum and maximum group size to scale between one and three instances. This will ensure that the group always has at least one instance but never more than three instances.

16. Under Scale Group Size, select the Metric Type Average CPU Utilization.

17. For the Target Value, enter **50**. This will cause Auto Scaling to attempt to keep the average CPU utilization of each instance at 50 percent. If the average CPU utilization falls below 50 percent, Auto Scaling will scale in, leaving only one instance in the group. If the average CPU utilization rises above 50 percent, Auto Scaling will add more instances to the group for a total of up to three.

18. Select the button titled Next: Configure Notifications.

19. Select the button titled Next: Configure Tags.

20. Select the Review button.

21. Review the settings, and select the Create Auto Scaling Group button.

22. Select the View Your Auto Scaling Groups link, and wait a few minutes for Auto Scaling to provision the instances.

23. Open a web browser, and browse to the DNS name of the application load balancer that you noted in Exercise 12.2. You should see the Apache Linux AMI test page, as shown in Figure 12.7.

FIGURE 12.7 The Apache Linux AMI test page

Amazon Linux AMI **Test Page**

This page is used to test the proper operation of the Apache HTTP server after it has been installed. If you can read this page, it means that the Apache HTTP server installed at this site is working properly.

If you are a member of the general public:

The fact that you are seeing this page indicates that the website you just visited is either experiencing problems, or is undergoing routine maintenance.

If you would like to let the administrators of this website know that you've seen this page instead of the page you expected, you should send them e-mail. In general, mail sent to the name "webmaster" and directed to the website's domain should reach the appropriate person.

For example, if you experienced problems while visiting www.example.com, you should send e-mail to "webmaster@example.com".

For information on Amazon Linux AMI , please visit the Amazon AWS website.

If you are the website administrator:

You may now add content to the directory /var/www/html/. Note that until you do so, people visiting your website will see this page, and not your content. To prevent this page from ever being used, follow the instructions in the file /etc/httpd/conf.d/welcome.conf.

You are free to use the image below on web sites powered by the Apache HTTP Server:

WARNING   When you're done experimenting, remember to delete the resources you created, including the Auto Scaling group, the instances it created, and the application load balancer.

Static Website Hosting Using S3

The next scenario you'll consider is a static website hosted on S3. Despite the term, a static website doesn't mean one that never changes. *Static* refers to the fact that the site's assets—HTML files, graphics, and other downloadable content such as PDF files—are just static files sitting in an S3 bucket. You can update these files at any time and as often as you want, but what's delivered to the end user is the same content that's stored in S3. This is in contrast to a dynamic website that uses server-side processing to modify the content on the fly just before sending it to the user. Some examples of dynamic websites are web-based email applications, database-backed ecommerce sites (like Amazon), and WordPress blogs. As a rule of thumb, if a website uses a database for storing any information, it's a dynamic website.

Setting up S3 to host a static website involves the following steps:

- Creating an S3 bucket
- Configuring it for static website hosting
- Uploading the web assets that contain the content you want to serve

By default, files in S3 buckets are not public and are accessible only by the account owner and any users the account owner has authorized. This has always been the case, but after several high-profile incidents of users unwittingly making files in their S3 buckets publicly available, AWS has taken steps to reduce this risk. This poses a challenge when you want everyone on the internet to be able to access your static website. Therefore, many of the steps you'll complete in Exercise 12.5 are there to overcome some of these important safeguards and ensure that your static website is in fact available to everyone.

EXERCISE 12.5

Create a Static Website Hosted Using S3

In this exercise, you're going to create a simple static website hosted by S3.

1. Browse to the S3 service console.

2. Choose the Create Bucket button.

3. Give the bucket a name of your choice. Try for something that's easy to type but unique (for this example, we used **benpiper2020**). Then choose the Next button.

4. Leave object versioning and encryption disabled by default. Enabling either won't impact your ability to use the bucket for hosting a static website. Choose the Next button.

---

5. Under Manage Public Access Control Lists (ACLs) For This Bucket, uncheck the check box labeled Block New Public ACLs And Uploading Public Objects (Recommended). This will allow you to grant public read access to files in this bucket.

6. Uncheck Remove Public Access Granted Through Public ACLs (Recommended). If you leave this box checked, S3 automatically removes any ACLs that grant public access to an object in this bucket. Even if you add back the ACL to allow public read access to an object, S3 will continue to remove it unless you uncheck this box. Choose the Next button.

7. Review your settings, and choose the Create Bucket button.

8. You should see your new bucket in the list of all your S3 buckets. Choose the bucket.

9. Choose the Properties tab.

10. Choose Static Website Hosting.

11. Choose the radio button titled Use This Bucket To Host A Website. S3 will display an endpoint URL (http://benpiper2020.s3-website-us-east-1.amazonaws.com in our example). Make a note of this, as it's the URL you'll browse to access the static website.

12. S3 will prompt you for an index document filename and an error document filename. Under Index Document, enter **index.html**.

13. Choose the Save button.

14. In your favorite text editor, create a new file and populate it with any content you like. For example, you can put "**Hello, world!**". Save the file as index.html.

15. In the S3 service console, choose the Overview tab.

16. Choose the Upload button.

17. Choose the Add Files button. On your local file system, locate and choose the index.html file you created earlier in this exercise. Then choose the Next button.

18. Under the Manage Public Permissions drop-down menu, choose Grant Public Read Access To This Object(s). You will see a warning that everyone will have read access to the object. This is necessary so that AWS will not require the person viewing the site to authenticate to AWS. (Incidentally, don't ever use this setting for files that you don't want to be made public!) This won't allow anyone else to modify the file.

19. On this screen and the screen that follows, choose the Next button.

20. Choose the Upload button, and wait for the file to upload.

21. Open your favorite web browser, and browse to the endpoint URL of the bucket you noted earlier. You should see the contents of the index.html file you created earlier.

Feel free to add more content if you'd like. Remember that you must grant public read access to each object that you want to make viewable using S3 static website hosting.

You're not stuck with the cumbersome URL that S3 gives you. If you have a custom domain name, you can forward it to your static website. The only caveat is that your bucket name must be the same as the domain name. For example, if the domain name is example.com, the bucket name must be example.com.

When you're browsing to a static website hosted on S3, your browser may display a message that the site is not secure. That's because static websites hosted on S3 do not use encrypted HTTPS, meaning the content you serve is not encrypted and can be read in transit. If you want to use HTTPS to secure your static website, you can do so by creating a CloudFront distribution. In addition to providing encryption in-transit, this can also improve the performance of your website by placing content in edge locations closer to your users.

Summary

You can use AWS to design, build, or run almost any application that you would in a traditional datacenter. But just treating AWS as a traditional data center would be a mistake. AWS allows you to implement a given scenario in a variety of ways, and each way comes with its own advantages and disadvantages.

Recall the shared responsibility model you learned about in Chapter 4, "Understanding the AWS Environment." Both you and AWS are responsible for different aspects of your application running on AWS. By adhering to the principles laid out in the five pillars of the Well-Architected Framework, you can clearly see where your responsibility begins and ends for each AWS resource that you plan to use.

Use the pillars to evaluate the trade-offs for different design decisions. For example, suppose you want to host a static website. On the one hand, you could host the site using S3, leaving AWS with the responsibility for ensuring its reliability, security, and performance. If the site receives a huge influx of visitors, it's the job of AWS to ensure that the S3 service scales to meet that demand.

On the other hand, you could host the same website using EC2 instances running the Apache web server. In that case, you'd be responsible for the reliability, security, and performance of the site. Given the same massive influx of visitors, it'd be up to you to ensure you have enough instances to handle the load.

Exam Essentials

Know the five pillars of the AWS Well-Architected Framework.   The five pillars are reliability, performance efficiency, security, cost optimization, and operational excellence. AWS describes these pillars at length in the AWS Well-Architected Framework white paper that you can find at https://d1.awsstatic.com/whitepapers/architecture/AWS_Well-Architected_Framework.pdf. You don't need to read the entire white paper for the exam, but you must know the five pillars.

Understand how AWS resources work together and separately to form the five pillars of the Well-Architected Framework.   Architecting AWS infrastructure from the ground up is beyond the scope of this book and the exam. But you should be able to look at an AWS Solution Architect's diagram and explain some of the ways the resources achieve reliability, cost optimization, performance efficiency, security, or operational excellence.

Be able to evaluate trade-offs between different design decisions.   If given two different implementation options for a given scenario, be able to identify some of the advantages and disadvantages of each. For example, you should know some of the trade-offs between using spot pricing for an EC2 instance versus on-demand pricing.

Review Questions

1. Which of the following is *not* one of the pillars of the Well-Architected Framework?

    A. Performance efficiency

    B. Reliability

    C. Resiliency

    D. Security

    E. Cost optimization

2. Which of the following are examples of applying the principles of the security pillar of the Well-Architected Framework? (Select TWO.)

    A. Granting each AWS user their own IAM username and password

    B. Creating a security group rule to deny access to unused ports

    C. Deleting an empty S3 bucket

    D. Enabling S3 versioning

3. You're hosting a web application on two EC2 instances in an Auto Scaling group. The performance of the application is consistently acceptable. Which of the following can help maintain or improve performance efficiency? (Select TWO.)

    A. Monitoring for unauthorized access

    B. Doubling the number of instances in the Auto Scaling group

    C. Implementing policies to prevent the accidental termination of EC2 instances in the same Auto Scaling group

    D. Using CloudFront

4. Which of the following can help achieve cost optimization? (Select TWO.)

    A. Deleting unused S3 objects

    B. Deleting empty S3 buckets

    C. Deleting unused application load balancers

    D. Deleting unused VPCs

5. Which of the following is a key component of operational excellence?

    A. Adding more security personnel

    B. Automating manual processes

    C. Making minor improvements to bad processes

    D. Making people work longer hours

6. Your default VPC in the us-west-1 Region has three default subnets. How many Availability Zones are in this Region?

   A. 2

   B. 3

   C. 4

   D. 5

7. Your organization is building a database-backed web application that will sit behind an application load balancer. You add an inbound security group rule to allow HTTP traffic on TCP port 80. Where should you apply this security group to allow users to access the application?

   A. The application load balancer listener

   B. The database instance

   C. The subnets where the instances reside

   D. None of these

8. How does an application load balancer enable reliability?

   A. By routing traffic away from failed instances

   B. By replacing failed instances

   C. By routing traffic to the least busy instances

   D. By caching frequently accessed content

9. Which of the following contains the configuration information for instances in an Auto Scaling group?

   A. Launch directive

   B. Dynamic scaling policy

   C. CloudFormation template

   D. Launch template

10. You've created a target tracking policy for an Auto Scaling group. You want to ensure that the number of instances in the group never exceeds 5. How can you accomplish this?

    A. Set the group size to 5.

    B. Set the maximum group size to 5.

    C. Set the minimum group size to 5.

    D. Delete the target tracking policy.

11. Which of the following is an example of a static website?

    A. A WordPress blog

    B. A website hosted on S3

    C. A popular social media website

    D. A web-based email application

12. Which of the following features of S3 improve the security of data you store in an S3 bucket? (Select TWO.)

   A. Objects in S3 are not public by default.

   B. All objects are readable by all AWS users by default.

   C. By default, S3 removes ACLs that allow public read access to objects.

   D. S3 removes public objects by default.

13. Which of the following is required to enable S3 static website hosting on a bucket?

   A. Enable bucket hosting in the S3 service console.

   B. Disable default encryption.

   C. Disable object versioning.

   D. Enable object versioning.

   E. Make all objects in the bucket public.

14. You've created a static website hosted on S3 and given potential customers the URL that consists of words and numbers. They're complaining that it's too hard to type in. How can you come up with a friendlier URL?

   A. Re-create the bucket using only words in the name.

   B. Use a custom domain name.

   C. Re-create the bucket in a different Region.

   D. Re-create the bucket using only numbers in the name.

15. Which of the following is true regarding static websites hosted in S3?

   A. The content served is not encrypted in transit.

   B. Anyone can modify the content.

   C. You must use a custom domain name.

   D. A website hosted on S3 is stored in multiple Regions.

16. Which of the following can impact the reliability of a web application running on EC2 instances?

   A. Taking EBS snapshots of the instances.

   B. The user interface is too difficult to use.

   C. Not replacing a misconfigured resource that the application depends on.

   D. Provisioning too many instances.

17. You have a public web application running on EC2 instances. Which of the following factors affecting the performance of your application might be out of your control?

   A. Storage

   B. Compute

   C. Network

   D. Database

18. An Auto Scaling group can use an EC2 system health check to determine whether an instance is healthy. What other type of health check can it use?

    A. S3

    B. SNS

    C. VPC

    D. ELB

19. You're hosting a static website on S3. Your web assets are stored under the Standard storage class. Which of the following is true regarding your site?

    A. Someone may modify the content of your site without authorization.

    B. You're responsible for S3 charges.

    C. You're charged for any compute power used to host the site.

    D. An Availability Zone outage may bring down the site.

20. You're hosting a static website on S3. Your web assets are stored in the US East 1 Region in the bucket named `mygreatwebsite`. What is the URL of the website?

    A. `http://mygreatwebsite.s3-website-us-east-1.amazonaws.com`

    B. `http://mygreatwebsite.s3.amazonaws.com`

    C. `http://mygreatwebsite.s3-website-us-east.amazonaws.com`

    D. `http://mygreatwebsite.s3-us-east-1.amazonaws.com`

Appendix A

Answers to Review Questions

Chapter 1: The Cloud

1. C. Having globally distributed infrastructure and experienced security engineers makes a provider's infrastructure more reliable. Metered pricing makes a wider range of workloads possible.

2. A, D. Security and virtualization are both important characteristics of successful cloud workloads, but neither will directly impact availability.

3. B, D. Security and scalability are important cloud elements but are not related to metered pricing.

4. A, B. Security and elasticity are important but are not directly related to server virtualization.

5. D. A hypervisor is software (not hardware) that administrates virtualized operations.

6. B. Sharding, aggregating remote resources, and abstracting complex infrastructure can all be accomplished using virtualization techniques, but they aren't, of themselves, virtualization.

7. C. PaaS products mask complexity, SaaS products provide end-user services, and serverless architectures (like AWS Lambda) let developers run code on cloud servers.

8. A. IaaS products provide full infrastructure access, SaaS products provide end-user services, and serverless architectures (like AWS Lambda) let developers run code on cloud servers.

9. B. IaaS products provide full infrastructure access, PaaS products mask complexity, and serverless architectures (like AWS Lambda) let developers run code on cloud servers.

10. A. Increasing or decreasing compute resources better describes elasticity. Efficient use of virtualized resources and billing models aren't related directly to scalability.

11. C. Preconfiguring compute instances before they're used to scale up an application is an element of scalability rather than elasticity. Efficient use of virtualized resources and billing models aren't related directly to elasticity.

12. A, D. Capitalized assets and geographic reach are important but don't have a direct impact on operational scalability.

Chapter 2: Understanding Your AWS Account

1. D. Only the t2.micro instance type is Free Tier–eligible, and any combination of t2.micro instances can be run up to a total of 750 hours per month.

2. B, C. S3 buckets—while available in such volumes under the Free Tier—are not necessary for an EC2 instance. Since the maximum total EBS space allowed by the Free Tier is 30 GB, two 20 GB would not be covered.

3. B, D. The API calls/month and ECR free storage are available only under the Free Tier.

4. A, B. There is no Top Free Tier Services Dashboard or, for that matter, a Billing Preferences Dashboard.

5. C. Wikipedia pages aren't updated or detailed enough to be helpful in this respect. The AWS CLI isn't likely to have much (if any) pricing information. The TCO Calculator shouldn't be used for specific and up-to-date information about service pricing.

6. A. Pricing will normally change based on the volume of service units you consume and, often, between AWS Regions.

7. B. You can, in fact, calculate costs for a multiservice stack. The calculator pricing is kept up-to-date. You can specify very detailed configuration parameters.

8. C, D. Calculate By Month Or Year is not an option, and since the calculator calculates only cost by usage, Include Multiple Organizations wouldn't be a useful option.

9. A. The calculator covers all significant costs associated with an on-premises deployment but doesn't include local or national tax implications.

10. D. The currency you choose to use will have little impact on price—it's all relative, of course. The guest OS and region will make a difference, but it's relatively minor.

11. B. The correct URL is `https://docs.aws.amazon.com/general/latest/gr/ aws_service_limits.html`.

12. A. Resource limits exist only within individual regions; the limits in one region don't impact another. There's no logistical reason that customers can't scale up deployments at any rate. There are, in fact, no logical limits to the ability of AWS resources to scale upward.

13. D. While most service limits are soft and can be raised on request, there are some service limits that are absolute.

14. D. The Cost Explorer and Cost and Usage Reports pages provide more in-depth and/or customized details. Budgets allow you to set alerts based on usage.

15. C. Reservation budgets track the status of any active reserved instances on your account. Cost budgets monitor costs being incurred against your account. There is no budget type that correlates usage per unit cost to understand your account cost efficiency.

16. D. You can configure the period, instance type, and start/stop dates for a budget, but you can't filter by resource owner.

17. A. Billing events aren't triggers for alerts. Nothing in this chapter discusses intrusion events.

18. C. Tags are passive, so they can't automatically trigger anything. Resource tags—not cost allocation tags—are meant to help you understand and control deployments. Tags aren't associated with particular billing periods.

19. A, C. Companies with multiple users of resources in a single AWS account would not benefit from AWS Organizations, nor would a company with completely separated units. The value of AWS Organizations is in integrating the administration of related accounts.

20. B. Budgets are used to set alerts. Reports provide CSV-formatted data for offline processing. Consolidated Billing (now migrated to AWS Organizations) is for administrating resources across multiple AWS accounts.

Chapter 3: Getting Support on AWS

1. C. The Basic plan won't provide any personalized support. The Developer plan is cheaper, but there is limited access to support professionals. The Business plan does offer 24/7 email, chat, and phone access to an engineer, so until you actually deploy, this will make the most sense. At a $15,000 monthly minimum, the Enterprise plan won't be cost effective.

2. B. Using the public documentation available through the Basic plan won't be enough to address your specific needs. The Business and Enterprise plans are not necessary as you don't yet have production deployments.

3. D. The lower three support tiers provide limited access to only lower-level support professionals, while the Enterprise plan provides full access to senior engineers and dedicates a technical account manager (TAM) as your resource for all your AWS needs.

4. C. Basic plan customers are given customer support access only for account management issues and not for technical support or security breaches.

5. B. The TAM is available only for Enterprise Support customers. The primary function is one of guidance and advocacy.

6. B. Only the Business and Enterprise plans include help with troubleshooting interoperability between AWS resources and third-party software and operating systems. The Business plan is the least expensive that will get you this level of support.

7. A. The Developer plan costs the greater of $29 or 3 percent of the monthly usage. In this case, 3 percent of the month's usage is $120.

8. D. The Business plan—when monthly consumption falls between $10,000 and $80,000— costs the greater of $100 or 7 percent of the monthly usage. In this case, 7 percent of a single month's usage ($11,000) is $770. The three month total would, therefore, be $2,310.

9. C. The AWS Professional Services site includes tech talk webinars, white papers, and blog posts. The Basic Support plan includes AWS documentation resources. The Knowledge Center consists of FAQ documentation.

10. A. The TAM is an AWS employee dedicated to guiding your developer and admin teams. There is no such thing as a network appliance for workload testing.

11. B, C. Although DOC and DocBook are both popular and useful formats, neither is used by AWS for its documentation.

12. A, C. The compare-plans page provides general information about support plans, and the professional-services site describes accessing that particular resource. Neither directly includes technical guides.

13. D. The Knowledge Center is a FAQ for technical problems and their solutions. The main documentation site is much better suited to introduction-level guides. The https:// forums.aws.amazon.com site is the discussion forum for AWS users.

14. B. The Knowledge Center is a general FAQ for technical problems and their solutions. The docs.aws.amazon.com site is for general documentation. There is no https://aws .amazon.com/security/encryption page.

15. A. Version numbers are not publicly available, and the word *Current* isn't used in this context.

16. C. Replication is, effectively, a subset of Fault Tolerance and therefore would not require its own category.

17. A. Performance identifies configuration settings that might be blocking performance improvements. Security identifies any failures to use security best-practice configurations. Cost Optimization identifies any resources that are running and unnecessarily costing you money.

18. B. Performance identifies configuration settings that might be blocking performance improvements. Service Limits identifies resource usage that's approaching AWS Region or service limits. There is no Replication category.

19. A. An OK status for a failed state is a false negative. There is no single status icon indicating that your account is completely compliant in Trusted Advisor.

20. B, D. Both the MFA and Service Limits checks are available for all accounts.

Chapter 4: Understanding the AWS Environment

1. B. The letter (a, b...) at the end of a designation indicates an Availability Zone. us-east-1 would never be used for a Region in the western part of the United States.

2. D. The AWS GovCloud Region is restricted to authorized customers only. Asia Pacific (Tokyo) is a normal Region. AWS Admin and US-DOD don't exist (as far as we know, at any rate).

3. D. EC2 instances will automatically launch into the Region you currently have selected. You can manually select the subnet that's associated with a particular Availability Zone for your new EC2 instance, but there's no default choice.

4. B, D. Relational Database Service (RDS) and EC2 both use resources that can exist in only one Region. Route 53 and CloudFront are truly global services in that they're not located in or restricted to any single AWS Region.

5. C. The correct syntax for an endpoint is `<service-designation>.<region-designation>`.amazonaws.com—meaning, in this case, `rds.us-east-1.amazonaws.com`.

6. B, C. For most uses, distributing your application infrastructure between multiple AZs within a single Region gives them sufficient fault tolerance. While AWS services do enjoy a significant economy of scale—bring prices down—little of that is due to the structure of their Regions. Lower latency and compliance are the biggest benefits from this list.

7. A. Sharing a single resource among Regions wouldn't cause any particular security, networking, or latency problems. It's a simple matter of finding a single physical host device to run on.

8. B. Auto Scaling is an important working element of application high availability, but it's not what most directly drives it (that's load balancing). The most effective and efficient way to get the job done is through parallel, load-balanced instances in multiple Availability Zones, not Regions.

9. A. "Data centers running uniform host types" would describe an edge location. The data centers within a "broad geographic area" would more closely describe an AWS Region. AZs aren't restricted to a single data center.

10. C. Imposing virtual networking limits on an instance would be the job of a security group or access control list. IP address blocks are not assigned at the Region level. Customers have no access to or control over AWS networking hardware.

11. B. AWS displays AZs in (apparently) random order to prevent too many resources from being launched in too few zones.

12. D. Auto Scaling doesn't focus on any one resource (physical or virtual) because it's interested only in the appropriate availability and quality of the overall *service*. The job of orchestration is for load balancers, not autoscalers.

13. C. Resource isolation can play an important role in security, but not reliability. Automation can improve administration processes, but neither it, nor geolocation, is the most effective reliability strategy.

14. A, C. RDS database instances and Lambda functions are not qualified CloudFront origins. EC2 load balancers can be used as CloudFront origins.

15. D. CloudFront can't protect against spam and, while it can complement your application's existing redundancy and encryption, those aren't its primary purpose.

16. B. Countering the threat of DDoS attacks is the job of AWS Shield. Protecting web applications from web-based threats is done by AWS Web Application Firewall. Using Lambda to customize CloudFront behavior is for Lambda Edge.

17. A, B. What's *in* the cloud is your responsibility—it includes the administration of EC2-based operating systems.

18. C. There's no one easy answer, as some managed services are pretty much entirely within Amazon's sphere, and others leave lots of responsibility with the customer. Remember, "if you can edit it, you own it."

19. D. The AWS Billing Dashboard is focused on your account billing issues. Neither the AWS Acceptable Use Monitor nor the Service Status Dashboard actually exists. But nice try.

20. B. The correct document (and web page `https://aws.amazon.com/aup/`) for this information is the AWS Acceptable Use Policy.

Chapter 5: Securing Your AWS Resources

1. A. Identity and Access Management (IAM) is primarily focused on helping you control access to your AWS resources. KMS handles access keys. EC2 manages SSH key pairs. While IAM does touch on federated management, that's not its primary purpose.

2. A, B, D. Including a space or null character is not a password policy option.

3. C, D. The root user should *not* be used for day-to-day admin tasks—even as part of an "admin" group. The goal is to protect root as much as possible.

4. D. MFA requires at least two ("multi") authentication methods. Those will normally include a password (something you know) and a token sent to either a virtual or physical MFA device (something you have).

5. B. The `-i` argument should point to the name (and location) of the key stored on the local (client) machine. By default, the admin user on an Amazon Linux instance is named `ec2-user`.

6. B. While assigning permissions and policy-based roles will work, it's not nearly as efficient as using groups, where you need to set or update permissions only once for multiple users.

7. C. An IAM role is meant to be assigned to a trusted entity (like another AWS service or a federated identity). A "set of permissions" could refer to a policy. A set of IAM users could describe a group.

8. A, D. Federated identities are for permitting authenticated entities access to AWS resources and data. They're not for importing anything from external accounts—neither data nor guidance.

9. C, D. Secure Shell (SSH) is an encrypted remote connectivity protocol, and SSO (single sign-on) is an interface feature—neither is a standard for federated identities.

10. D. The credential report focuses only on your users' passwords, access keys, and MFA status. It doesn't cover actual activities or general security settings.

11. B. The credential report is saved to the comma-separated values (spreadsheet) format.

12. A. Your admin user will need broad access to be effective, so AmazonS3FullAccess and AmazonEC2FullAccess—which open up only S3 and EC2, respectively—won't be enough. There is no AdminAccess policy.

13. D. "Programmatic access" users don't sign in through the AWS Management Console; they access through APIs or the AWS CLI. They would therefore not need passwords or MFA. An access key ID alone without a matching secret access key is worthless.

14. B. When the correct login page (such as `https://291976716973.signin.aws.amazon.com/console`) is loaded, an IAM user only needs to enter a username and a valid password. Account numbers and secret access keys are not used for this kind of authentication.

15. C. In-transit encryption requires that the data be encrypted on the remote client before uploading. Server-side encryption (either SSE-S3 or SSE-KMS) only encrypts data within S3 buckets. DynamoDB is a NoSQL database service.

16. A. You can only encrypt an EBS volume at creation, not later.

17. D. A client-side master key is used to encrypt objects before they reach AWS (specifically S3). There are no keys commonly known as either SSH or KMS master keys.

18. C. SSE-KMS are KMS-managed server-side keys. FedRAMP is the U.S. government's Federal Risk and Authorization Management Program (within which transaction data protection plays only a relatively minor role). ARPA is the Australian Prudential Regulation Authority.

19. B. SOC isn't primarily about guidance or risk assessment, and it's definitely not a guarantee of the state of your own deployments. SOC reports are reports of audits *on* AWS infrastructure that you can use as part of your own reporting requirements

20. A, B. AWS Artifact documents are about AWS infrastructure compliance with external standards. They tangentially can also provide insight into best practices. They do *not* represent internal AWS design or policies.

Chapter 6: Working with Your AWS Resources

1. D. You can sign in as the root user or as an IAM user. Although you need to specify the account alias or account ID to log in as an IAM user, those are not credentials. You can't log in to the console using an access key ID.

2. B. Once you're logged in, your session will remain active for 12 hours. After that, it'll expire and log you out to protect your account.

3. A. If a resource that should be visible appears to be missing, you may have the wrong Region selected. Since you're logged in as the root, you have view access to all resources in your account. You don't need an access key to use the console. You can't select an Availability Zone in the navigation bar.

4. C. Each resource tag you create must have a key, but a value is optional. Tags don't have to be unique within an account, and they are case-sensitive.

5. A. The AWS CLI requires an access key ID and secret key. You can use those of an IAM user or the root user. Outbound network access to TCP port 443 is required, not port 80. Linux is also not required, although you can use the AWS CLI with Linux, macOS, or Windows. You also can use the AWS Console Mobile Application with Android or iOS devices.

6. A, D. You can use Python and the pip package manager or (with the exception of Windows Server 2008) the MSI installer to install the AWS CLI on Windows. AWS SDKs don't include the AWS CLI. Yum and Aptitude are package managers for Linux only.

7. B. The `aws configure` command walks you through setting up the AWS CLI to specify the default Region you want to use as well as your access key ID and secret key. The `aws --version` command displays the version of the AWS CLI installed, but running this command isn't necessary to use the AWS CLI to manage your resources. Rebooting is also not necessary. Using your root user to manage your AWS resources is insecure, so there's no need to generate a new access key ID for your root user.

8. C. The AWS CLI can display output in JSON, text, or table formats. It doesn't support CSV or TSV.

9. B, D, E. AWS offers SDKs for JavaScript, Java, and PHP. There are no SDKs for Fortran. JSON is a format for representing data, not a programming language.

10. A, B. The AWS Mobile SDK for Unity and the AWS Mobile SDK for .NET and Xamarin let you create mobile applications for both Android and Apple iOS devices. The AWS SDK for Go doesn't enable development of mobile applications for these devices. The AWS Mobile SDK for iOS supports development of applications for Apple iOS devices but not Android.

11. A, B. AWS IoT device SDKs are available for C++, Python, Java, JavaScript, and Embedded C. There isn't one available for Ruby or Swift.

12. A, B. The AWS CLI is a program that runs on Linux, macOS, or Windows and allows you to interact with AWS services from a terminal. The AWS SDKs let you use your favorite programming language to write applications that interact with AWS services.

13. B. CloudWatch metrics store performance data from AWS services. Logs store text-based logs from applications and AWS services. Events are actions that occur against your AWS resources. Alarms monitor metrics. Metric filters extract metric information from logs.

14. D. A CloudWatch alarm monitors a metric and triggers when that metric exceeds a specified threshold. It will not trigger if the metric doesn't change. Termination of an EC2 instance is an event, and you can't create a CloudWatch alarm to trigger based on an event. You also can't create an alarm to trigger based on the presence of an IP address in a web server log. But you could create a metric filter to look for a specific IP address in the log and increment a custom metric when that IP address appears in the log.

15. A, C. SNS supports the SMS and SQS protocols for sending notifications. You can't send a notification to a CloudWatch event. There is no such thing as a mobile pull notification.

16. C, D. CloudWatch Events monitors events that cause changes in your AWS resources as well as AWS Management Console sign-in events. In response to an event, CloudWatch

Events can take an action including sending an SNS notification or rebooting an EC2 instance. CloudWatch Events can also perform actions on a schedule. It doesn't monitor logs or metrics.

17. B, D. Viewing an AWS resource triggers an API action regardless of whether it's done using the AWS Management Console or the AWS CLI. Configuring the AWS CLI doesn't trigger any API actions. Logging into the AWS Management Console doesn't trigger an API action.

18. A. The CloudTrail event history log stores the last 90 days of management events for each Region. Creating a trail is overkill and not as cost-effective since it would involve storing logs in an S3 bucket. Streaming CloudTrail logs to CloudWatch would require creating a trail. CloudWatch Events doesn't log management events.

19. A, D. Creating a trail in the Region where the bucket exists will generate CloudTrail logs, which you can then stream to CloudWatch for viewing and searching. CloudTrail event history doesn't log data events. CloudTrail logs global service events by default, but S3 data events are not included.

20. B. Log file integrity validation uses cryptographic hashing to help you assert that no CloudTrail log files have been deleted from S3. It doesn't prevent tampering or deletion and can't tell you how a file has been tampered with. Log file integrity validation has nothing to do with CloudWatch.

21. D. The costs and usage reports show you your monthly spend by service. The reserved instances reports and reserved instance recommendations don't show actual monthly costs.

22. A. RDS lets you purchase reserved instances to save money. Lambda, S3, and Fargate don't use instances.

23. B. The reservation utilization report shows how much you have saved using reserved instances. The reservation coverage report shows how much you could have potentially saved had you purchased reserved instances. The daily costs and monthly EC2 running hours costs and usage reports don't know how much you've saved using reserved instances.

24. D. Cost Explorer will make reservation recommendations for EC2, RDS, ElastiCache, Redshift, and Elasticsearch instances. You need to select the service you want it to analyze for recommendations. But Cost Explorer will not make recommendations for instances that are already covered by reservations. Because your Elasticsearch instances have been running continuously for at least the past seven days, that usage would be analyzed.

Chapter 7: The Core Compute Services

1. C. An instance's hardware profile is defined by the instance type. High-volume (or low-volume) data processing operations and data streams can be handled using any storage volume or on any instance (although some may be better optimized than others).

2. A. The Quick Start includes only the few dozen most popular AMIs. The Community tab includes thousands of publicly available AMIs—whether verified or not. The My AMIs tab only includes AMIs created from your account.

3. B, C. AMIs can be created that provide both a base operating system and a pre-installed application. They would not, however, include any networking or hardware profile information—those are largely determined by the instance type.

4. B, D. c5d.18xlarge and t2.micro are the names of EC2 instance types, not instance type families.

5. D. A virtual central processing unit (vCPU) is a metric that roughly measures an instance type's compute power in terms of the number of processors on a physical server. It has nothing to do with resilience to high traffic, system memory, or the underlying AMI.

6. A. An EC2 instance that runs on a physical host reserved for and controlled by a single AWS account is called a dedicated host. A dedicated host is not an AMI, nor is it an instance type.

7. C. A virtualized partition of a physical storage drive that is directly connected to the EC2 instance it's associated with is known as an instance store volume. A software stack archive packaged to make it easy to copy and deploy to an EC2 instance describes an EC2 AMI. It's possible to encrypt EBS volumes, but encryption doesn't define them.

8. C, D. Instance store volumes cannot be encrypted, nor will their data survive an instance shutdown. Those are features of EBS volumes.

9. B. Spot instances are unreliable for this sort of usage since they can be shut down unexpectedly. Reserved instances make economic sense where they'll be used 24/7 over long stretches of time. "Dedicated" isn't a pricing model.

10. D. Reserved instances will work here because your "base" instances will need to run 24/7 over the long term. Spot and spot fleet instances are unreliable for this sort of usage since they can be shut down unexpectedly. On-demand instances will incur unnecessarily high costs over such a long period.

11. A. There's no real need for guaranteed available capacity since it's extremely rare for AWS to run out. You choose how you'll pay for a reserved instance. All Upfront, Partial Upfront, and No Upfront are available options, and there is no automatic billing. An instance would never be launched automatically in this context.

12. A, C. Because spot instances can be shut down, they're not recommended for applications that provide any kind of always-on service.

13. C, D. Elastic Block Store provides storage volumes for Lightsail and Beanstalk (and for EC2, for that matter). Elastic Compute Cloud (EC2) provides application deployment, but no one ever accused it of being simple.

14. A. Beanstalk, EC2 (non-reserved instances), and RDS all bill according to actual usage.

15. B, D. Ubuntu is an OS, not a stack. WordPress is an application, not an OS.

16. B, C. Elastic Block Store is, for practical purposes, an EC2 resource. RDS is largely built on its own infrastructure.

17. A, C. While you could, in theory at least, manually install Docker Engine on either a Lightsail or EC2 instance, that's not their primary function.

18. **A, B.** Both Lambda and Lightsail are compute services that—while they might possibly make use of containers under the hood—are not themselves container technologies.

19. **D.** Python is, indeed, a valid choice for a function's runtime environment. There is no one "primary" language for Lambda API calls.

20. **A.** While the maximum time was, at one point, 5 minutes, that's been changed to 15.

Chapter 8: The Core Storage Services

1. **B.** Bucket names must be globally unique across AWS, irrespective of Region. The length of the bucket name isn't an issue since it's between 3 and 63 characters long. Storage classes are configured on a per-object basis and have no impact on bucket naming.

2. **A, C.** STANDARD_IA and GLACIER storage classes offer the highest levels of redundancy and are replicated across at least three Availability Zones. Due to their low level of availability (99.9 and 99.5 percent, respectively), they're the most cost-effective for infrequently accessed data. ONEZONE_IA stores objects in only one Availability Zone, so the loss of that zone could result in the loss of all objects. The STANDARD and INTELLIGENT_TIERING classes provide the highest levels of durability and cross-zone replication but are also the least cost-effective for this use case.

3. **A, D.** S3 is an object storage service, while EBS is a block storage service that stores volumes. EBS snapshots are stored in S3. S3 doesn't store volumes, and EBS doesn't store objects.

4. **A, B, D.** Object life cycle configurations can perform transition or expiration actions based on an object's age. Transition actions can move objects between storage classes, such as between STANDARD and GLACIER. Expiration actions can delete objects and object versions. Object life cycle configurations can't delete buckets or move objects to an EBS volume.

5. **A, B.** You can use bucket policies or access control lists (ACLs) to grant anonymous users access to an object in S3. You can't use user policies to do this, although you can use them to grant IAM principals access to objects. Security groups control access to resources in a virtual private cloud (VPC) and aren't used to control access to objects in S3.

6. **C, D.** Both S3 and Glacier are designed for durable, long-term storage and offer the same level of durability. Data stored in Glacier can be reliably retrieved within eight hours using the Expedited or Standard retrieval options. Data stored in S3 can be retrieved even faster than Glacier. S3 can store objects up to 5 TB in size, and Glacier can store archives up to 40 TB. Both S3 or Glacier will meet the given requirements, but Glacier is the more cost-effective solution.

7. **B.** You can create or delete vaults from the Glacier service console. You can't upload, download, or delete archives. To perform archive actions, you must use the AWS Command Line Interface, an AWS SDK, or a third-party program. Glacier doesn't use buckets.

8. **D.** The Standard retrieval option typically takes 3 to 5 hours to complete. Expedited takes 1 to 5 minutes, and Bulk takes 5 to 12 hours. There is no Provisioned retrieval option, but you can purchase provisioned capacity to ensure Expedited retrievals complete in a timely manner.

9. **A.** A Glacier archive can be as small as 1 byte and as large as 40 TB. You can't have a zero-byte archive.

10. **B, D.** The tape gateway and volume gateway types let you connect to iSCSI storage. The file gateway supports NFS. There's no such thing as a cached gateway.

11. **B.** All AWS Storage Gateway types—file, volume, and tape gateways—primarily store data in S3 buckets. From there, data can be stored in Glacier or EBS snapshots, which can be instantiated as EBS volumes.

12. **A, B, D, E.** The AWS Storage Gateway allows transferring files from on-premises servers to S3 using industry-standard storage protocols. The AWS Storage Gateway functioning as a file gateway supports the SMB and NFS protocols. As a volume gateway, it supports the iSCSI protocol. AWS Snowball and the AWS CLI also provide ways to transfer data to S3, but using them requires installing third-party software.

13. **A, C, E.** The volume gateway type offers two configurations: stored volumes and cached volumes. Stored volumes store all data locally and asynchronously back up that data to S3 as EBS snapshots. Stored volumes can be up to 16 TB in size. In contrast, cached volumes locally store only a frequently used subset of data but do not asynchronously back up the data to S3 as EBS snapshots. Cached volumes can be up to 32 TB in size.

14. **C.** The 80 TB Snowball device offers 72 TB of usable storage and is the largest available. The 50 TB Snowball offers 42 TB of usable space.

15. **A, B.** AWS Snowball enforces encryption at rest and in transit. It also uses a TPM chip to detect unauthorized changes to the hardware or software. Snowball doesn't use NFS encryption, and it doesn't have tamper-resistant network ports.

16. **C.** If AWS detects any signs of tampering or damage, it will not replace the TPM chip or transfer customer data from the device. Instead, AWS will securely erase it.

17. **B.** The Snowball Client lets you transfer files to or from a Snowball using a machine running Windows, Linux, or macOS. It requires no coding knowledge, but the S3 SDK Adapter for Snowball does. Snowball doesn't support the NFS, iSCSI, or SMB storage protocols.

18. **A, D.** Snowball Edge offers compute power to run EC2 instances and supports copying files using the NFSv3 and NFSv4 protocols. Snowball devices can't be clustered and don't have a QFSP+ port.

19. **B.** The Snowball Edge—Compute Optimized with GPU option is optimized for machine learning and high-performance computing applications. Although the Compute Optimized and Storage Optimized options could work, they aren't the best choices. There's no Network Optimized option.

20. **B.** Snowball Edge with the Compute Optimized configuration includes a QSFP+ network interface that supports up to 100 Gbps. The Storage Optimized configuration has a QSFP+ port that supports only up to 40 Gbps. The 80 TB Snowball supports only up to 10 Gbps. A storage gateway is a virtual machine, not a hardware device.

Chapter 9: The Core Database Services

1. B. A relational database stores data in columns called attributes and rows called records. Nonrelational databases—including key-value stores and document stores—store data in collections or items but don't use columns or rows.

2. B. The SQL INSERT statement can be used to add data to a relational database. The QUERY command is used to read data. CREATE can be used to create a table but not add data to it. WRITE is not a valid SQL command.

3. D. A nonrelational database is schemaless, meaning that there's no need to predefine all the types of data you'll store in a table. This doesn't preclude you from storing data with a fixed structure, as nonrelational databases can store virtually any kind of data. A primary key is required to uniquely identify each item in a table. Creating multiple tables is allowed, but most applications that use nonrelational databases use only one table.

4. C. A no-SQL database is another term for a nonrelational database. By definition, nonrelational databases are schemaless and must use primary keys. There's no such thing as a schemaless relational database. No-SQL is never used to describe a relational database of any kind.

5. B. RDS instances use EBS volumes for storage. They no longer can use magnetic storage. Instance volumes are for temporary, not database storage. You can take a snapshot of a database instance and restore it to a new instance with a new EBS volume, but an RDS instance can't use a snapshot directly for database storage.

6. B, D. PostgreSQL and Amazon Aurora are options for RDS database engines. IBM dBase and the nonrelational databases DynamoDB and Redis are not available as RDS database engines.

7. A, B. Aurora is Amazon's proprietary database engine that works with existing PostgreSQL and MySQL databases. Aurora doesn't support MariaDB, Oracle, or Microsoft SQL Server.

8. B, C. Multi-AZ and snapshots can protect your data in the event of an Availability Zone failure. Read replicas don't use synchronous replication and may lose some data. IOPS is a measurement of storage throughput. Vertical scaling refers to changing the instance class but has nothing to do with preventing data loss.

9. B. Amazon Aurora uses a shared storage volume that automatically expands up to 64 TB. The Microsoft SQL Server and Oracle database engines don't offer this. Amazon Athena is not a database engine.

10. A. Multi-AZ lets your database withstand the failure of an RDS instance, even if the failure is due to an entire Availability Zone failing. Read replicas are a way to achieve horizontal scaling to improve performance of database reads but don't increase availability. Point-in-time recovery allows you to restore a database up to a point in time but doesn't increase availability.

11. B, D. A partition is an allocation of storage backed by solid-state drives and replicated across multiple Availability Zones. Tables are stored across partitions, but tables do not

contain partitions. A primary key, not a partition, is used to uniquely identify an item in a table.

12. A. The minimum monthly availability for DynamoDB is 99.99 percent in a single Region. It's not 99.95 percent, 99.9 percent, or 99.0 percent.

13. D. Items in a DynamoDB table can have different attributes. For example, one item can have five attributes, while another has only one. A table can store items containing multiple data types. There's no need to predefine the number of items in a table. Items in a table can't have duplicate primary keys.

14. C, E. Increasing WCU or enabling Auto Scaling will improve write performance against a table. Increasing or decreasing RCU won't improve performance for writes. Decreasing WCU will make write performance worse.

15. C. A scan requires reading every partition on which the table is stored. A query occurs against the primary key, enabling DynamoDB to read only the partition where the matching item is stored. Writing and updating an item are not read-intensive operations.

16. D. A primary key must be unique within a table. A full name, phone number, or city may not be unique, as some customers may share the same name or phone number. A randomly generated customer ID number would be unique and appropriate for use as a primary key.

17. B. Dense compute nodes use magnetic disks. Dense storage nodes use SSDs. There are no such nodes as dense memory or cost-optimized.

18. A. Redshift Spectrum can analyze structured data stored in S3. There is no such service as Redshift S3. Amazon Athena can analyze structured data in S3, but it's not a feature of Redshift. Amazon RDS doesn't analyze data stored in S3.

19. B. A data warehouse stores large amounts of structured data from other relational databases. It's not called a data storehouse or a report cluster. Dense storage node is a type of Redshift compute node.

20. A. Dense storage nodes can be used in a cluster to store up to 2 PB of data. Dense compute nodes can be used to store up to 326 TB of data.

Chapter 10: The Core Networking Services

1. B, D. For each account, AWS creates a default VPC in each Region. A VPC spans all Availability Zones within a Region. VPCs do not span Regions.

2. A. A VPC or subnet CIDR can have a size between /16 and /28 inclusive, so 10.0.0.0/28 would be the only valid CIDR.

3. B, C. A subnet exists in only one Availability Zone, and it must have a CIDR that's a subset of CIDR of the VPC in which it resides. There's no requirement for a VPC to have two subnets, but it must have at least one.

4. C. When you create a security group, it contains an outbound rule that allows access to any IP address. It doesn't contain an inbound rule by default. Security group rules can only permit access, not deny it, so any traffic not explicitly allowed will be denied.

5. B, D. A network access control list is a firewall that operates at the subnet level. A security group is a firewall that operates at the instance level.

6. B. A VPC peering connection is a private connection between only two VPCs. It uses the private AWS network, and not the public internet. A VPC peering connection is different than a VPN connection.

7. A, B. A Direct Connect link uses a dedicated link rather than the internet to provide predictable latency. Direct Connect doesn't use encryption but provides some security by means of a private link. A VPN connection uses the internet for transport, encrypting data with AES 128- or 256-bit encryption. A VPN connection doesn't require proprietary hardware.

8. B, D. When you register a domain name, you can choose a term between 1 year and 10 years. If you use Route 53, it will automatically create a public hosted zone for the domain. The registrar and DNS hosting provider don't have to be the same entity, but often are.

9. B. A Multivalue Answer routing policy can return a set of multiple values, sorted randomly. A simple record returns a single value. A Failover routing policy always routes users to the primary resource unless it's down, in which case it routes users to the secondary resource. A Latency routing policy sends users to the resource in the AWS Region that provides the least latency.

10. C. All Route 53 routing policies except for Simple can use health checks.

11. C. An Endpoint health check works by connecting to the monitored endpoint via HTTP, HTTPS, or TCP. A CloudWatch alarm health check simply reflects the status of a CloudWatch alarm. A Calculated health check derives its status from multiple other health checks. There is no such thing as a Simple health check.

12. A. A Weighted routing policy lets you distribute traffic to endpoints according to a ratio that you define. None of the other routing policies allows this.

13. B. A private hosted zone is associated with a VPC and allows resources in the VPC to resolve private domain names. A public hosted zone is accessible by anyone on the internet. Domain name registration is for public domain names. Health checks aren't necessary for name resolution to work.

14. A. Route 53 private hosted zones provide DNS resolution for a single domain name within multiple VPCs. Therefore, to support resolution of one domain names for two VPCs, you'd need one private hosted zone.

15. B. CloudFront has edge locations on six continents (Antarctica is a hard place to get to).

16. B. A CloudFront origin is the location that a distribution sources content from. Content is stored in edge locations. A distribution defines the edge locations and origins to use.

17. B. The RTMP distribution type is for delivering streaming content and requires you to provide a media player. A Web distribution can also stream audio or video content but doesn't require you to provide a media player. Streaming and Edge are not distribution types.

18. A. The more edge locations you use for a distribution, the more you'll pay. Selecting the minimum number of locations will be the most cost effective.

19. B. There are more than 150 edge locations throughout the world.

20. A, B. An origin can be an EC2 instance or a public S3 bucket. You can't use a private S3 bucket as an origin.

Chapter 11: Automating Your AWS Workloads

1. C. CloudFormation can create AWS resources and manages them collectively in a stack. Templates are written in the CloudFormation language, not Python. CloudFormation can't create resources outside of AWS. It also doesn't prevent manual changes to resources in a stack.

2. B, D. CloudFormation templates are written in the YAML or JSON format.

3. A. Parameters let you input customizations when creating a CloudFormation stack without having to modify the underlying template. Parameters don't prevent stack updates or unauthorized changes. A template can be used to create multiple stacks, regardless of whether it uses parameters.

4. A, B. Resources CloudFormation creates are organized into stacks. When you update a stack, CloudFormation analyzes the relationships among resources in the stack and updates dependent resources as necessary. This does not, however, mean that any resource you create using CloudFormation will work as you expect. Provisioning resources using CloudFormation is not necessarily faster than using the AWS CLI.

5. A, C. CodeCommit is a private Git repository that offers versioning and differencing. It does not perform deployments.

6. B. Differencing lets you see the differences between two versions of a file, which can be useful when figuring out what change introduced a bug. Versioning, not differencing, is what allows reverting to an older version of a file. Differencing doesn't identify duplicate lines of code or tell you when an application was deployed.

7. D. Continuous integration is the practice of running code through a build or test process as soon as it's checked into a repository. Continuous delivery and continuous deployment include continuous integration but add deployment to the process. Differencing only shows the differences between different versions of a file but doesn't perform any testing.

8. B, D. Build.general1.medium and build.general1.large support Windows and Linux operating systems. Build.general1.small supports Linux only. The other compute types don't exist.

9. A, B. A CodeBuild build environment always contains an operating system and a Docker image. It may contain the other components but doesn't have to.

10. A, B, C. CodeDeploy can deploy application files to Linux or Windows EC2 instances and Docker containers to ECS. It can't deploy an application to smartphones, and it can't deploy files to an S3 bucket.

11. B. At the very least, a CodePipeline must consist of a source stage and a deploy stage.

12. D. A launch template can be used to launch instances manually and with EC2 Auto Scaling. A launch configuration can't be used to launch instances manually. An instance role is used to grant permissions to applications running on an instance. Auto Scaling can't provision instances using a CloudFormation template.

13. A, D. The maximum and minimum group size values limit the number of instances in an Auto Scaling group. The desired capacity (also known as the group size) is the number of instances that Auto Scaling will generally maintain, but Auto Scaling can launch or terminate instances if dynamic scaling calls for it.

14. B. Auto Scaling will use self-healing to replace the failed instance to maintain the desired capacity of 7. Terminating an instance or failing to replace the failed one will result in 6 instances. Auto Scaling won't ever change the desired capacity in response to a failed instance.

15. A. Predictive scaling creates a scheduled scaling action based on past usage patterns. Scheduled scaling and dynamic scaling do not create scheduled scaling actions. There is no such thing as pattern scaling.

16. B. A Command document can execute commands on an EC2 instance. An Automation document can perform administrative tasks on AWS, such as starting or stopping an instance. There is no such thing as a Script document or a Run document.

17. D. An Automation document can perform administrative tasks on AWS, such as starting or stopping an instance. A Command document can execute commands on an EC2 instance. There is no such thing as a Script document or a Run document.

18. B. AWS OpsWorks Stacks uses Chef recipes, while AWS OpsWorks for Puppet Enterprise uses Puppet modules. There is no service called AWS OpsWorks Layers or AWS OpsWorks for Automation.

19. B, D. OpsWorks supports the Puppet Enterprise and Chef configuration management platforms. It doesn't support SaltStack, Ansible, or CFEngine.

20. C. Only an OpsWorks layer contains at least one EC2 instance. There's no such thing as an EC2 Auto Scaling layer.

Chapter 12: Common Use-Case Scenarios

1. C. The five pillars of the Well-Architected Framework are reliability, performance efficiency, security, cost optimization, and operational excellence. Resiliency is not one of them.

2. A, D. Security is about protecting the confidentiality, integrity, and availability of data. Granting each AWS user their own IAM username and password makes it possible to ensure the confidentiality of data. Enabling S3 versioning protects the integrity of data by maintaining a backup of an object. Deleting an empty S3 bucket doesn't help with any of these. It's not possible to create a security group rule that denies access to unused ports since security groups deny any traffic that's not explicitly allowed.

3. C, D. Preventing the accidental termination of an EC2 instance in the Auto Scaling group can avoid overburdening and causing performance issues on the remaining instance, especially during busy times. Using CloudFront can help improve performance for end users by caching the content in an edge location close to them. Doubling the number of instances might improve performance, but because performance is already acceptable, doing this would be inefficient. Monitoring for unauthorized access alone won't improve performance or performance efficiency.

4. A, C. Deleting unused S3 objects and unused application load balancers can reduce costs since you're charged for both. Deleting unused VPCs and empty S3 buckets won't reduce costs since they don't cost anything.

5. B. Operational excellence is concerned with strengthening the other four pillars of reliability, performance efficiency, security, and cost optimization; automation is the key to achieving each of these. Improving bad processes and making people work longer hours run counter to achieving operational excellence. Adding more security personnel may be a good idea, but it isn't a key component of operational excellence.

6. B. In a default VPC, AWS creates a subnet for each Availability Zone in the Region. Hence, if there are three subnets in the default VPC, there must be three Availability Zones.

7. A. Application load balancer listeners use security groups to control inbound access, so you need to apply a security group that has an inbound rule allowing HTTP access. Applying the security group rule to the database instance won't help, since users don't connect directly to the database instance. You can't apply a security group to a subnet, only a network access control list.

8. A. An application load balancer can use health checks to identify failed instances and remove them from load balancing. This can prevent a user from ever reaching a failed instance. A load balancer can't replace a failed instance, but Auto Scaling can. An application load balancer distributes traffic to instances using a round-robin algorithm, not based on how busy those instances are. An application load balancer doesn't cache content.

9. D. A launch template tells Auto Scaling how to configure the instances it provisions. A dynamic scaling policy controls how Auto Scaling scales in and out based on CloudWatch metrics. There's no such thing as a launch directive. Auto Scaling does not reference a CloudFormation template, but you can use a CloudFormation template to create a stack that contains a launch template.

10. B. The maximum group size limits the number of instances in the group. Setting the group size (also known as the desired capacity) or minimum group size to 5 would increase the number of instances to 5 but would not stop Auto Scaling from subsequently adding more instances. Deleting the target tracking policy would not necessarily prevent the number of instances in the group from growing, as another process such as a scheduled scaling policy could add more instances to the group.

11. B. A static website serves content just as it's stored without changing the content on the fly. A WordPress blog, a social media website, and a web-based email application all compile content from a database and mix it in with static content before serving it up to the user.

12. A, C. Objects you upload to an S3 bucket are not public by default, nor are they accessible to all AWS users. Even if you try to make an object public using an ACL, S3 will immediately remove the ACL, but you can disable this behavior. S3 never removes objects by default.

13. A. To have S3 host your static website, you need to enable bucket hosting in the S3 service console. It's not necessary to disable or enable default encryption or object versioning. There's also no need to make all objects in the bucket public, but only those that you want S3 to serve up.

14. B. Purchasing and using a custom domain name is the best option for a friendly URL. You need to name the bucket the same as the domain name. Creating a bucket name with only words is unlikely to work, regardless of Region, as bucket names must be globally unique. A bucket name can't start with a number.

15. A. Websites hosted in S3 are served using unencrypted HTTP, not secure HTTPS. The content is publicly readable, but that doesn't mean the public can modify it. You don't have to use a custom domain name, as S3 provides an endpoint URL for you. A website hosted in S3 is stored in a bucket, and a bucket exists in only one Region.

16. C. The reliability of an application can be impacted by the failure of resources the application depends on. One way a resource can fail is if it's misconfigured. Taking EBS snapshots of an instance or provisioning more instances than you need won't impact reliability. The user interface being difficult to use might be an annoyance for the user but doesn't affect the actual reliability of the application.

17. C. You may have control over your VPC, but the rest of the network between your application and users on the internet is not under your control. Compute, storage, and any database your application uses are, or at least theoretically could be, under your control.

18. D. An Auto Scaling group can use an ELB health check to determine whether an instance is healthy. There is no such thing as an S3 health check, a VPC health check, or an SNS health check.

19. B. You're responsible for S3 charges related to your static website. You're not charged for compute with S3. No one may modify the content of your site unless you give them permission. The S3 Standard storage class keeps objects in multiple Availability Zones, so the outage of one won't affect the site.

20. A. The format of the URL is the bucket name, followed by s3-website-, the Region identifier, and then amazonaws.com.

Appendix

B

Additional Services

You've learned a lot about the key AWS services that you're most likely to see covered on the exam and encounter in the real world. But AWS has well over 100 services, and it's important that you be familiar with some of the services that haven't been covered in the preceding chapters. This appendix briefly introduces 15 important services that are likely to come up on the exam.

Athena

Athena lets you use SQL queries to find data stored in S3. If you have data stored in CSV, JSON, ORC, Avro, or Parquet format, simply upload it to S3 and use Athena to query it. Athena is serverless, so there's no need to provision your own database or import your data into it. For more information, visit https://aws.amazon.com/athena/.

AWS Backup

AWS Backup lets you centrally configure backup policies and monitor backup activity for all of your data stored on AWS. It supports EBS volumes, RDS databases, DynamoDB tables, EFS file systems, and Storage Gateway volumes. For more information, visit https://aws.amazon.com/backup/.

AWS Glue

Data can live in a variety of places on AWS. AWS Glue can discover, clean, and bring this data together in one place for analysis using the Apache Spark big data framework. It can extract and analyze data from S3 objects and relational databases such as MySQL, Oracle, and Microsoft SQL Server. For more information, visit https://aws.amazon.com/glue/.

Batch

Batch computing jobs are used for performing complex analysis on large data sets. Some examples of batch computing include financial risk modeling, graphics processing, simulations, and even analyzing genomes. Batch allows you to run thousands of batch computing jobs on AWS without having to build any infrastructure. Simply define your batch job as a Docker container and submit it, and AWS takes care of the rest. For more information, visit `https://docs.aws.amazon.com/batch/`.

Cognito

Cognito lets you add user access control to your application. Cognito integrates with many identity providers including Amazon, Google, Microsoft Active Directory, and Facebook. You can also use Cognito to provide your users access to AWS resources without having to give them their own IAM credentials. For more information, visit `https://aws.amazon.com/cognito/`.

Database Migration Service

Database Migration Service (DMS) makes it easy to migrate data from one database to another, whether it's in the cloud or on-premises. DMS supports both relational databases such as Aurora, Oracle, Microsoft SQL Server, MariaDB, and PostgreSQL, as well as nonrelational databases including MongoDB, DocumentDB, and DynamoDB. DMS also supports migrating data to S3, Elasticsearch, and Kinesis Data Streams. For more information, visit `https://docs.aws.amazon.com/dms/`.

Elastic File System

The Elastic File System (EFS) is a scalable file system for Linux instances. You can attach multiple instances to a single EFS volume so that they can all share the same files. EFS volumes are highly available, spanning multiple Availability Zones in a single VPC. EFS can scale up to petabytes in size without disruption and automatically scales down so you're not charged for space you're not using. Unused files are automatically moved to a cost-optimized storage class. For more information, visit `https://aws.amazon.com/efs/`.

Elastic MapReduce

Elastic MapReduce (EMR) lets you analyze enormous amounts of data stored in the cloud. EMR supports the Apache Hadoop, Apache Spark, HBase, Presto, and Flink big data platforms. For more information, visit `https://aws.amazon.com/emr/`.

Inspector

Inspector analyzes your EC2 instances for security vulnerabilities and common misconfigurations. For more information, visit https://aws.amazon.com/inspector/.

Kinesis

Kinesis can ingest and process large amounts of data in real time. It's useful for analyzing large amounts of streaming data including access logs, video, audio, and telemetry. For more information, visit https://aws.amazon.com/kinesis/.

Macie

Macie automatically finds and classifies sensitive data stored in AWS. It uses machine learning to recognize sensitive data such as personally identifiable information or trade secrets and shows you how that data is being used in AWS. For more information, visit https://aws.amazon.com/macie/.

Neptune

Neptune is a graph database that you can use to store and query highly connected data sets. It's useful for recommendation engines, social networks, fraud detection, and network security. For more information, visit https://aws.amazon.com/neptune/.

Simple Queue Service

Simple Queue Service (SQS) enables developers to create decoupled, distributed applications in the cloud. SQS is a message broker that different components of your application can use to send messages to each other. SQS scales automatically to accommodate any volume. For more information, visit https://aws.amazon.com/sqs/.

WorkDocs

WorkDocs is a secure content sharing and collaboration service. You can store any type of file in WorkDocs, and it provides preview and commenting functionality for documents such as Microsoft Office files, PDFs, and text files. For more information, visit https://aws.amazon.com/workdocs/.

WorkSpaces

Workspaces lets you provision Linux or Windows virtual desktops in the cloud. AWS manages the operating system, patching, and virtual desktop infrastructure. Users can connect to their virtual desktops from any PC and a variety of mobile devices. For more information, visit https://aws.amazon.com/workspaces/.

Index

S

Comprehensive Online Learning Environment

Register to gain one year of FREE access to the online interactive learning environment and test bank to help you study for your AWS certification exam—included with your purchase of this book!

The online test bank includes the following:

- **Assessment Test** to help you focus your study to specific objectives
- **Chapter Tests** to reinforce what you've learned
- **Practice Exams** to test your knowledge of the material
- **Digital Flashcards** to reinforce your learning and provide last-minute test prep before the exam
- **Searchable Glossary** to define the key terms you'll need to know for the exam

Register and Access the Online Test Bank

To register your book and get access to the online test bank, follow these steps:

1. Go to bit.ly/SybexTest.
2. Select your book from the list.
3. Complete the required registration information, including answering the security verification to prove book ownership. You will be emailed a PIN code.
4. Follow the directions in the email or go to https://www.wiley.com/go/sybextestprep.
5. Enter the pin code you received and click the "Activate PIN" button.
6. On the Create an Account or Login page, enter your username and password, and click Login. A "Thank you for activating your PIN!" message will appear. If you don't have an account already, create a new account.
7. Click the "Go to My Account" button to add your new book to the My Products page.